The U.S. Supreme Court
and the Judicial Review
of Congress

PETER LANG
New York • Washington, D.C./Baltimore • Bern
Frankfurt am Main • Berlin • Brussels • Vienna • Oxford

Linda Camp Keith

The U.S. Supreme Court
and the Judicial Review
of Congress

Two Hundred Years in the Exercise
of the Court's Most Potent Power

PETER LANG
New York • Washington, D.C./Baltimore • Bern
Frankfurt am Main • Berlin • Brussels • Vienna • Oxford

Library of Congress Cataloging-in-Publication Data

Keith, Linda Camp.
The U.S. Supreme Court and the judicial review of Congress: two hundred years
in the exercise of the court's most potent power / Linda Camp Keith.
p. cm.
Includes bibliographical references and index.
1. Judicial review—United States—History.
2. United States. Supreme Court. I. Title.
KF4575.Z9K45 347.73'12—dc22 2008000226
ISBN 978-0-8204-8880-6

Bibliographic information published by **Die Deutsche Bibliothek**.
Die Deutsche Bibliothek lists this publication in the "Deutsche
Nationalbibliografie"; detailed bibliographic data is available
on the Internet at http://dnb.ddb.de/.

Cover design by Joni Holst

Cover art by Joe Prescher (joetheartist.com), "Truth"
Mixed media on canvas, 24"x 30"

The paper in this book meets the guidelines for permanence and durability
of the Committee on Production Guidelines for Book Longevity
of the Council of Library Resources.

© 2008 Peter Lang Publishing, Inc., New York
29 Broadway, 18th floor, New York, NY 10006
www.peterlang.com

Printed in the United States of America

To my life partner, Joseph Prescher

Contents

Acknowledgments   ix

CHAPTER 1   Introduction   1
             Counter-Majoritarian Difficulty   2
             Preference-Based Theories of Judicial Decision Making   7
                 The Justices' Ideology   8
                 Strategic Considerations and Institutional Context   11
             Outline of the Book   13

CHAPTER 2   Judicial Review: The Norm of Deference and its Contours   23
             Cases of Supreme Court Review of Congress   23
             The Norm of Supreme Court Deference to Congress   26
                 Judicial Review Across Time   27
                 Supreme Court Deference to Congress Over Time   34
             The Issue of Ideological Direction of Judicial Decisions   37
             Chief Justice Courts and the Exercise of Judicial Review   40
             Major Legal Issues and Constitutional Provisions   45
             Conclusions   51

CHAPTER 3   "Activist" or "Restraintist"? The Justices on the Bench   59
             Introduction   59
             The Justices' Votes on the Constitutionality
                 of Congressional Statutes   60
             Conclusions   98

CHAPTER 4   Majoritarian Issues: An Initial Exploration   103
             Introduction   103
             Hypotheses and Initial Tests of the Early
                 Counter-Majoritarian Studies   107

	Majoritarian Hypotheses from Recent Empirical Studies	112
	The Court as Protector against "Tyranny of the Majority" Hypothesis	117
	Conclusions	121
CHAPTER 5	The Decision to Nullify or Uphold: Exploratory and Explanatory Models of Individual Justices' Judicial Review Votes	127
	Theoretical Expectations and Hypotheses	128
	The Attitudinal Model	128
	Strategic and Institutional Influences	130
	Issue Areas and Policy Direction of the Statute	136
	Data and Methods	140
	Dependent Variable: Justices Votes to Nullify or Uphold Congressional Statute	140
	Independent Variables: Justice's Policy Preferences and Personal Attributes	140
	Political Factors	142
	Cleavages	143
	Career Experiences and Socialization	146
	Other Independent Variables	148
	Results	152
	Conclusions	164
CHAPTER 6	Conclusions	175
Bibliography		183
Index		193

Acknowledgments

This research would not have been possible were it not for the dedication of Collin College to engaged scholarship. Early portions of this work were funded by a Collin study grant and then subsequently a sabbatical grant. I am grateful to have been the beneficiary of the foresight of my colleagues David Cullen and Larry Stern who established the faculty grant program. And I am grateful to have had the support of a dean, Gary Hodge, and a president, Cary Israel, who valued and supported scholarly research in a two-year institution, and who ultimately forgave my sabbatical debt so I could teach at the University of Iowa. I am also grateful to Mike Lewis-Beck, and the political science department at the University of Iowa, for the year there that enabled me to pursue components of this project as well as my human rights research with the benefits and resources of a major university, which included the able support of research assistants Emily Buckel, Erin Waitz, and Drew Henning. And I am grateful for the support and encouragement of my colleagues at the University of Texas at Dallas the past two years.

The interest and the origins of this research, however, actually began at the University of North Texas, as I wrote my Master's thesis on the Supreme Court's nullification of congressional statutes under the direction of Neal Tate, to whom I am indebted for fostering my intellectual interest and analytical skills in engaging in empirical research on judicial behavior. I also am grateful to have been a part of a research group established by Sandra Wood (joined by Ayo Ogundele and Drew Lanier) that sought to expand our understanding of the earlier Supreme Court and that ultimately replicated part of the Spaeth dataset backwards in time. Much of my understanding of the Supreme Court comes from endless hours spent in a conference room pouring over Supreme Court volumes and engaged in lively discussion with these colleagues. I am also indebted to the late Steve Poe, who along with Neal Tate brought me into their research project on global human rights, which overtime extended my research more broadly into rule of law and judicial independence issues. I would be remiss if I did not also thank Tony Champagne and Loren Miller who piqued my curiosity and provided my initial understanding of the Supreme Court as an undergraduate student at the University of Texas at Dallas.

Finally, there are important personal acknowledgements that I must also make. My twin sister, Brenda, for her boundless friendship and wise counsel. My son Adam, for his unique insights and continuing encouragement. My parents who have helped me move back and forth across the country and still have found the energy to support my work from nearby and faraway. And last, Joe, to whom I dedicate this book, who was there to remind me to take it one day at a time, and who had the faith to follow me across the country.

1

Introduction

Introduction

Judicial review has long been touted as a significant component of American constitutionalism, one which has been exported in various forms to increasing numbers of newly independent or democratizing states across the globe. In the United States, however, this power has been both praised and criticized—praised as a "powerful barrier erected against the tyranny of political assemblies" (de Tocqueville, 1966, 261) but also criticized as being inherently undemocratic by some constitutional scholars (e.g., Bickel 1962; Ely 1980; Parker 1981). Regardless of the normative debates, judicial review is arguably the U.S. Supreme Court's most potent power vis-à-vis the popularly elected branches of government, at both the federal and state level. In two centuries the Supreme Court has overturned as unconstitutional, in whole or in part, over 1500 laws and ordinances passed by elected bodies across the United States. Over 160 of the laws overturned were congressional statutes. The extent of this power is further illustrated by the finality of the Court's decisions in these nullifications. Congress has only succeeded in directly overturning four of these cases, by passing an amendment to undo the Court's decision.[1] The magnitude of importance of this judicial power has not been reflected in the level empirical attention given to it by political scientists. Much of the early attention to this behavior has not extended beyond the context of constitutional case studies, doctrinal analysis, or normative theory. Until recently, relatively few rigorous, systematic, empirical studies of the behavior were published, with a few notable exceptions, as we will see below. In part, this lack of attention was due to the unavailability of the necessary data; lists of cases in which the Supreme Court exercised its power of review to nullify congressional or state statutes were widely published, but no lists are available that identify the Court's exercise of judicial review to *uphold* laws. With the increasing attention to the competition between the attitudinal approach and the strategic approach as explanatory models of Supreme Court behavior, scholars have turned their attention back to the Supreme Court's exercise of judicial review, and as we will see below, scholars have begun to fill in this gap in the literature. In addition, some scholars have attempted to fill in the data gap as well, creating the appropriate data, as searchable electronic copies of the Court's opinions, and even Court briefs, have become more widely accessible. In writing this book, I seek to contribute the effort to fill in this gap in our understanding of the Court's exercise of this potent power, specifically in regard to its review of congressional statutes. The work of this book is significant in that it examines this power across two-hundred years of its exercise and attempts to answer important questions in regard to the counter-majoritarian nature of the power and the competing explanatory theories of judicial behavior, while at the same time providing a full descriptive analysis of the Court's and its individual justices' voting behavior, offering insights along many dimensions. The benefits of the longitudinal nature of the book, of course, are offset by some trade-offs, such as data limitations on some measures. The book seeks to identify those limitations openly, and to deal with them appropriately, given the practical constraints of academic research. In the sections that follow I will discuss the relevant theories of judicial behavior, and assess the state of the literature that has empirically examined the questions generated by the theory. And finally, I will present the outline of the book, as it attempts to address these questions, and at the same time present a preliminary glimpse of the findings for each chapter.

Counter-Majoritarian Difficulty

Much of the early theoretical exploration of the power of judicial review has been normative, addressing the question of whether judges in a democratic system of governance should engage in behavior that is inherently undemocratic, at least in terms of procedural or majoritarian models of democracy (e.g., Dillard 1959; Weschler 1959; Bickel 1962). Contemporary scholars continue the normative debate (e.g., Ely 1980; Bork 1996; Ackerman 1998; Tushnet 1999) with some of these scholars continuing to express dismay at the counter-majoritarian nature of this power. Ironically, in the international community the power of judicial review, considered a component of judicial independence, is perceived somewhat differently in terms of democratization. The establishment of judicial or constitutional review is perceived to be a significant tool to protect human rights and a potential check against the arbitrary exercise of power by political and social actors (e.g., Becker 1970; International Commission of Jurists 1983; Rosenn 1987; Chowdury 1989; Ackerman 1989; Stotzky 1993; Garro 1993; Larkins 1996), and concomitantly is often a significant component of rule of law programs supported by bilateral and multilateral aid. However, for many comparativists and human rights scholars, including me, the role judicial review plays in protecting human rights remains an empirical question to be tested (Blasi and Cingranelli 1996; Keith 2002; Keith, Tate and Poe 2007; Keith and Ogundele 2007).[2] Although the interest of this book lies beyond the normative issues, perhaps the normative debate will be informed to the extent that we more fully understand the United States Supreme Court's exercise of this power through the analyses reported here.

A significant body of quantitative research has examined empirically the question of whether the U.S. Supreme Court's exercise of judicial review has countered the popularly elected branches of government, and if so under what circumstances.[3] These efforts began with Dahl (1957, 1967), who examined the influence of the Court on national policy and the antimajoritarian nature of judicial activism. Dahl concluded that the Court does not have significant policy influence because it had been unable to hold out against the national majority or the other branches of the government for long, and in only a few important cases was it able to thwart or delay the national will. In 1976 Casper updated Dahl's original analysis which he criticized for its narrow focus that ignored statutes that were overturned after four years. Taking into consideration the longer tenure of members of Congress, and the fact that Dahl ignored the much larger body of state statutes and local ordinances that Congress has nullified, Casper's analysis concluded that the Court was more influential and counter-majoritarian than Dahl believed it to be. Funston (1975), on the other hand, found that the Court was not likely to perform a counter-majoritarian role over long periods of time but rather only during a transitional period in party realignments. Handberg and Hill's more extensive analysis judged the high level of congressional court-curbing attempts to be an indicator of the Court's influence, consistent with Casper's research and countering Dahl's notion of the Court exercising its power of judicial review largely as a legitimator of current majorities (1980). Although, not specifically addressing the counter-majoritarian issue, more recent studies of congressional attempts at court-curbing demonstrate that overall Congress is not likely to take any action against the Court's nullifications, and when it does, rarely is it successful (Ignagni and Meernik 1994; Meernik and Ignagni 1997; Friedman and Harvey 2003) or the studies demonstrate that when Congress does take action it is not always even to challenge the Court's constitutional holdings but instead it is most frequently to modify legislation to fit within the Court's holding, at least to some degree (Pickerill 2005). I will return to the issue of congressional response and norms, but before moving to that issue, we need to consider another counter argument to the counter-majoritarian difficulty.

Graber (1993) has argued that the issue really is a "nonmajoritarian difficulty" (or more descriptively an "ineffective-majority difficulty") rather than a counter-majoritarian one; he argues "historically, the justices have most often exercised their power to declare state and federal practices unconstitutional only when the dominant national coalition is unable or unwilling to settle some public dispute" (36). He notes that many prominent cases stem from public disputes that crosscut existing political alignments, and that elected officials consciously invite, facilitate or bless the judiciary's attempt to resolve those political controversies that elected officials "cannot or would rather not address," and the judiciary is in turn more willing to declare statutes unconstitutional after receiving these explicit or implicit invitations (36–71). Graber casts doubt on the presupposition that when justices declare laws unconstitutional they overturn the policies preferred by the current lawmaking majorities, and instead concludes that the American political and legal history does not support the assumption. But rather "with the important exception of the New Deal, whenever a prevailing national majority clearly supported a policy, the Supreme Court declared that policy constitutional [and] whenever the Supreme Court declared a law unconstitutional, no prevailing majority clearly supported that policy" (71). Whereas Graber's analysis is limited to case studies of three key historical issue areas, more recent systematic empirical analyses, as we will see below, have also suggested that Congress is not necessarily upset with the Supreme Court's exercise of judicial review and indeed exhibits a strong norm of respect for the Court's independence in these matters.

Ferejohn's (1999) work, while primarily focusing on the separation of powers issues, reaches somewhat similar conclusions to Graber's, concerning the difficulty of forming majorities; although, he assumes Congress *wants* to curb the Court but the "diversity and heterogeneity of American political parties usually makes it difficult to form constitutional majorities capable of infringing on judicial powers" (382). Yet he argues that the popular branches are also willing to restrain from using their ample constitutional powers to curb the Court because of the "success of the appellate structure in keeping independent judges within politically acceptable bounds" (382). He argues, though, that there are periods of time in which a party experiences unity and there is temporary discipline within the parties that present dangerous times for the Court, especially on issues relating to politically weak minorities, such as criminal defendants or third world immigrants where the Court's jurisprudence may be unpopular throughout the political spectrum. Ultimately, though Ferejohn concludes that the Court's jurisprudence is not out of sync with the preferences of the elected branches for long periods of time for two reasons:

> First, judicial preferences tend to be fairly stable and resistant to change. This is so because turnover of federal bench is quite low, especially at the higher levels, and general respect for legal values of stability and predictability work to make doctrine evolve quite slowly in most areas of the law. Second, elected officials learn to be quite effective in using official resources to stabilize their hold on office for fairly long periods of time.

He identifies five periods of stable political rule, characterized by a dominant majority party or by divided government, in which he believes the Court has tended to "come into alignment with the dominant political configuration," and four periods of imbalance in which a decisive electoral shift leaves the Court out of alignment and suddenly vulnerable to attempts to alter its jurisprudence (383).[4]

Friedman and Harvey (2003), whose work primarily belongs within strategic approach, also challenge the assumption that "Congress *wants* to do anything about the Supreme Court" arguing that it is a misconception to assume that "because the Court is striking down congressional statutes, Congress disagrees with what the Court is doing" (125). In their examination of the Rehnquist Court they counter this conception, arguing that the current Court's unusually high level of nullification could instead be a "clear signal that the Court faces an ideologically congenial sitting Congress" (125). They note that despite the high level of nullification and rhetorical response to the Court's actions, Congress generally has acquiesced to the Court's rulings, and thus their ultimate premise is that "given all the actions Congress could take against the Court, the fact it is not taking those actions suggested congressional contentment with the situation" (128). They then turn their attention to the Court's behavior, and find that there is no evidence of the Court being sensitive to the ideological congruence of the *enacting* Congress but instead find that the Court is sensitive to the ideological distance from the *sitting* Congress, meaning that the Court is more likely to strike congressional action when facing a friendly Congress. Pickerill's (2005) research, on the other hand, shows that Congress does respond to judicial review in a variety of ways beyond which the work of Meernik and Ignagni (see above) or Friedman and Harvey would suggest. However, his conclusions parallel Friedman and Harvey's in that he argues that these congressional responses are not necessarily *challenges* to the Court's constitutional holdings. He posits that Congress may react to a nullification ruling in five ways: (1) do nothing, (2) amend the Constitution, (3) pass new legislation to override the Court, (4) pass legislation to circumvent the Court, or (5) pass legislation to comply with the Court. He finds that, overwhelmingly, the most common response Congress makes is to modify the legislation in a manner that complies with or makes concessions to the Court's constitutional holding, while at the same time still preserving the statutory policy in some form (162). Ultimately, Pickerill concludes that the only congressional responses that truly amounted to challenges of the Court's constitutional holdings were the congressional responses to *Oregon v. Mitchell* and *INS v. Chadha* (167).[5] Whittington's (2005) regime enforcement argument and historical analysis fits well with these scholars' conclusions. He argues that the Court sometimes engages in "friendly judicial review" that enforces the current regime's attempt to overcome obstructions to its policy goals, such as the entrenched interests of conservative legislators on the congressional reapportionment issue, the fractious party coalitions on the federal income tax issue, and the cross-pressured political coalitions on the civil rights issues. And while he does not test his theory with systematic empirical analysis, his case studies of three key historical issue areas do strongly support his expectations.

Finally, Geyh (2006) argues that Congress has largely been acquiescent to the Court, giving it oversight of the Constitution, through a gradual establishment of the customary judicial independence which became increasingly entrenched toward the end of the nineteenth century. He notes, as many of these authors do, that despite the variety of tools at Congress' disposal with which they could react to an unfavorable decision, Congress has either historically declined to use the tool or only rarely (especially in contemporary times) used their powers to respond to a case. He does point out that there has been one significant exception in which Congress has been willing to manipulate judicial decision making—the nomination process, which has been "intensely partisan and politicized since the Washington administration" (11).[6] Geyh identifies five periods when Congress curbed or attempted to rein in the Court, but his comprehensive lengthy analysis of each period and the intervening calm leads him to conclude that "although the level of criticism across the cycles may have been comparably shrill, the political branches' responses to such criticism diminished over time" (80).[7] He ultimately concludes that each cycle became less extreme, came to comparatively little, or was less significant or less destructive to customary judicial independence than it appeared (80–1). He argues that the restraint shown by Congress towards the Court, in most contexts has been reciprocated by the Court in three ways: (1) the Court has developed conflict-avoidance doctrines to sidestep retaliation; (2) the

Court has acquiesced when hostility reached its peak; and (3) the Court has exercised its powers of self-government deferentially (223). Geyh's historical analyses lead him to conclude:

> When, however, the judiciary's occasional genuflections to the legislature are reexamined in tandem with the evolution of independence norms in Congress, a more nuanced explanation emerges, in which the courts' occasional, short-term displays of deference, offered in a spirit of comity, have promoted long-term congressional acceptance of customary judicial independence (224).

Geyh cautions however that the increasingly confrontational Court may be "turning a new page on its relationship with Congress—one that is considerably less deferential" (243). But Friedman and Harvey would likely counter that the Court frequently faces an ideologically congruent Congress who may have no reason to be hostile to the court's jurisprudence.

The scholarly inquiry into the antimajoritarian nature of the Court's exercise of judicial review has evolved substantially beyond the original work of Dahl and Casper and beyond the simple extrapolation of legislative majorities forward in time to determine if the Court was acting against a sitting legislative majority. There is some evidence that Court acts, or is called upon to act, when a majority coalition is unable to form a deal with a policy issue satisfactorily and we also find some evidence that Court acts to enforce or enable policy when a sitting "friendly" Congress is obstructed in the legislative process. In addition, we find fairly strong evidence that Congress has largely acquiesced to the Court's exercise of this power and its independence generally, with relatively few periods of instability or court curbing—in part due the Court's careful exercise of the power and in part due to the stability of the legislative and judicial systems. Some of the majoritarian issues are beyond the scope of this book, but I will address some of the key hypotheses in Chapter Four, and we will also see that some of the theoretical issues raised here are a part of the dominant theoretical discourse among judicial behavioralists—the debate between the attitudinal and strategic models.[8] And thus the hypotheses that are suggested by the work of Ferejohn, Friedman, Harvey, and Geyh will be revisited in that context in the empirical chapters that follow.

Preference-Based Theories of Judicial Decision Making

Two categories of preference-based theories dominate current behavioralist research on U.S. Supreme Court decision-making: social psychological theories that focus on the justices' ideological attitudes and economic theories that focus on the justices' strategic interactions within their institutional contexts (Epstein, Hoekstra, Segal, and Spaeth 1998, 802). In the sections that follow I review these theories and their implications for understanding the Court's exercise of judicial review, and then I examine the growing body of empirical research that has sought to test the competing theories' ability to explain the justices' behavior in judicial review decisions.

The Justices' Ideology

The attitudinal model, which has its origins in the legal realist movement (Llewellyn 1931; Frank 1949) and the behavioralist movement (Pritchett 1948, 1954; Schubert 1965; Goldman 1966), generally posits that "the Supreme Court decides disputes in light of the facts of the case vis-à-vis the ideological attitudes and values of the justices" (Segal and Spaeth 1993, 65). In other words, as Segal and Spaeth explain, Rehnquist voted the way he did because he was extremely conservative and conversely, Thurgood Marshall voted the way he did because he was extremely liberal (65). Supreme Court justices are perceived to be goal-oriented actors who want case outcomes, and ultimately the law, to reflect as closely as possible their particular policy preferences, and the justices are assumed generally to be able to vote their individual policy preferences because "they lack electoral or political accountability, ambition for higher office, and comprise a court of last resort that controls its own jurisdiction" (69). Overtime measures of judicial attitudes have proven to be good predictors of the justices' votes in economic cases and in civil rights and liberties cases, the two main issue areas before the Court in the last half century (Segal and Cover 1989; Segal, Epstein, Cameron, and Spaeth 1995). Surrogate measures for the justices' ideology, such as partisan identification and appointing president, have also been used successfully to explain the justices' votes in these key issue areas, extending back to the earlier part of the last century in one study (Tate 1981; Tate and Handberg 1991).

As we examine the Supreme Court's review of congressional statutes the attitudinal model would predict, in the most simple terms, that a justice would vote to uphold those statutes that are consistent with his or her policy preferences and conversely would vote to strike those statutes which are inconsistent with his or her policy preferences. Schubert (1965, 1974) and subsequently Segal and Spaeth (1993, 2002) outlined the model more formally in terms of ideological space positing that the justices' values could be placed in ideological space or on a continuum from liberal to conservative. As an illustration, in Figure 1.1 we could place three

Figure 1.1 Justices and statutes in ideological space

justices on a continuum with Justice 1 being the most liberal and Justice 3 being the least liberal with moderate Justice 2 somewhere in between. Concomitantly, the model assumes that case stimuli can also be placed along the same continuum, and thus in congressional review cases, the policy content of a challenged congressional statute could be placed along the scale in Figure 1.1 based upon the degree to which the statute promotes liberal values. Schubert referred to the justices' positions on the scale as their "ideal points" but Segal and Spaeth more correctly identified them as "indifference points" because, continuing with our example below, a justice would vote to uphold all congressional statutes to the left of his or her "ideal point," would vote to nullify all statutes to the right of his or her "ideal point," and would be *indifferent* to whether a statute is upheld or nullified at the "ideal point."

Early empirical tests of the Court's exercise of judicial review have largely supported these expectations, repeatedly demonstrating the dominant observable influence of the justices' political preferences, even if these values have not been the sole influence on the justices' vote. While Champagne and Nagel's 1982 analysis was limited to four justices with strong reputations for judicial restraint, their empirical analysis found that the justices' nullification votes varied according to the political preference that would benefit from the decision, and the results led them to conclude that the rhetoric of judicial restraint of these four justices was primarily "a smoke screen to mask political alliances and ideologies" (316). Segal and Spaeth's systematic analysis of the Warren and Burger Court justices' exercise of judicial review demonstrated that in fact liberal justices were more likely to strike laws that infringe on individuals civil liberties and that conservative justices were more likely to strike laws that infringe on business interests (1993, 321–22).[9] These findings found support in their subsequent analysis of the Rehnquist Court's nullification of federal, state, and local laws which demonstrated that with only two exceptions "every justice displays an attitudinal pattern: They vote to uphold either conservative or liberal laws, but never both" (2002, 415). Sala and Spriggs (2004) in their rigorous examination of the separation of powers model, which I will discuss below, found that the justices' ideology was the strongest predictor of the justices' votes on the constitutionality of federal statutes from 1946 to 1999, once again with liberal justices more likely to strike conservative laws and vice versa. These results were supported by Solberg and Lindquist's extensive analysis of the Rehnquist Court's review of federal, state, and local statutes (2006), which led the authors to conclude that even though the justices' votes depended to some degree on whether a federal or state statute was under review, the votes depended "far more profoundly on the underlying ideological dimension reflected in the statute at issue" (259). While Lindquist and Solberg's study of both the Burger and Rehnquist Courts' constitutional review of federal, state, and local statutes found that the justices' votes in these cases are "the product of a nuanced process" in which the justices' behavior was also influenced by institutional and contextual factors, they again concluded that the process is "strongly governed by the justices' policy preferences" (2007, 88). Keck's (2007) examination of cases striking federal statutes from 1981–2005 finds some support for the attitudinal model but finds substantial evidence that institutional roles must be at work as well. He finds that most nullification decisions are mixed coalitions of liberals and conservatives in almost two-thirds of all the congressional nullification decisions in that period and in almost one-half of those that are nonunanimous decisions. Thus he concludes that there are some distinct judicial motivations or there is a sense of duty in some conflicts which divide judges from legislators rather than, or perhaps more than, it divides Democrats from Republicans or liberals from conservatives (331). Most of the recent empirical studies of the Supreme Court's exercise of the power of judicial review have focused on either the justices' votes in nullification decisions or their votes in the full set of constitutional review cases. However, Howard and Segal's (2004) work extends empirical research beyond the Court's opinions as they examine all briefs filed by litigants over a ten-term period requesting judicial review. Although they find a strong level of deference for Congress, particularly in that the Court never strikes laws *sua sponte,* they, too, conclude that "clearly, ideological considerations predominate the decision to strike legislation" (138). Fewer researchers have examined the justices' exercise of judicial review of presidential action, and the focus of these inquiries has tended toward the "two presidencies" hypothesis examining the issue area success of the president (Yates and Whitford 1998; King and Meernik 1999). Even so, the strong influence of the justices' political preferences (both the justice's political party and ideology) continues to be observed in these votes as well (Yates and Whitford, 544).[10] Taken as whole, the systematic empirical research has clearly demonstrated strong support for attitudinal effects, but as we will see in the sections that follow, many of these studies have also suggested that our understandings of the Court's exercise of its power is not complete without a consideration of institutional influences. It is those concerns that I turn to next.

Strategic Considerations and Institutional Context

The attitudinal model assumes that the Supreme Court justices are primarily seekers of legal policy who are largely unconstrained by the political system in voting their individual ideological attitudes (Rhode and Spaeth 1976; Segal and Spaeth 1993; Segal and Spaeth 2002). The strategic account of judicial behavior, derived in part from the early work of Walter Murphy (1964) and more formally from the rational choice model, also assumes the justices to be primarily seekers of legal policy; however, the justices are not perceived as unconstrained actors, but rather are seen as "strategic actors who realize that their ability to achieve their goals depends on a consideration of the preferences of other actors, the choices they expect others to make, and the institutional context in which they act" (Epstein and Knight 1998, 10). The justices may be constrained by external institutional features such as the separation of powers system (Marks 1988) or by internal institutional constraints such as formal rules or informal norms that limit the justices' choices (Epstein and Knight 1998; Maltzman, Spriggs, and Wahlbeck 2000).

Of particular relevance here, separation of powers models argue that other political actors, Congress in particular, possess a variety of tools to curb the Court's rulings, especially in statutory interpretation cases, and therefore, the justices must act strategically to defuse possible negative consequences (Ferejohn and Shipan 1990; Eskridge 1991; Spiller and Gely 1992; Hansford and Damore 2000). Indeed, Ignagni and Meernik (1994) found that Congress reacted to Supreme Court overruling of congressional statutes in almost thirty percent of the instances.[11] Most proponents of the strategic approach, however, argue that the justices will be less constrained, and therefore less strategic, in their votes in constitutional cases where Congress has infrequently overturned the Court's decisions (Eskridge 1991; Epstein and Knight 1998). Even though Epstein and Knight expect that the justices will thus be "less attentive to the preferences and likely actions of other actors in constitutional disputes than statutory cases," they argue that we should not expect the Court to ignore completely the inter-branch constraint in these cases for three reasons (142). Even though Congress may not often override constitutional rulings, the mere fact that Congress may do so in the future may be sufficient to cause the justices to pay some attention to Congress' preferences. In addition, Congress has other weapons that it has used in the past to punish justices, such as removing the Court's jurisdiction or punishing the justices by holding their salaries constant. Finally, the other branches may simply refuse to implement the Court's policies. Interestingly, Epstein and Knight found in their analysis of the justices' papers that the justices actually discussed the preferences of other actors in 46 percent of the constitutional cases, while not as prevalent as in nonconstitutional cases—70 percent—it is still close to half of the cases.[12] Although the strategic approach has strong theoretical appeal, empirical evidence to support the separation of powers model has been rather weak thus far (e.g., Eskridge 1991; Hansford and Damore 2000; Spriggs and Hansford 2001; Howard and Segal 2004; see, Segal and Spaeth 2002, for comprehensive summary). Most notable here, recent large-*N* studies of the Court's exercise of constitutional review have found no observable evidence of strategic influences (Howard and Segal 2004; Sala and Spriggs 2004; Segal and Westerland 2005) but, as we saw above, Friedman and Harvey (2003) did find evidence of the strategic influence rather than attitudinal influence, and Lindquist and Solberg (2007) did find cross-institutional influences in that the Court was less likely to nullify statutes when the ideological direction of the law more closely matched the ideological direction of Congress and when the solicitor argued against nullification as amicus in the case. I will explore some of these findings and the inconsistency in the empirical evidence in Chapters Three and Five.

The institutional context that constrains or influences the justices' behavior is not limited to the formal structure of government and actors external to the Court, but rather it also encompasses informal institutions such as the norm of *stare decisis* and informal rules and procedures such as the requirement that the chief justice or senior most just assigning the majority opinion when in the conference majority or the requirement that precedent have the support of a majority of the sitting justices (Maltzman, Wahlbeck, and Spriggs 2000, 14). These influences can constrain the justices' ability to achieve their preferred goals, such as the collegial requirements of the Rule of Four and for a majority of the justices to be in agreement with their preferred jurisprudence in a particular case. Empirical research, relying on the justices' private papers, has demonstrated convincingly that at every stage of the decision-making processes the justices' decisions, while affected by their own ideological preferences, are also shaped by consideration of their colleagues' preferences and expected actions (Brenner 1989; Epstein and Knight 1998; Maltzman, Spriggs, and Wahlbeck 2000). On the other hand the institutional context may actually present the justice with a contravening goal, such as adhering to the norms of *stare decisis* or judicial restraint, or the goal of protecting or enhancing institutional legitimacy (especially for the chief justice), that weighs against the justices' individual policy goals (Epstein and Knight 1998). Empirical research has demonstrated that some norms, such as *stare decisis* are undeniably present on the bench (Brenner and Spaeth 1995; Knight and Epstein 1996; Epstein and Knight 1998).[13] Although these empirical studies have shown that precedents do influence the justices' decision making (Epstein and Knight 1998; Spriggs and Hansford 2001), much of the evidence suggests that adherence to precedence is a function of the justices' ideology. Of course, the interest of this book here involves the alleged norm of judicial restraint, or deference to the elected branches. Its existence remains somewhat of an empirical question at this point, but the descriptive data of Chapter Two strongly demonstrates that the justices do behave as though the norm exists, at least in regard to Congress—striking congressional action less than 20 percent of the time it is presented opportunity to do so. However, we will also see that this norm has varied across Courts and across justices. The work of Lindquist and Solberg (2007) illustrated that the norm may be less viable in terms of state and local statutes than congressional ones; the Rehnquist and Burger Courts nullified congressional statutes in only approximately 30 percent of the review cases but the rate rose to almost 50 percent in terms of state and local statutes (80). Of course, the crux of the analysis here is to explain under what circumstances the Court or individual justices are willing to act or vote against this norm of deference. As mentioned above, to ferret much of the informal institutional context, we must rely primarily upon the justices' private papers such as docket books and memoranda, or in regard to some norms, such as *sua sponte,* we must rely upon the case briefs (e.g., Howard and Segal 2004), or rare interviews with court personnel (Perry 1991), each of which is certainly prohibitive, if not impossible, in terms of two hundred years of the Court's history. In Chapter Five, I will present the major hypotheses and alternative hypotheses that may be gleaned from these competing theoretical accounts, and then specify and estimate multivariate models to test the expectations empirically.

Outline of the Book

In **Chapter Two** I will present the process through which I identified the cases under study here, and will present a descriptive analysis of the Court's behavior over time. In this chapter we will see that the Court exhibits a strong norm of deference to Congress across the entire history over review here, much higher even than the level that the president receives even in national security and foreign policy matters. The number of Supreme Court cases challenging Congress increases gradually following the Civil War and Reconstruction, with a concomitant increase in the number of nullifications of Congress. However, the dominant trend across the Court's history remains one of supporting Congress, with exceptions primarily during the decades of the 1960s and the 1990s. There is also a decline in the proportion of cases nullifying Congress during times of national crises, specifically the two world wars. Not only does the level of judicial review and nullification rates vary across chief justice courts, the ideological outcomes produce a significant pattern of the Courts supporting primarily one ideological position or other, but not usually both. Some Courts such as the Taney Court, the Stone Court, and the Burger Court also show the particularly high levels of ideological consistency associated with the Warren and Rehnquist Courts. In this chapter we also see an interesting pattern when the ideological direction of the outcomes are delineated according to whether the Court is acting to nullify or acting to uphold Congress—when the Court does decide to go against the norm of deference it usually does so in a single ideological direction that is quite extreme from the direction of its votes to uphold congressional statutes. Finally, the Court treats the issue-areas before it somewhat differently, at least at the aggregate level. The Court is most likely to nullify Congress on First Amendment and criminal procedure issues, followed by issues of judicial power and federalism. We find that counter to normative expectations, in the broad category of civil rights and civil liberties (criminal procedure, First Amendment, civil rights and due process issue-areas) the Court is much more likely to vote against rather than support rights claims. In this set of cases, the Court is also much more likely to support judicial power and federal power over state rights, and is more likely to vote in the liberal direction on economic issues. But when the analysis is limited to the rarer occasions when the Court nullifies Congress, then we will find the Court more likely to support rights claims, business interests, and property rights.

In **Chapter Three** I present an initial examination of the justices' congressional review votes and we will be able to observe several significant patterns across the justices' votes. First, even though the justices on average are highly deferential to Congress, we are able to identify significant numbers of justices who depart from the norm. We also find among the justices who are most willing to challenge Congress both liberals and conservatives, and both Democrats and Republicans. We also see that after Warren joins the bench very few justices have extremely deferential scores, and more specifically we find that all of the recent justices on the bench (excluding Roberts and Alito who are not included here) place within the top thirteen nullification rates of the justices to have served on the bench. When we examine the ideological dimension of these votes we will find several significant patterns as well. First, we see that the majority of the justices' votes fall in the moderate range, with only small proportions of the justices earning scores that could be considered consistently liberal or conservative. However, this finding also has an over-time caveat, in that as we move into the appointees of Franklin Roosevelt and beyond, the moderate tendency disappears rather quickly. Overall, the ideological dimension of the justices' votes in congressional review cases tends to be moderate in comparison to the liberalism scores based on the full set of the justices' decisions or key issue areas across the justices' tenure. We also will see that when we separate out the justices' votes to nullify from those to uphold, the nullification votes were more likely to be more extreme. However, it is interesting to note that the movement in ideology was in the liberal direction. In fact when we examine justices with large differences between their upheld votes and votes to nullify, we find that the difference was primarily with justices being more liberal in their nullifying votes than in their votes to uphold Congress.

When we examine the votes across issues, again, we will find several important trends as well. We find that on average, the justices were much less likely to support civil rights and civil liberties claims, despite the claim that judicial review is most legitimately exercised in regard to rights-based claims. We will see that the justices were much more likely to support national government claims over states' rights claims and against tax-payer claims. We also find that justices on average were much more likely to vote against business claims in favor of government regulation.

Chapter Four will examine the key majoritarian issues that arise in Court's exercise of judicial review. We see that at least in regard to the Court's exercise of this power in congressional review cases, it is some somewhat more majoritarian than counter-majoritarian, along multiple dimensions. We see that the overwhelming majority of the statutes are old enough that their enacting majorities would seem to represent a significantly different Congress than the sitting majority in Congress. And while we will find that nullifying decisions appear to be less majoritarian than those that uphold Congress, the level is not nearly as much as we might expect. In regard to the development of constitutional jurisprudence, we will see that only a small percentage of these review cases can be considered landmark, particularly those upholding congressional statutes, and still even among the nullification cases less than half are considered landmark cases. Overall, the chapter will find that Dahl's assessment is more accurate than his critics. However, it will be demonstrated that the Court in these decisions, whether nullifying or upholding, is not acting consistently in the general policy direction of the sitting Congress, unless the sitting Congress is at least in part controlled by Democrats. In regard to the final majoritarian issue, we will also find that the Court largely acts in a majoritarian role, not as the bulwark against intrusions against minority rights by the political majority.

In **Chapter Five** I will present the major hypotheses that can be derived from the dominant theories with judicial behavior and empirically test them in full multivariate models of the justices' individual votes. The models will examine the justices' behavior across the full time period and in smaller historic time periods as well. Overall, we will see that when we examine the full set of votes across the entire time period, the attitudinal and institutional influences are better explanators than those associated with the strategic model. Even as we break down the analyses by historic periods, we will continue to see that overall the factors associated with the attitudinal model perform much better than those associated with the strategic approach. However, we will also see that with one significant exception the explanations for the justices' behavior that are currently accepted do not tend to transfer backwards in time as robustly.

Chapter Six will present the final conclusions we can draw across the broad set of analyses presented in the book and will discuss the implications in terms of theories of judicial behavior, and in regard to the global expectations for judicial independence and the exercise of judicial review. The chapter will also consider the limitations of these analyses and their implications for future study.

Notes

1. The Eleventh Amendment undid *Chisholm v. Georgia*, 2 Dall. (2 U.S.) 419 (1793), which had ruled that citizens could sue a state other than their own state; the Fourteenth Amendment undid *Dred Scott v. Sandford*, 19 How. (60 U.S.) 393 (1857); the Sixteenth Amendment undid *Pollock v. Farmers' Loan and Trust Company*, 157 U.S. 429 (1895), which had declared a federal income tax unconstitutional; and the Twenty-Sixth Amendment, which gave 18 year-olds the right to vote, undid *Oregon v. Mitchell*, 400 U.S. 112 (1970). See Segal and Spaeth (1993).

2. Initial empirical tests have suggested that formal judicial review is not a factor in reducing human rights abuse, but rather is associated with increased levels of abuse. Current efforts are under way to refine and extend these studies in order to more rigorously further test the relationship.

3. While the body of research that is specifically relevant here has dealt with the counter-majoritarian nature in relationship to either the partisan or ideological make-up of Congress and the executive, other studies have examined public opinion or mood as an indication of majority will (e.g., Barnum 1985; Marshall 1989; Mishler and Sheehan 1996; Flemming and Wood 1997). Clearly, the lack of public opinion data back into the eighteenth and nineteenth centuries makes it impossible to consider that dimension directly in this work, except to the extent that public

opinion is reflected indirectly through elections of presidents and congresses affiliated with party parties and the policy preferences they represent.

4. The stable periods of dominant majority party are the Democrats (1828–1860 and 1932–1968) and the Republicans (1898–1930) and divided government (1876–1896 and 1968–1994). The imbalance occurred following Jefferson's first election in 1800, during the post-Civil War period, during the early years of the New Deal period, and following the 1994 congressional elections.

5. Pickerill notes that Congress may respond differently to the Court's nullification of state statutes and even to the court's votes to uphold congressional statutes.

6. Ferejohn (1999) also makes this assertion.

7. These include: (1) the court packing, unpacking and impeachment when the Federalists lose power and Jefferson becomes president; (2) altercations between the Marshall Court and the Jackson administration; (3) confrontations with the Republicans before, during and after the Civil War; (4) Populist, Progressive and New Deal criticisms of the Supreme Court; and (5) the backlash against the Warren Court in the mid-twentieth century.

8. I mentioned at the beginning of the chapter that there is an additional dimension to the majoritarian issue of judicial review—its role in preventing "tyranny of the majority," especially in regard to fundamental rights. I will address this issue in the next chapter.

9. Their analysis also included the first four terms of the Rehnquist Court.

10. Ducat and Dudley who examined federal district judges rather than the Supreme Court justices also found a relationship with the appointing president but not with the justices' political party. The difference in results is likely due to the different institutional context which I will discuss in the next section. Segal, Howard, and Timpone (2000), while not examining support for presidential action, examined support for the president's policy positions and found that the justices tended to vote in sync with their appointing president but generally the affect only lasted the first four terms on the bench for civil liberties issues and the first ten to twelve years for economic issues.

11. But it should be noted that it was in only 13 of 19 attempts (68 percent) where Congress reported a bill out of committee, and the legislation was signed and passed into law, which means Congress was only successful its reaction nineteen percent of the time. I will return to this issue in Chapters Three and Five and examine other theoretical and empirical expectations concerning congressional reaction.

12. And they found that the cases in which there was no discussion of the other political actors' preferences were in large part criminal due process cases (18 out of 37), and they note that it is a given that Congress goes against the criminal defendant's rights. If these cases are removed, then they find the justices referred to other political actors' preferences in approximately 60 percent of the constitutional cases (150).

13. Epstein and Knight report that only 196 cases decided through 1990 overturned Court precedent (Epstein and Knight 1998, 175–76). Brenner and Spaeth (1995) found only 154 precedents that were overruled on the Vinson through Rehnquist Courts (average of 2.5 cases per term). Knight and Epstein examined cases overruled as a percentage of all cases available for overruling and found less than .007 across the entire history of the Court (.002 percent or less from 1811 forward) (1996, 176). Even though, the authors use somewhat varying measurement for overruling precedent, they still reach the same conclusion about the existence of the norm of stare decisis if not agreement on the level of the norm.

References

Ackerman, Bruce. 1998. *We The People: Transformations*. Cambridge: Harvard University Press.

Becker, Theodore. 1970. *Comparative Judicial Politics*. Landham, MD: University Press of America.

Bickel, Alexander. 1962. *The Least Dangerous Branch: The Supreme Court at the Bar of Politics*. Indianapolis: Bobbs-Merrill.

Blasi, Gerard J., and David L. Cingranelli. 1996. "Do Constitutions and Institutions Help Protect Human Rights?" In *Human Rights and Developing Countries*, ed. David Cingranelli. Greenwich, CT: JAI Press.

Bork, Robert. 1996. *Slouching to Gomorrah: Modern Liberalism and American Decline*. New York: Regan Books.

Brenner, Saul. 1989. "Ideological Voting on the Vinson Court: A Comparison of Original & Final Votes on the Merits." *Polity* 22: 157–64.

Brenner, Saul and Harold J. Spaeth. 1995. *Stare Indecisis: The Alteration of Precedent on the Supreme Court, 1946–1992*. New York: Cambridge University Press.

Casper, Jonathan D. 1976. "The Supreme Court and National Policy Making." *American Political Science Review* 70: 50–63.

Champagne, Anthony and Stuart S. Nagel. 1982. "The Advocates of Restraint: Holmes, Brandeis, Stone, and Frankfurter." In *Supreme Court Activism and Restraint*, eds. Stephen C. Halpern and Charles M. Lamb. Lexington, MA: Lexington Books.

Chowdhury, Subrata Roy. 1989. *Rule of Law in a State of Emergency*. New York: St. Martin's Press.

Dahl, Robert A. 1957. "Decision-Making in a Democracy: The Supreme Court as a National Policy Maker." *Journal of Public Law* 6: 279–95.

Dahl, Robert A. 1967. *Pluralist Democracy in the United States*. Chicago: RAND McNally and Company.

De Tocqueville, Alexis. 1966. *Democracy in America*, ed. J.P. Mayer. New York: Harper and Row.

Devins, Neal and Keith E. Whittington, eds. 2005. *Congress and the Constitution*. Durham: Duke University Press.

Dilliard, Irving. 1959. *The Spirit of Liberty Papers and Addresses of Judge Learned Hand*. New York: Knopf.

Ducat, Craig and Robert L. Dudley. 1989. "Federal District Judges and Presidential Power During the Postwar Era." *The Journal of Politics* 51: 98–118.

Ely, John Hart. 1980. *Democracy and Distrust: A Theory of Judicial Review*. Cambridge: Harvard University Press.

Epstein, Lee and Jack Knight. 1998. *The Choices Judges Make*. Washington, DC: Congressional Quarterly Press.

Epstein, Lee, Valerie Hoekstra, Jeffrey A. Segal, and Harold J. Spaeth. 1998. "Do Political Preferences Change? A Longitudinal Study of US Supreme Court Justices." *Journal of Politics* 60: 801–18.

Epstein, Richard. 2000. "Undue Restraint: Why Judicial Activism Has Its Place." *National Review* 52: 26.

Eskridge, William N. 1991. "Overriding Supreme Court Statutory Interpretation Decisions." *Yale Law Journal* 101: 331–455.

Ferejohn, John. 1999. "Independent Judges, Dependent Judiciary: Explaining Judicial Independence." 72: 353–84.

Ferejohn, John A. and Charles Shipan. 1990. "Congressional Influence on Bureaucracy." *Journal of Law, Economics, and Organization* 6: 1–20.

Frank, Jerome. 1949. *Law and the Modern Mind*. New York: Coward-McCann.

Friedman, Barry and Anna Harvey. 2003. "Electing the Supreme Court." *Indiana Law Journal* 78: 123–39.

Funston, Richard. 1975. "The Supreme Court and Critical Elections." *American Political Science Review* 69: 795–811.

Garro, Alejandro. 1993. "Nine Years to Democracy in Argentina: Partial Failure or Qualified Success?" *Columbia Journal of Transnational Law* 31: 1–102.

George, Tracey E., and Lee Epstein. 1992. "On the Nature of Supreme Court Decision Making." *American Political Science Review* 86(3): 323–37.

Geyh, Charles Gardner. 2006. *When Courts and Congress Collide: The Struggle for Control of America's Judicial System*. Ann Arbor: University of Michigan Press.

Goldman, Sheldon. 1966. "Voting Behavior of the United States Courts of Appeals, 1961–1964." *American Political Science Review* 60: 374–84.

Graber, Mark A. 1993. "The Non-Majoritarian Difficulty: Legislative Deference to the Judiciary." *Studies in American Political Development* 7: 35–73.

Hansford, Thomas and David F. Damore. 2000. "Congressional Preferences, Perceptions of Threat, and Supreme Court Decision Making." *American Politics Quarterly* 28: 490–510.

Howard, Robert M., and Jeffrey A. Segal. 2004. "A Preference for Deference? The Supreme Court and Judicial Review." *Political Research Quarterly* 57(1): 131–43.

Ignagni, Joseph and James Meernik. 1994. "Explaining Congressional Attempts to Reverse Supreme Court Decisions." *Political Research Quarterly* 47: 353-71.

International Commission of Jurists. 1983. *States of Emergency: Their Impact on Human Rights.* Geneva: International Commission of Jurists.

Keck, Thomas. 2007. "Party, Policy, or Duty: Why Does the Supreme Court Invalidate Federal Statutes?" *American Political Science Review* 101: 321–39.

Keith, Linda Camp. 2002. "International Principles for Formal Judicial Independence: Trends in National Constitutions and Their Impact (1976 to 1996)." *Judicature* 85: 194–200.

Keith, Linda Camp. 2002. "Constitutional Provisions for Individual Human Rights (1976–1996): Are They More than Mere 'Window Dressing?'" *Political Research Quarterly* (March) 55: 111–43.

Keith, Linda Camp and Ayo Ogundele. 2007. "Legal Systems and Constitutionalism in Sub-Saharan Africa: An Empirical Examination of Colonial Influences on Human Rights." *Human Rights Quarterly* 29(4): 1065–1097.

Keith, Linda Camp, C. Neal Tate, and Steven C. Poe. 2007. "Is the Law a Mere Parchment Barrier to Human Rights Abuse?" Unpublished manuscript.

King, Kimi and James Meernik. 1999. "The Supreme Court and the Powers of the Executive: The Adjudication of Foreign Policy." *Political Research Quarterly* 52: 801–24.

Knight, Jack and Lee Epstein. 1996. "On the Struggle for Judicial Supremacy." *Law and Society Review* 30: 87–120.

Larkins, Christopher M. 1996. "Judicial Independence and Democratization: A Theoretical and Conceptual Analysis." *American Journal of Comparative Law* 44: 605–26.

Lindquist, Stephanie A. and Rorie Spill Solberg. 2007. "Judicial Review by the Burger and Rehnquist Courts: Explaining Justices' Responses to Constitutional Challenges." *Political Research Quarterly* 60: 71–90.

Llewellyn, Karl. 1931. "Some Realism about Realism—Responding to Dean Pound." *Harvard Law Review* 44: 1222–64.

Maltzman, Forest, James F. Spriggs III, and Paul Wahlbeck. 2000. *Crafting Law on the Supreme Court: The Collegial Game.* Cambridge, UK: Cambridge University Press.

Marks, Brian. 1988. "A Model of Judicial Influence on Congressional Policymaking: *Grove City College v. Bell,*" working papers in Political Science, 88–7, Hoover Institution, Stanford University.

Meernik, James and Joseph Ignagni. 1997. "Congressional Attacks on Supreme Court Rulings Involving Unconstitutional State Laws." *Political Research Quarterly* 48(1): 43–59.

Murphy, Walter F. 1964. *Elements of Judicial Strategy.* Chicago: University of Chicago Press.

Parker, Richard. 1981. "The Past of Constitutional Theory—And Its Future." *Ohio State Law Review* 43: 233.

Perry, H.W. Jr. 1991. *Deciding to Decide.* Cambridge, MA: Harvard University Press.

Pickerill, J. Mitchell. 2005. "Congressional Responses to Judicial Review." In *Congress and the Constitution,* eds. Neal Devins and Keith E. Whittington. Durham: Duke University Press.

Pritchett C. Herman. 1948. *The Roosevelt Court: A Study in Judicial Politics and Values.* New York: McMillan Press.

Pritchett C. Herman. 1954. *Civil Liberties and the Vinson Court.* Chicago: University of Chicago Press.

Rohde, David W. and Harold J. Spaeth. 1976. *Supreme Court Decision Making.* San Francisco, CA: W.H. Freeman.

Rosenn, Keith S. 1987. "The Protection of Judicial Independence in Latin America." *University of Miami Inter-American Law Review* 19: 1–35.

Sala, Brian R. and James F. Spriggs. 2004. "Designing Tests of the Supreme Court and the Separation of Powers." *Political Research Quarterly* 57: 197–208.

Schubert, Glendon A. 1965. *The Judicial Mind.* Evanston: Northwestern University Press.

Schubert, Glendon A. 1974. *The Judicial Mind Revisited: Psychometric Analysis of the Supreme Court Ideology.* New York: Oxford Press.

Schwartz, Bernard. 1993. *A History of the Supreme Court.* New York: Oxford University Press.

Segal, Jeffrey A. and Albert Cover. 1989. "Ideological Values and the Votes of U.S. Supreme Court Justices." *American Political Science Review* 83: 557–65.

Segal, Jeffrey A., Lee Epstein, Charles M. Cameron, and Harold D. Spaeth. 1995. "Ideological Values and the Votes of U.S. Supreme Court Justices Revisited." *Journal of Politics* 57: 812–23.

Segal, Jeffrey A. and Harold J. Spaeth. 1993. *The Supreme Court and the Attitudinal Model.* Cambridge: Cambridge University Press.

Segal, Jeffrey A., Robert M. Howard, and Richard J. Timpone. 2000. *Political Research Quarterly* 53: 557–73.

Segal, Jeffrey A. and Harold J. Spaeth. 2002. *The Supreme Court and the Attitudinal Model Revisited.* Cambridge: Cambridge University Press.

Segal, Jeffrey A. and Chad Westerland. 2005. "The Supreme Court, Congress, and Judicial Review." *North Carolina Law Review* 83: 101–66.

Solberg, Rorie Spill, and Stephanie Lindquist. 2006. "Activism, Ideology, and Federalism: Judicial Behavior in Constitutional Challenges Before the Rehnquist Court, 1986–2000." *Journal of Empirical Legal Studies* 3: 237–61.

Spiller, Palo T. and Emerson H. Tiller. 1996. "Invitations to Override: Congressional Reversals of Supreme Court Decisions." *International Review of Law and Economics* 16: 503–21.

Spriggs, James F. III and Thomas G. Hansford. 2001. "Explaining the Overruling of U.S. Supreme Court Precedent." *Journal of Politics* 63: 1091–1111.

Stotzky, Irwin P. 1993. "The Tradition of Constitutional Adjudication." In *Transitions to Democracy in Latin America: The Role of the Judiciary*, ed. Irwin P. Stotzky. Boulder, CO: Westview.

Tate, C. Neal. 1981. "Personal Attribute Models of the Voting Behavior of U.S. Supreme Court Justices: Liberalism in Civil Liberties and Economic Decisions, 1946–1978." *American Political Science Review* 75: 355–67.

Tate, C. Neal and Roger Handberg. 1991. "Time Building and Theory Building in Personal Attribute Models of Supreme Court Voting Behavior, 1916–88." *American Journal of Political Science* 35: 460–80.

Tushnet, Robert. 1999. *Taking the Constitution Away from the Courts.* Princeton: Princeton University Press.

Weschler, Herbert. 1959. "Toward Neutral Principles of Constitutional Law." *Harvard Law Review* 73:1–35.

Whittington, Keith. 2005. "Interpose Your Friendly Hand: Political Supports for the Exercise of Judicial Review by the United States Supreme Court." *American Political Science Review* 99: 583–96.

Yates, Jeff and Andrew Whitford. 1998. "Presidential Power and the United States Supreme Court." *Political Research Quarterly* 51: 539–50.

Judicial Review:
The Norm of Deference
and its Contours

Cases of Supreme Court Review of Congress

As we saw in the first chapter most empirical studies and case studies alike have tended to focus only on the instances of the Supreme Court exercising judicial review to nullify congressional statutes, ignoring the larger body of decisions in which the Court upholds Congress.[1] This limited focus has been driven in part by normative or theoretical concerns, such as the counter-majoritarian difficulty, which are not as obviously linked to the Court's decisions to uphold Congress as perhaps they should be. In part, the incomplete attention to the full variation in the Court's judicial review behavior, especially in systematic empirical analyses, has stemmed from a lack of readily available data. Comprehensive lists of Supreme Court cases overturning congressional statutes are widely available but no such lists exist that catalog cases in which congressional statutes faced constitutional challenges but were upheld rather than nullified. Harold Spaeth's widely used *U.S. Supreme Court Judicial Data Base* does include a variable that can be searched to identify cases from the 1946 term forward in which the Supreme Court determined the constitutionality of national government action; Spaeth's source is the individual case syllabus. In the last few years political scientists have belatedly begun to use this database to explore this fuller dimension of the Court's judicial review behavior, at least in the Rehnquist or Burger Courts.

I began my effort to build a dataset of the Court's entire history of exercising judicial review with Spaeth's dataset. For the years 1947–2001 I was able to identify 336 such cases in the database.[2] I then expanded backwards the dataset to cover all years prior to 1947, closely following Spaeth's guidelines so that my data will be consistent with his data.[3] I conducted LEXIS key word searches of all Supreme Court syllabi prior to 1947 to identify cases in which the Court determined the constitutionality of Congress's actions.[4] In order to do the most comprehensive and appropriate word searches, I generated a list of key–word pairings by reading (1) the syllabi of cases identified from the Spaeth dataset as determining constitutionality of congressional statutes and (2) cases identified in Library of Congress lists as congressional nullification cases.[5] Using LEXIS I ran key word searches on case syllabi to identify *potential* congressional review cases until I reached the point that multiple word searches repeatedly failed to produce any new hits. I personally read all cases that these searches identified as hits and I culled out the cases where the Supreme Court actually determined the constitutionality of congressional action. Ultimately I examined the Supreme Court's own words in the arguments of the opinion to answer the question—did the "majority determine the constitutionality" of the congressional statute at issue in disposing of the case? This follows Spaeth's specific coding rules. Thus, cases in which the Court dismissed on technicalities (lack of jurisdiction, lack of standing, lack of actual controversy) were not included in the dataset here.

In regard to *Ashwander*-type principles, which the Court actually discusses in many cases prior to the *Ashwander* decision with Brandeis giving full citation of these cases in his *Ashwander* concurring footnote, I followed as consistently as possible the language of the Court's opinion itself and Spaeth's coding rule. Obviously, in regard to the Spaeth data, he and his coders made the final call, and I cannot know how many cases they rejected in their coding. However, in regard to the pre-Spaeth data I personally made the final call, and I tried to employ logic that was consistent with the intent of the Spaeth rule. For the 1803–1946 period I had a relatively small number of cases, 31 cases in 567 cases, in which I had to deal with *Ashwander*-type issues. Of these 31 cases, 16 ultimately were rejected from the dataset and 15 were accepted, a fairly even split.

Of the 16 cases that were rejected, there were generally 3 or 4 types of reasoning in the opinion that I felt did not fit the decision rule here. First, the Court argues that it cannot or will not deal with the constitutional issue because the Court below made no mention of the constitutional questions; for example *Duignan v. U.S.* (1927). In addition, I rejected cases in which the Court dismisses the constitutional issue as a frivolous federal question; for example, *United Surety Co. v. American Fruit* (1915). I also rejected cases in which the Court *digged* the case—dismissing as improvidently granted; for example, *Moor v. Texas* (1936). Finally, I rejected cases in which even though the constitutionality of a congressional statute is raised, the Court says that it does not consider it here because there are other grounds upon which the case may be disposed of; for example, *McCurdy v.*

U.S. (1918). I believe these decisions are consistent with Spaeth's standard of the majority "determined the constitutionality of the statute."

Of the fifteen cases that were accepted in the dataset, the cases were generally dealing with *Ashwander*-type reasoning, in which Court has said that "when the validity of an act of the Congress is drawn into question, and even if a serious doubt of constitutionality is raised, it is the cardinal principle that this Court will ascertain whether a construction of the statute is fairly possible by which the question may be avoided." If we take this principle literally, it appears that such language would put a case in the category above. The cases would be rejected as *McCurdy* above was. However, in regard to these fifteen specific cases, when the *language of the opinion* is examined closely, what the Court is ultimately deciding is whether the statute can be construed to avoid the claim of *un*constitutionality— construed to be constitutional. Thus we see language in which a judgment of constitutionality is actually expressed by the Court. For example, the opinion in *Bingham v. U.S.* (1935) says that "acts of Congress are to be construed, if possible to avoid grave doubts of their constitutionality" and then goes on to conclude its argument with the language "So construed, Section 402(f) is constitutional." In *Becker v. Cummings Steel* (1935) we see the Court use the language: "any other construction … would raise grave doubts of the constitutionality of the statute as applied to non-enemies." This language implies a judgment that as constructed the act is constitutional and upheld. And in *Reineche v. Northern Trust Company* (1929) we actually see the language referring to the statute being upheld: "Doubts of constitutionality of the statute, if construed as contended by the government, would require us to adopt the construction, at least reasonably possible here, which would uphold the act." Again, the guiding practice was to examine and follow fully the language of the Court used throughout the opinion. In this set of fifteen cases, the Court was construing a statute to avoid finding a statute *unconstitutional*, and in construing the statute thusly, was in fact "determining the statute to be constitutional" which fits the Spaeth rule.

The case-by-case examination of the LEXIS search-produced hits resulted in the identification of 560 congressional review cases. Upon completion of this step, I then conducted a double check based on LEXIS *headnotes* rather than syllabi to insure that my search was exhaustive enough and not biased against earlier years of the Court's history. I selected random years in each decade and then reviewed the LEXIS headnotes for *all cases* in each of those individual years. Through this process I verified that for each of the random years no constitutional cases were missed by using the syllabus search method. Combining my set of cases with those identified through the Spaeth data base produces a set of 896 Supreme Court cases that review congressional statutes. I believe the rigorous search process and reliability checks on the search results gave me a dataset in which we can be highly confident that I have the complete set of constitutional review cases of Congress for the first two-hundred years of the Court's history.[6]

The Norm of Supreme Court Deference to Congress

As we saw in Chapter One, Geyh (2006) noted that Congress has established a norm of judicial independence or "customary judicial independence" as he terms it, in which Congress is largely deferential towards the Court's constitutional holdings. He bases his conceptualization on Glennon's (1984) work on the establishment of customs that regulate the relationship between government branches under a separation of powers system. Glennon identifies six factors that contribute to the establishment of custom which could be extended and applied just as well to the Supreme Court's level of deference to Congress: (1) CONSISTENCY: the similarity of the unrelated historical events that constitute a custom; (2) NUMEROSITY: the number of times a custom has been repeated; (3) DURATION: the period of time over which an act has been repeated; (4) DENSITY: the number of times an act has been repeated over its duration; (5) CONTINUITY: the regularity with which the act is repeated over its duration; and (6) NORMALCY: the extent to which the act has been performed across different Courts, so as to exist independently of the personalities or political agendas of particular decision makers (128–33). When we examine the Supreme Court's constitutional review of congressional statutes we find significant evidence of these indicators of a strong norm for deference to Congress. Across its two-hundred-year history, the Court votes to uphold Congress 83.0 percent of the time, nullifying congressional action in less than 17 percent of the cases. On average, the Court has nullified Congress at a rate of less than one statute a year (.76). As I examine below, the patterns of judicial review and the level of deference across time, we will observe substantial variation across time and across chief justice courts, and even by individual justices, but we will continue to see a strong custom of deference to congressional action at each juncture with only a couple of exceptions. And thus while Geyh and others find strong levels of inter–branch support for the Court's independence or at least acquiescence toward the *Court's* constitutional holdings, here we see a similar level of deference from the Court toward *Congress*. Although it may be premature to conclude definitively at this point, the evidence does seem to support Geyh's and

Glennon's suggestion that one branch's informal acquiescence to the established practices of another branch will over time authorize the actions of the latter (Geyh, 13). But given the Court's norm of deference as well, it appears that it is *each* branch to some extent acquiescing to the other's powers while at the same time protecting its own powers in the very act of doing so. I will explore this possibility more in the chapters that follow, and I will examine the variation in the levels of deference in the sections that follow.

Before turning to that analysis it is interesting to note that the Court's level of support for congressional action is significantly higher than the level of deference given by Court to presidential action. King and Meernik's 1999 examination of 347 Supreme Court cases from 1790–1996 that reviewed presidential power issues on foreign policy, which is presumably the executive's strongest prerogative, found that the Court had deferred to the executive at substantially lower rate than here at only 69 percent. Yates and Whitford (1998) found even lower levels of presidential success before the Supreme Court from 1949–1993: the Court deferred to the president at a rate of 62 percent on foreign policy issues but only 55 percent on domestic issues. We will see below that in only three of the decades does the level of deference to Congress drop below even the highest levels of deference the president earns on his foreign policy issues.

Judicial Review Across Time

Figure 2.1 presents the annual number of Supreme Court opinions reviewing the constitutionality of congressional action. The first observable trend is the rise in the number of congressional review cases following the end of the Civil War. The mean number of congressional review cases prior to 1865 is only 0.2 cases per year, while in the following period (1865 through 2001) the mean is remarkably higher at 6.58 cases per year. Although the data here represents all congressional review opinions rather than just nullification votes, the observable patterns still parallel those of Caldeira and McCrone's (1982) more limited analysis, finding here that the Supreme Court became increasingly willing to taking on cases that challenged congressional legislation following the Civil War. This result fits with Ackerman's (1991) claim that it was during this period that the Supreme Court began to review regularly the national legislation. The periods of increased judicial review we see here generally parallel the periods of increased nullifications that Caldeira and McCrone identify: "the late 1860s; during the administration of Theodore Roosevelt; after World War I; during the 1920s and 1930s; and during the 1960s, a cycle that has not yet begun its decline" (113). I also find that the general trend

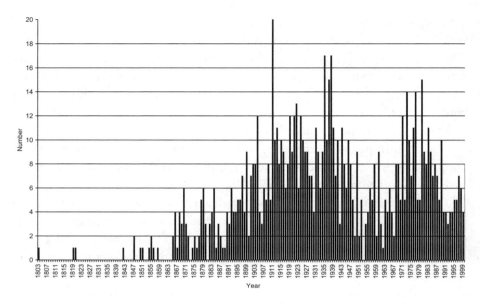

Figure 2.1 The Annual Number of Cases of Judicial Review of Congress (1803–2001)

has been toward overall growth in judicial review as Caldeira and McCrone found in regard to growth in nullifications; however, unlike in their study, the data here do not indicate that the cycles of judicial review become more and more extreme. It should be noted though that their study did not extend beyond 1973.

Figures 2.2 through 2.8 provide a closer examination of the judicial review cases by dividing the cases into those that nullified congressional action and those that upheld congressional action and by examining each of the time periods more closely. Figure 2.2 depicts the period 1803–1864. As is commonly known, the Supreme Court, after establishing judicial review in *Marbury v. Madison* in 1803, did not use the power of judicial review again to nullify a congressional statute until *Dred Scott* in 1956. Less well known is the fact that during this period the Supreme Court did consider questions of constitutionality in eleven other cases challenging congressional action. In each of these cases, the Court upheld the congressional statute. Thus we find additional evidence of the restraint exercised by both the Marshall and Taney Courts.[7] McCloskey argues that despite rather bold actions by Chief Justice Marshall, he exercised substantial restraint, recognizing that the Court must slowly gain national acceptance for the power of judicial review—that the power had to "be nourished and cultivated" in order to grow into a nationally accepted doctrine of judicial sovereignty (60). McCloskey also posits that the Taney Court, too, for a long time "recognized the need to slow the pace of [the Court's]

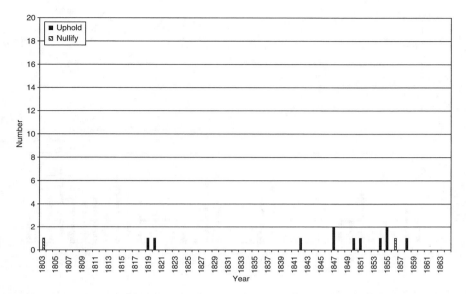

Figure 2.2 Frequencies of Supreme Court Judicial Review of Congress by Votes to Nullify or Votes to Uphold (1803–1864)

constitution–making process so that America could grow used to the house that John Marshall had built" and in order for the judicial power to be "consolidated" (69). With the *Dred Scott* decision the Taney Court abandoned this protective restraint and severely weakened the foundation of the Court's power, the principle of national sovereignty. During the Civil War the Supreme Court ducked salient constitutional issues, such as presidential war powers and civilians being tried in military courts, based on jurisdictional grounds. McCloskey argues that the Civil War demonstrated that "the experiment of an independent and influential national judiciary had failed" (64). He accepts this outcome as inevitable, arguing that "war is never a favorable environment for judicial power" because "war is characterized by emotion and quick, drastic actions and courts are not well equipped to deal with either" (64). Human rights scholars would take issue with this assertion and instead argue that an independent judiciary is most suited to stand between the passions and emotions of the majority and the Constitution, especially during times of threat (e.g., International Commission of Jurists 1983; Ackermann 1989; Chowdhury 1989; Keith, Poe, and Tate 2007). This issue is both a normative question and an empirical question that will be addressed in the following chapters. Later in this chapter, I will also compare the chief justice courts more fully.

Figure 2.3 depicts 1865–1900, the period McCloskey labels as "Constitutional Evolution in the Gilded Age." The mean number of cases challenging congressional

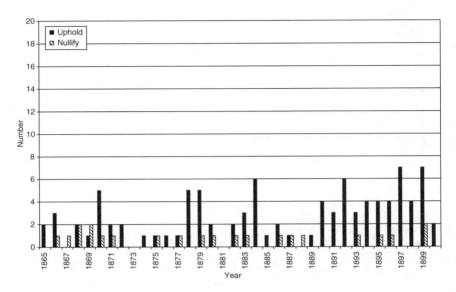

Figure 2.3 Frequencies of Supreme Court Judicial Review of Congress by Votes to Nullify or Votes to Uphold (1865–1900)

statutes during this period is 3.22, a remarkable increase over the previous period's mean of .2 cases per year. If we take into consideration the size of the Court's docket during this period we see that the cases range from approximately 0 to 4 percent of the Court's caseload, on average 1.7 percent of the caseload. Towards the end of this period, we find five outliers, years in which the annual number of cases is well beyond the mean of 3.22: 1879 (6), 1884 (6), 1892 (6), 1897 (7), and 1899 (9). The annual number of review cases in these five years is more in line with the mean of the next period we will examine. In the 1865–1900 period the Supreme Court nullifies congressional action in 21 cases of 116 cases, an average of .58 cases per year. As Caldeira and McCrone point out, the substantial increase in nullification cases following the Civil War marks the solidification or "institutionalization of the Court's power to negate actions of the legislative departments" (106). McCloskey (1994) recognizes this period as one of increased but moderated activism, arguing that the Court had realized that the "ambiguity of its mandate is both its limitation and its opportunity" (89). His assertion is supported by Caldeira and McCrone's empirical analysis which identifies a significant but gradual growth in Supreme Court nullifications after the Civil War. In the following sections I will identify the issues driving these cases and the Court's actions.

Figure 2.4 depicts 1901–1937, the period McCloskey refers to as the "Judiciary and the Regulatory State." McCloskey's analysis of this period becomes somewhat

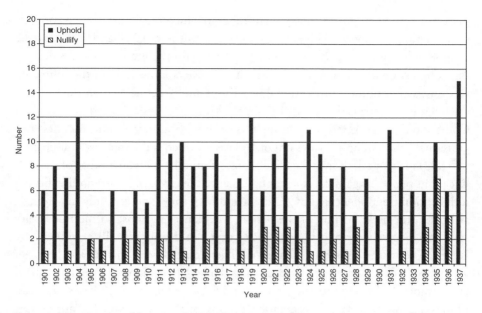

Figure 2.4 Frequencies of Supreme Court Judicial Review of Congress by Votes to Nullify or Votes to Uphold (1901–1937)

trapped in his metaphor of medieval knights slaying the dragons of socialism to protect the maidens of capitalism, but ultimately he settles upon the label of "judicial dualism" to describe a Court that at times was "determined to halt the regulatory movement in its tracks" and one that "ratified many inroads on the free enterprise ideal" (91). This period overlaps with four of the five periods of activism identified in Caldeira and McCrone's work which were all linked to "such economic phenomena as industrialization, depression, and the rise of corporations" (91). During the 1901–1937 period the Supreme Court decides 347 cases in which congressional actions are challenged constitutionally. The Court hears an average of 9.38 of these cases per year during this period, which again represents a rather substantial increase in the review of the last period, 3.22. If we take into consideration the size of the Court's docket during this period we see that the cases range from approximately 1.5 to 11.7 percent of the Court's caseload, on average 4.3 percent of the caseload, which is a significant increase over the percentage in the last period, 1.7. Fifty-seven of the review cases in this period result in nullification of a congressional statute, with an average of 1.54 nullifications per year. Although the number of nullifications increases substantially in this period, the proportion of cases resulting in nullifications is actually smaller than in the previous period: .16 compared to .18 per year. In not a single year does the number of cases nullifying Congress surpass the number in which the Court upheld congressional action. A few individual years appear as outliers: 1911 and 1937 for the number of congressional cases reviewed and 1935 for the number of cases nullifying congressional action. I will discuss these outliers more fully in the following sections, as I examine constitutional provisions and issues at stake in the cases.

Figure 2.5 depicts the years 1937–1957, which McCloskey called the "Modern Court and Postwar America."[8] During this period the Supreme Court nullifies congressional action in only 5 cases out of 148 cases, which is the smallest nullification rate (.03) of any period since the Civil War. This number nets an average of .23 nullifications per year, again the smallest figure since the Civil War. This finding fits the nullification trend identified by Caldeira and McCrone, and certainly may reflect, at least in the early portion of the period, the Court's response to the Roosevelt's court-packing scheme and the exigencies of a world war. We will examine these issues more in the subsequent chapters. The Court during this period hears an average 6.73 cases per year constitutionally challenging actions of Congress, which is substantially lower than the previous period's average of 9.38 cases per year. However, if we take into consideration the size of the Court's docket during this period we see that the cases range from approximately none in 1953 to 12.2 percent of the Court's caseload, on average 5.5 percent of the caseload, which is actually an

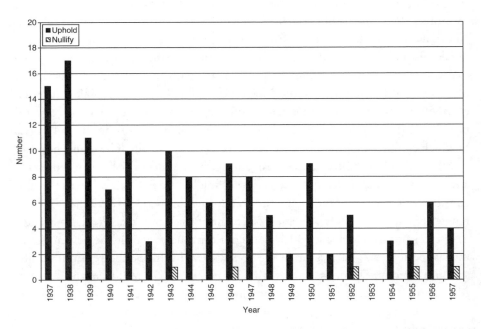

Figure 2.5 Frequencies of Supreme Court Judicial Review of Congress by Votes to Nullify or Votes to Uphold (1937–1957)

increase over the last period, 4.3, thus the lower percentage of review cases is in part a function of a lower caseload. In Chapters Four and Five I formally test the impact of congressional statutes changing the jurisdiction of the Court. Three years emerge as outliers in this period, in that the Court decides more than ten cases challenging congressional statutes: 1937 (fifteen), 1938 (seventeen), 1939 (twelve). Clearly, during the period encompassing World War II, the Court was much less likely to challenge Congress, even though it was hearing rather substantial numbers of such challenges. I will return to the issue of the Supreme Court's restraint during times of national crises in the following sections that examine the data by decade and in Chapters Four and Five, which present multivariate explanatory models.

Figure 2.6 depicts the remaining years, 1958–2001. During this period the Court hears 299 cases reviewing the constitutionality of congressional action, an average of 6.8 cases per year, which is approximately the same average as the previous period. Four years are outliers, with the Court hearing more than ten cases in each of these years: 1973 (11), 1977 (13), and 1981 (14). Again, if we take into consideration the size of the Court's docket during this period we see that the cases range from approximately .8 to 11.7 percent of the Court's caseload, on average 5.6 percent of the caseload, which is approximately equal to the last period, 5.5. This period, however, produces several notable records. First, the Court hands down

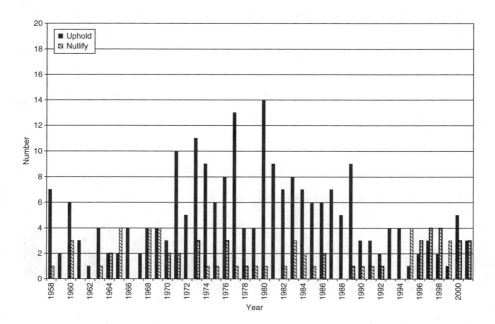

Figure 2.6 Frequencies of Supreme Court Judicial Review of Congress by Votes to Nullify or Uphold 1958–2001

seventy-four cases that nullify Congress, at a rate of 1.68 nullifications per year, the highest rate of any period. The proportion of nullifications is .25, the highest of any period. Additionally in five years the Court nullifies Congress in four cases: 1965, 1968, 1969, 1995, and 1998. Finally, it is significant that for the first time, we have years in which the cases resulting in nullification outnumber the cases upholding Congress: 1965 (four nullifying Congress to two upholding Congress), 1967 (two to zero), 1995 (four to one), 1996 (three to two), 1998 (four to two), 1999 (three to one). Four of the six years occur in the Rehnquist Court and the other two in the Warren Court. Though Caldeira and McCrone's study extended only to 1973, they do identify the 1960s as a cycle of activism "that had not yet begun its decline" (113). The number of nullifications here seems to support their conclusion. In the next section, I continue the analysis with the nullification rates.

Supreme Court Deference to Congress Over Time

Figure 2.7 depicts the annual number of cases of nullifying congressional action across the entire 1803–2001 period. Here, of course, we see clearly the increase following the Civil War. Although the Supreme Court only overturns two congressional statutes between 1803 and 1864, in the period between1865–2001 the

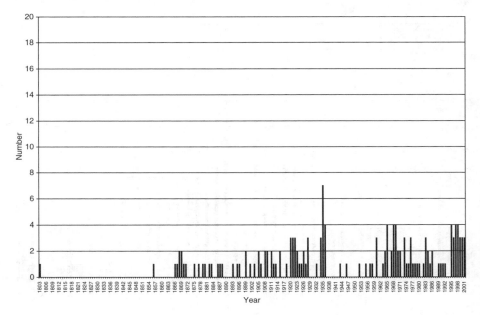

Figure 2.7 Annual Number of Cases of Judicial Review of Congress Resulting in Nullification (1803–2001)

Court nullifies on average one congressional statute per year. This result parallels those of Caldeira and McCrone's study which concluded that the Civil War was a watershed in the "development of the Court's use of judicial review to declare state and federal enactments invalid" (106). Examining the figure we can see a second increase in nullifications occur in 1920. For the period 1920–2001, the Court nullifies congressional action an average 1.3 cases per year. Then again in 1965, we see a third increase in nullifications, with the mean number of nullifications rising to 1.8 for the period 1965–2001. We can observe several outliers, years with four or more nullifications. Two years of the New Deal produced four or more cases that nullified congressional action: 1935 (7), and 1936 (4). In the Warren Court three years produce four nullification cases: 1965, 1968, and 1969 and in the Rehnquist Court we find two years with four nullifications cases: 1995 and 1998. The Court's opportunity to nullify cases will vary by the number of cases on the docket that consider constitutional challenges to congressional action. The next graph controls for that data.

Figure 2.8 presents the annual percentage of cases reviewing congressional action that resulted in nullification from 1865 to 2001. On average the Court nullified congressional action in only 26 percent of the cases challenging Congress. The overwhelming norm is to support Congress rather than to nullify its actions. This high overall level of deference supports Lamb's (1982) observation that the Court is "primarily a Court of restraint—or at least of mild and infrequent activism"

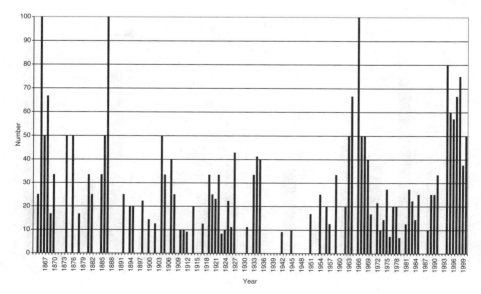

Figure 2.8 Percentage of Cases that Nullify Congress (1865–2001)

and the statistic is in keeping with recent empirical studies of the Vinson through Rehnquist Courts (Howard and Segal 2004; Lindquist and Solberg 2007). The level of deference does fall away in several periods: the post-Cold War period, the 1960s, and following the 1994 congressional elections. These cycles fit somewhat with the expectations of Ferejohn and Geyh, but not as clearly as they predict. I will examine these expectations more formally in the chapters that follow. Here, I found only eight years to be extreme outliers—with percentages higher than 60 percent. In three of these years the Court nullified in 100 percent of the case: 1867, 1888, and 1967. But it should be noted that the number of cases is quite small, only one case in 1867 and 1888 and only two cases in 1967. The more significant outliers are Warren Court's 1965 (67 percent) and the Rehnquist Court's 1995 (80 percent), 1998 (67 percent), and 1999 (75 percent). In these years the Court considered four or more cases of constitutional challenges to Congress. We will discuss the issues in these peak years with the decade by decade analysis in the next figure.

Figure 2.9 examines the Court by decade rather than year referenced against the mean percentage of cases that nullify Congress in the post-Civil War period. The mean decade nullification rate across the entire period is 26 percent. The rates for four of the thirteen decades reach levels well above the mean. The Rehnquist Court during the decade of the 1990s earns the highest average percentage; 42 percent nullification rate in cases primarily dealing with civil rights and civil liberties, as well as federalism and interstate economic activity issues. Approximately

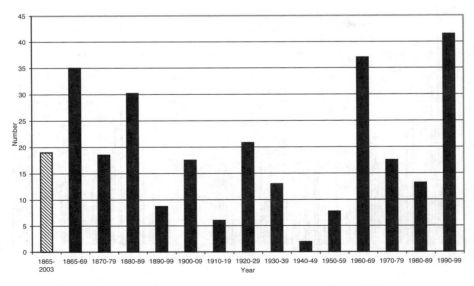

Figure 2.9 Decade Percentages of Judicial Review Cases that Resulted in Nullification

two-thirds of this decade's nullification cases are decided in the conservative direction (63.5 percent), which is consistent with general perceptions of the conservative activism of the Rehnquist Court (e.g., Savage 1992; Schwartz 2002; Keck 2004). The Warren Court during the 1960s earns the second highest average at 37 percent. Civil rights and civil liberties dominate in these nullification cases, with 74 percent of the cases decided in the liberal direction, which fits Powe's (2000) assessment that it was from 1962 forward that the Warren Court, with Frankfurter's retirement and Goldberg's appointment to the bench, demonstrated "aggressive willingness to implement liberal values" (498). The half decade following the Civil War produces the third largest mean score with a set of decisions dominated by taxation, interstate commerce, and federalism issues. The Court of the 1880s produces an average of 30 percent with cases primarily dealing with interstate commerce, federalism, and economic activity issues, with a few cases dealing with civil rights issues for Indians and immigrants. The two lowest decade-nullification rates occur during the two world wars. During World War II and the period immediately following the war only 2 percent of the cases challenging Congress were nullified. In eight of these ten years the Court upheld Congress in 100 percent of the cases. The second lowest average is during World War I, with the Court nullifying Congress in only 2 percent of the cases. In four of these years, the Court upholds Congress 100 percent of the time. This result supports McCloskey's expectation that "judicial review is to be weakest during grave national emergencies" (135). Born out in this analysis is Chief Justice Rehnquist's (1998) assertion that "there is some truth to the maxim *Inter arma silent leges*" (221). The data could also support Schwartz' (1993) criticism of the Court's failure to defend fundamental rights during times of external threat, but of course, here we do not know what portion of the cases are rights–based claims. I will test these hypotheses more rigorously in subsequent chapters. Before we turn to the next set of analyses, I need to take an aside and deal with the issue of ideology introduced in my comments about the Rehnquist and Warren Courts.

The Issue of Ideological Direction of Judicial Decisions

Most political scientists' assessment of the ideological direction of Supreme Court votes follows Spaeth's delineation of liberal and conservative outcomes and is based on the primary issue area of each case (see Segal and Spaeth 1993, 243 but also Goldman 1966, 1975). A liberal justice under this demarcation would be one that supports civil rights, civil liberties, and criminal procedure claims.[9] He or she would be pro-economic regulation and pro-economic underdog, pro-judicial power, pro-federal power, and pro-federal taxation. Although this delineation is quite justifiable for the more recent Court, it becomes potentially more problematic to accept unquestionably as we move backwards in time across the Court's two century history, particularly in terms of the federalism issue and the use of the label "conservative." In looking for an American ideological schema and ultimately a delineation of American party politics, I rely on the work of Reichley (1992) who identifies two ideological traditions of American politics extending back at least as far as the ratification battle over the federal Constitution, and probably as far back as the party battles under the Articles of Confederation (4). Reichley calls the two ideological traditions "republican" and "liberal" giving both terms their twentieth-century meaning, although noting that some of the connotations from the eighteenth and early-nineteenth centuries are retained in their current usage (4). Although Reichley identifies important areas of agreement across the two traditions, such as commitment to representative government and constitutional protection of personal liberties, he identifies consistent, albeit not extreme, differences in the traditions in "the priorities they assign public order and economic growth on one hand and economic and social equality on the other hand." He delineates the republican and liberal traditions along the following dimensions:

> The republican tradition upholds equality of the law and equal access to public goods (although the traditions disagree on how public goods should be defined); and the liberal tradition recognizes the need to maintain a certain amount of public order and favors economic growth when it can be achieved without aggravating inequality. But when order and growth clash with equality, the republican tradition has usually come down on the side of the former and the liberal tradition on the side of the latter.

> Both traditions cherish individual freedom as a fundamental human value ... but the republican tradition has particularly advocated freedoms that are less likely to conflict with order, specifically economic freedoms; and the liberal tradition has specifically championed freedoms that are most likely to be compatible with equality, notably freedoms of personal behavior and expression.

> The traditions agree that government in a democratic society has a responsibility to "promote the general welfare," but the liberal tradition, particularly in the twentieth century has tended to identify such promotion with direct government intervention and support, while the republican tradition has emphasized government's role in securing economic and social conditions favorable to individual, family and community achievement.

Republicans accept substantial inequality as a necessary source of investment and motivation for economic growth, while liberals are prepared to take risks with disorder and pay some price in economic inefficacy in return for almost unlimited right to socially unrestrained expression and behavior not physically harmful to others (4–5).

Reichley further notes that each of the traditions has "given rise to a series of major political parties in American national politics:"

REPUBLICAN TRADITION: Federalists (before and after the ratification of the Constitution), National Republicans, Whigs, and modern Republicans.

LIBERAL TRADITION: Antifederalists, Democratic-Republicans, and modern Democrats (6).

Ultimately, Reichley's dichotomy overlaps almost completely with Spaeth's dichotomy of liberal and conservative. And Reichley himself notes that the republican tradition now is often labeled simply "conservative." However, he argues that the label does not fit for several reasons: (1) identification of conservatism with the resistance to change, while the republican tradition has been the most dynamic source of change in American life, (2) the application of the label to hard-line Stalinists who are not free-market ideologues, and (3) the association of conservatism with feudalism when the republican tradition is an inclusive not exclusive hierarchy, based on individualist rather than collectivist ideology. For the ease of presentation and discussion, I will primarily use the term "conservative" as Reichley himself, ultimately does.

Although these traditions as defined above, fit the traditionally accepted Spaeth delineation, Spaeth's delineation of liberal and conservative on the issue of federalism does not hold up over time.[10] As Reichley notes, "the two traditions have sometimes switched sides on issues that once seemed fundamental, such as states' rights and the power of the executive in the federal government—stealing each others' clothes as Lincoln said," but in the context of political parties, he asserts that "if Hamilton and Jefferson, whom many regard as the founders of the two traditions, were restored to life today, each would quickly know ... to which party he should belong" (6). If we look at the original party in the republican tradition, the Federalists, we find it to be the "party of the national idea" as Ladd (1970) terms it. In addition, we find one of the early parties of the liberal tradition, the Democratic-Republicans, who espouse "the 'parochial idea' of state autonomy" (86). Generally, as we examine Ladd's analysis, we find this dimension of American ideology or party alignment to be almost a matter of where the tradition or the party's interests would be better protected at that particular time in history; Ladd ultimately asserts that its mostly Federalists who "held forth a bold and coherent vision of a national union, strong politically, and integrated economically, who saw their interests better protected and promoted by national than by state and local authority" (86). He argues that this alignment on national versus state power slowly shifts after the Great Depression, during the partisan conflict of the 1930s. He notes the 1928 Democratic platform reiterates their historic commitment to states' rights and but then shifts in 1935 with the emergence of the second New Deal, and thus, he concludes that "long the parochials, the Democrats became the proponents of a new nationalism" (207–09). Because of this shift, I decided to deviate from the Spaeth delineation on the federalism issue and switch the coding of ideological direction on federalism votes prior to 1935 where appropriate. For most of the analysis that I present, I try to report the analysis with federalism coded each way. My goal is to be as accurate as possible in identifying the ideological direction of the votes without complicating the analysis beyond what is reasonable. Empirically, the analysis of each chapter suggests that the time-modified delineation is most supportable.

Chief Justice Courts and the Exercise of Judicial Review

Figure 2.10 and Table 2.1 describe the Court's behavior in congressional review cases by chief justice court. Due to the small number of cases in the Marshall Court

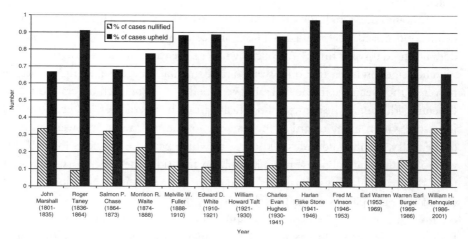

Figure 2.10 Judicial Review by Chief Justice Court (Percentage Nullified and Upheld)

Table 2.1 Ideological Direction of the Chief Justice Court's Judicial Review Decisions (Percentage Liberal)

	Percentage Liberal Traditional Coding	Percentage Liberal Adjusted Direction on Federalism
Roger Taney (1836–1864)	81.8	27.3
Salmon P. Chase (1864–1873)	60.0	40.0
Morrison R. Waite (1874–1888)	69.2	64.1
Melville W. Fuller (1888–910)	64.6	49.6
Edward D. White (1910–1921)	65.2	39.2
William Howard Taft (1921–1930)	76.2	58.7
Charles Evan Hughes (1930–1941)	76.1	54.0
Harlan Fiske Stone (1941–1946)	81.8	–
Fred M. Vinson (1946–1953)	57.8	–
Earl Warren (1953–1969)	66.2	–
Warren Earl Burger (1969–1986)	38.2	–
William H. Rehnquist (1986–2001)	44.7	–

I have not included that Court in the ideological analysis as it would be rather problematic to draw conclusions from such a limited number of cases. In the table I report the ideological direction of the votes with both codings of federalism. The importance of this distinction is rather evident in that the results are more clearly in keeping with anecdotal and historical evidence of the Court's ideological leanings in each of the chief justice eras. Just as we saw in the decade-analysis above the Taney Court seems to fit scholar's description of a Court exercising restraint in its use of this power as it consolidated its power and prestige, and interestingly the Taney Court is the most conservative of the chief justice courts, with a liberalism score of 27.3 percent with the modified federalism score and over 80 percent with the Spaeth coding (Swisher 1974; Schwartz 1993; McCloskey 1994), indicating the strong presence of national supremacy sentiments. McCloskey notes that within a few years of Taney's accession, the concept of judicial sovereignty was more secure than ever, and he argues that "now [that] the Chief and a majority of his associates were Jackson-approved ... the anti-judicial tradition of the Democrats lost much of its edge" (55). He also posits that as a result of Taney's pragmatism and non-doctrine course, the Court repeatedly upheld the national government's supremacy over the states' and thus for a long time the Taney Court exercised "temperance and reason against extremism that threaten to dissever the Republic" (55–9).

The Chase Court nullifies a significantly larger percentage of congressional statutes than did the Taney Court, 32 percent compared to only 9 percent, and in fact, the Chase Court has the highest nullification rate of any chief justice court except the Rehnquist Court, if we discount the Marshall Court due to its small number of cases. These results runs somewhat counter to the traditional view of the Supreme Court during the Civil War and Reconstruction which holds that the Court has during this period "played a more subdued role than at any other time in history—that it had been weakened, if not impotent, ever since the *Dred Scott* decision" (Schwartz 1993, 154). McCloskey, though, asserts that *Milligan* and other Chase Court decisions illustrated the Court's "eagerness to impose its wisdom on the government in connection with momentous issues, and more particularly, a growing compulsion to defend property rights against all who assail them" (75). However, as Schwartz points out, even though the Court was exercising a much higher level of nullification, the majority of the nullifications "were of little of practical importance and received scant notice either at the time or from constitutional historians since then" (154).[11] The two most notable cases here are the two legal tender cases, *Hepburn v. Griswold* and *The Legal Tender Cases*, in which the Supreme Court overturns itself within one year due to Grant's packing of the Court, but as Segal and Spaeth (2002) point out the Court "managed to escape relatively unscathed, however, because the criticism fell on President Grant for interfering with the independence of the judiciary by 'packing' the Court" (127). The Chase Court's level of liberalism in these cases is rather low at 40 percent, and is in keeping with analysis of this Court's overall conservative ideology, particularly in support of property rights in an agenda that largely dealt with the government-business relationship (McCloskey 1960, 1994; Schwartz 1993; Ogundele and Keith 2006).

The Waite Court's nullification rate of 23 percent is only slightly higher than the average chief justice court rate of 18.1 percent, which is more in keeping with the traditional expectations in regard to post-Civil War and Reconstruction deference to Congress than the Chase Court is, and likely contributes to Schwartz's assessment that under the somewhat mediocre Chief Justice Waite "the Court's tarnished reputation was refurbished" and it was then "ready to take its place as a fully coordinate department of government" (162). The Waite Court's moderate level of liberalism (64.1) is somewhat higher than its moderate to conservative scores in the full set of cases handed down by the Waite Court—Ogundele and Keith (2006) found that the Court to be rather conservative on economic, federalism, and rights and liberties issues, ranging from 47 percent liberalism on the rights issues and 45 percent on economic activity issues to less than 30 percent on federalism issues. They do note however, that the federalism cases constituted only 1.6 percent of the Waite Court's decisional agenda.

Despite Schwartz's assertion that the Court emerges from the Waite Court as a fully coordinate department of government, the Fuller Court nullifies at a rate quite below average (a nullification rate of 12 percent). This court falls clearly within the moderate range at 49.6 percent liberal, although Wood, Keith, Lanier and Ogundele (1998) found that the early Fuller Court (1888–1892) was slightly more conservative (45 percent), and they found the Fuller Court's strongest level of conservatism was expressed in civil rights and liberties cases, in which the Fuller Court earned as low as 15 percent liberalism during the natural Court of 1902–1905.[12] However, most of the Court's agenda was comprised of economic decisions and the Court largely acted to protect the economy, corporate power, and property rights from government restrictions (Lanier 2003).

The White Court's level of nullification also falls quite below average (11 percent), which is not surprising since its later years encompass World War I. Its liberalism score of 39.2 percent, which is the third lowest of the chief justice courts, is somewhat more conservative than the ideological direction exhibited in the full set of cases the Court handed down; the overall liberalism score for the White Court is 48 percent; however, there was significant variation, with its liberalism in civil liberties cases 20 percent, compared to 60 percent liberalism in economic cases (Wood, Keith, Lanier and Ogundele 1998, 215).[13] Of course, it is the White Court that upholds national security interests over civil liberties claims, upholding the Espionage Act and the Selective Service Act during the Red Scare.

The Taft Court's level of nullification increases over the two previous courts to 18 percent, but still is right at the overall mean of the chief justice courts. Its liberalism score here is fairly moderate at 58.7 percent and is comparable to the Wood, Keith, Lanier, and Ogundele's (1998) analysis of the Taft Court's full set of decisions. Here, the Taft Court's cases primarily deal with economic and taxation issues, which is representative of the Court's agenda at that time (Lanier 2003, 98–9).

The Hughes Court falls within the liberal range (76.1 percent) when federalism cases are coded under Spaeth's rule and falls within the moderate range (54 percent) when coded with the modified federalism delineation. This distinction is important since it was posited that in 1935 the federalism position shifted in the U.S. political parties; this date splits the Hughes Court (1929–1940). The 76.1 percent liberalism score seems to fit best for this Court level of liberalism. Wood, Keith, Lanier, and Ogundele (1998) found that an overall liberalism rate of 74 percent, but as I have noted above, their coding relied on the Spaeth coding; however, Lanier (2003) found that federalism issues made up an extremely low annual proportion of the Hughes Court's decisional agenda, ranging from substantially below 1 percent to 10 percent. Neither studies reports the liberalism scores on federalism issues, but the studies show the Hughes Court becoming more liberal in both economic and civil liberties issues beginning in 1932 and consolidating in 1935 somewhat prior to Robert's so called "switch in time." I will examine the individual justices' liberalism scores in Chapter Three.

We find the Stone and Vinson Court's with the lowest nullification rates of any chief justice courts. These Courts overlap with the World War II and post-war period in which the Court has tended to restrain itself from overruling Congress. However, if when we examine the ideological direction of the review votes, we find rather different directions in the Court's deference to Congress: the Stone Court ruled in the liberal direction 81.8 percent of the time, the highest level of liberalism of any chief justice court, but the ideological direction of the Vinson Court is in the moderate range at 57.8 percent. The Stone Court's level of liberalism in the congressional review is somewhat higher than its overall liberalism scores. Lanier found annual highs in economic liberalism as high as 73.8 and civil liberties liberalism as high as 64.5 percent; again, he does not report liberalism in federalism cases. Here, we find eleven cases in which federalism was a main issue, and the Stone Court ruled liberally in each of these cases. The Vinson Court's moderate scores here reflect those Lanier found, although he found the Vinson Court to be less moderate in civil liberties cases than in economic cases.

The last three chief justice courts have already received much empirical attention due to the availability of the Spaeth dataset. The Rehnquist Court has the highest nullification rate of the Court's history (34 percent) and Warren has the third highest rate (30 percent), discounting Marshall's Court, results which are not surprising given the statistics we saw for the decades of the 1990s and the 1960s. However, Rehnquist's historical high does run counter to assumption of critics of *liberal* "activism." The Warren Court's liberalism score of 66.2 percent in this limited set of cases is slightly lower than its overall liberalism score of 68 percent (Wood, Keith, Lanier, and Ogundele 1998). The Burger Court, which has a lower than average nullification rate of 15 percent is quite conservative at 38.2 percent liberalism, which roughly fits this chief justice court's overall conservatism; Wood et al. found a liberalism score of 45 percent. Schwarz (2002) concludes that the Burger Court turned out not to be as conservative as expected, and he even finds the Burger Court to fit within his moderate to liberal Supreme Court of "half a century from 1937 until as late as 1987" (13); however, at least in terms of the Court's review of congressional action, the Burger Court is strongly conservative, in fact it is the second most conservative in the Court's history. Schwartz also criticizes the Rehnquist Court as being the most conservative court since before the New Deal, but in this narrow set of judicial decisions we find the Rehnquist Court to be the fifth most conservative chief justice court, with a liberalism score of 44.7 percent, which could be interpreted as moderately conservative. This score roughly fits Epstein, Segal, Spaeth and Walker (2003) report in which we find the Rehnquist Court's liberalism during this period of time ranged from the low to high forties on due process, privacy, civil liberties, and economic activity and slightly over 50 percent on civil rights (230).[14] Here, the Rehnquist Court's somewhat moderate liberalism is likely due more to its economic decisions (66.7 percent liberal) than its civil rights and liberties decisions (39.2 percent). The moderate conservatism of the Rehnquist Court fits somewhat with Keck's assessments of the Rehnquist Court (2002) and his broader analysis of the "O'Connor Court" (2007). Although he argues that three of the conservatives on the Court (Scalia and Thomas, and Rehnquist, perhaps to a somewhat lesser extent) have "simply abandoned restraint in order to promote their own preferences wherever possible" and "to constitutionalize their New Right commitments" (140), he notes, however, the other two conservatives—the swing voters on the Rehnquist Court, Kennedy and O'Connor—"in contrast, have generally supported judicial activism in defense of both liberal and conservative ends" (141). We will examine the justices' individual ideological patterns in the next chapter. The final section of this chapter examines the extent to which the congressional review decisions varied across the key legal issue areas.

Major Legal Issues and Constitutional Provisions

Table 2.2 presents the analysis of the cases according to the major issue area that forms the legal basis of the decision. This variable is obtained from Spaeth's U.S. Supreme Court Database for the cases decided since 1953.[15] For cases preceding Spaeth I coded the issues following Spaeth's guidelines, with an eventual further delineation in regard to due process. Spaeth's category for due process is rather problematic in that it combines economic due process, such as cases involving the takings clause with non-economic due process issues. When coding liberalism the scores become rather complicated as the direction of liberalism is not consistent across the two types of due process cases. For my analyses here, I have separated out economic due process cases and combined those cases with the economic activity issue area. The first column of Table 2.2 shows the percentage of cases by key legal issue area. Federalism is the most prevalent issue area, accounting for almost

Table 2.2 Analysis by Major Legal and Constitutional Issues

	Percentage of Cases of Judicial Review of Congress	Percentage of the Cases within the Issue Area that Upheld Congressional Action	Percentage of the Cases within the Issue Area that Nullified Congressional Action
Criminal Procedure	10.5	77.8	22.2
Civil Rights	13.5	77.7	22.3
First Amendment	10.5	88.9	27.7
Non-economic Due Process	3.7	90.9	9.1
Privacy	0.7	83.3	16.7
Attorneys	0.2	100.0	0.0
Unions	1.0	88.9	11.1
Economic Activity including Economic Due Process	16.6	95.3	4.7
Judicial Power	5.2	73.3	26.7
Federalism	19.2	84.3	15.7
Taxation	14.1	84.1	15.9
Miscellaneous (primarily separation of power)	5.0	82.2	17.8

20 percent (19.2 percent) of the cases. Next in size is the economic activity issue area which represents 16.6 percent of the cases. Two issue-areas roughly tie with the third and fourth– highest percentage, taxation cases (14.1 percent) and civil rights cases (13.5 percent). Two issue areas fall into the fourth–highest percentage: criminal procedure (10.5 percent) and First Amendment issues (10.5 percent). Judicial power cases are tied for the lowest percentage of cases at 5.2 percent, along with the miscellaneous category (5.0 percent) which consists mostly cases dealing with separation of powers issues such as the constitutional challenge to the Line Item Veto Act or the War Revenue Act of 1898. Three issue areas, those dealing with unions, attorneys and privacy issues, each represent 1 percent or less of the cases under study here and make it difficult to draw generalizations across that set of issues.

The second and third columns in Table 2.2 present the nullification and uphold rates within each issue area. Examining these summary statistics, we can see that over the course of the Court's history it is most likely to nullify congressional statutes in cases dealing with First Amendment issues (27.7 percent), followed by statutes dealing with issues of judicial power (26.7 percent). The next most likely categories of issues where the Court is likely to nullify Congress are civil rights

(22.3 percent) or criminal procedure (21.3 percent). This analysis does not tell us whether the Court is striking down congressional statutes to uphold rights or to curb them. I will address that question in the next analysis. The fifth and sixth highest nullification rates occur in the miscellaneous category (17.8 percent) and privacy (16.7 percent). Federalism and taxation cases have roughly the same nullification rates at 15.7 and 15.9 percent. Non-economic due process cases have a nullification rate of 9.1 percent. The economic activity issue area has one of the lowest nullification rates at 4.7 percent. We should keep in mind that this analysis examines only the dominant issue of each case but in some cases there is a second issue as well. For example, *Bob Jones University v. U.S.* (1982) involved a First Amendment issue as well as the civil rights issue, so Spaeth has coded the first issue area as 2, civil rights and the second issue area as 3, First Amendment. Sometimes these distinctions between a first and second issue can be rather difficult to make. In the majority of cases only one key issue is identified; nonetheless, in the cases under study here 369 of the 896 cases have a second key legal issue. Table 2.3 presents an analysis by issue that includes second issues as well as the first issue area. There are only a few significant changes, however, the most significant being

Table 2.3 Analysis by Major Legal and Constitutional Issues (Includes First and Second Issues)

	Percentage of Cases of Judicial Review of Congress	Percentage of the Cases within the Issue Area that Upheld Congressional Action	Percentage of the Cases within the Issue Area that Nullified Congressional Action
Criminal Procedure	10.4	77.9	22.1
Civil Rights	12.9	81.6	18.4
First Amendment	8.4	74.5	25.5
Non-economic Due Process	4.9	82.3	17.7
Privacy	0.5	85.7	14.3
Attorneys	0.2	100.0	0.0
Unions	1.0	92.3	7.7
Economic Activity including Economic Due Process	23.6	90.6	9.4
Judicial Power	4.8	80.3	19.7
Federalism	17.6	82.1	17.9
Taxation	11.5	84.3	15.7
Miscellaneous (primarily separation of power)	4.2	81.1	18.9

that the percentage of cases involving an economic activity issue goes from 16.6 percent to 23.6 percent—129 of the 369 cases with second key issues had an economic activity issue as the second issue area. This finding fits much of the analysis of the early Supreme Court that I did with other colleagues (Wood, Keith, Lanier, and Ogundele 1998) in which we frequently found inter-connected economic activity issues with another key issue, especially federalism. Most other issue areas experience a minimal decrease, due primarily to the shift in the economic activity issue areas. Including the second key area does however produce some significant changes in the nullification rates in some of the issue areas. The nullification rate on civil rights issues goes down from 23.3 percent to 18.4 percent. The nullification rate in the First Amendment and privacy issue areas drops a couple of points but the level of nullification in non-economic due process increases significantly, going from 9.1 to 17.7 when the second issue area is added. Not surprisingly a large number of cases have a due process issue as a second key issue: 73 out of the 369 cases with second issues, which is the second largest area. The nullification rate in the economic activity issue area goes up substantially, 4.7 to 9.4 percent, which is more in line with historical expectations. Nullification on judicial power issues goes down substantially, from 26.7 to 19.7, and the federalism nullification rate goes down by a couple of points. As I mentioned earlier, what we do not know is the direction of the nullifications. Is the Court nullifying congressional statutes largely to support the federal government's power or to protect states' rights? Is the Court nullifying congressional statutes to support or to curb civil rights and civil liberties? The next analysis looks at this question.

Table 2.4 presents the ideological direction of the case outcome within these issue areas. The economic due process cases are reported within the broad economic activity issue area rather than in the due process issue area because of the conflicting ideological direction. And the ideological direction of the federalism votes is reported in both delineations. The mean liberalism score across the eight issue areas is 61 percent, which would be on the high end of most delineations of a moderate range. However, when the direction of the votes on federalism issue was switched in 1935 to reflect the partisan switch, the mean liberalism score drops to 52.5 percent, which is dead center of the moderate range. Still, there is much variation across the issue areas. The Court is most conservative in the non-economic due process area, with a liberalism score of 21 percent. The Court is second most conservative, not surprisingly, in cases dealing primarily with criminal procedure (only 27 percent liberal), followed by First Amendment (33 percent liberalism) and civil rights (34 percent liberalism) issues. Thus, we find that across all four issue areas that comprise the broader category of civil rights and civil liberties, the

Table 2.4 Ideological Direction of the Outcomes by Issue Area

	Percent that Supported Conservative Values	Percent that Supported Liberal Values
Criminal Procedure	72.3	27.6
Civil Rights	66.1	33.9
First Amendment	67.0	33.0
Non-economic Due Process	78.8	21.2
Economic Activity Including Economic Due Process	19.7	80.3
Judicial Power	21.4	78.6
Federalism (Spaeth coding)	16.9	83.1
Federalism (modified coding)	57.5	42.4
Taxation	11.3	88.7
Mean (with Spaeth coding)	39.0	61.0
Mean (with modified federalism)	47.5	52.5

Court is *not* exercising its power of judicial review to protect rights claims but rather the opposite. In three issue areas we find outcomes to fall clearly within the liberal range: economic activity (80 percent), judicial power (79 percent), and national taxation (89 percent). The liberalism on the federalism issue varies substantially, depending upon the federalism delineation. In 83.1 percent of the cases, the Court supported the national government over the states' rights issue. If the Spaeth coding is followed, the Court is then quite liberal in these cases with an 83 percent liberalism score; however, when using the modified coding the Court is liberal in only 42.4 percent of the federalism cases. The latter delineation seems to most closely fit the historical review of the Court. The analysis still does not tell us the Court's ideological tendencies distinguishing between nullification and uphold decisions.

Table 2.5 reports the ideological tendencies while distinguishing between votes to nullify Congress and votes to uphold Congress. One of the most interesting general patterns to observe is that the Court tends to flip ideological direction in its decision, based on whether it is upholding or whether it is nullifying Congress; this pattern holds true across all but one issue area—judicial power. The Court consistently votes in the liberal direction on judicial power issues, meaning that the Court votes to uphold laws that support or enhance judicial power (76.7 percent) and to nullify laws that diminish judicial power (83.3 percent). Thus the Court clearly exercises its power of judicial review to protect the

Table 2.5 Ideological Direction of the Nullification Votes and Votes to Uphold by Issue Area

	Votes to Nullify Statutes		Votes to Uphold Statutes	
	Percentage in Conservative Direction	Percentage in Liberal Direction	Percentage in Conservative Direction	Percentage in Liberal Direction
Criminal Procedure	5.0	95.5	90.5	9.5
Civil Rights	29.6	70.4	76.6	23.4
First Amendment	15.4	84.6	86.8	13.2
Non-economic Due Process	33.3	67.3	83.3	16.7
Economic Activity Including Economic Due Process	85.7	14.3	16.4	83.6
Judicial Power	16.7	83.3	23.3	76.7
Federalism (Spaeth coding)	100.0	0.0	1.4	98.6
Federalism (modified coding)	33.3	66.7	62.1	37.9
Taxation	73.4	26.3	0.0	100.0
Overall (with Spaeth coding)	45.5	54.5	37.2	62.8
Overall (with modified federalism)	32.9	67.1	49.7	50.3

judiciary's own powers in general. If we look at the civil liberties issue areas—criminal procedure, civil rights, First Amendment, and due process—we see that the Court acts in quite a conservative manner, ruling against the rights claims when it is ruling to uphold Congress (ranging 76.6 percent to 90.5 percent); however, when the Court does act outside the norm of uphold Congress, it does so to protect the rights claims at rather high levels (ranging from 67.3 percent to 95.5 percent). Although we cannot say the power of judicial review generally is used to support rights claims, as human rights proponents might expect, we can say that when the Court exercises the power of judicial review to challenge Congress it does so overwhelmingly to protect the rights claims. We see the opposite pattern in regard to economic activity. There when the Court steps outside the norm of deference, it does so in the conservative direction to generally protect business interest and property rights (85.7 percent), but when it has upheld congressional statutes they have predominantly been statutes that went against the business interests (83.6 percent). I have again reported both codings of federalism. When we look at the modified coding it is of course more complicated to discuss in descriptive terms because at times upholding Congress is the liberal position and at times it is the conservative position. Perhaps here the simple descriptive delineation gives us more substantive information. We can see that when the Court adheres to its norm of deference it has overwhelmingly voted to support national over state power; but when it does move against the norm of deference, it does so to support state over national power.

If we look at the Court's overall patterns we see a Court that across two centuries has been rather balanced in its ideological leanings when upholding Congress (50.3 percent liberal), and this in part may be due to the balanced ideological nature of the set of statutes produced by Congress. When the Court has moved outside the norm of deference it still has acted in the moderate range, but at a rather higher end of that range (67.1 percent) that would be considered moderately liberal.[16] In Chapter Three, we will return to the ideological direction of the votes in reference to the ideological preferences or patterns of the individual justices, and in Chapter Five, we will examine the ideological component of the Court's decision making in controlled models that test various explanations of the Court's behavior.

Conclusions

In this chapter we have seen the Court exhibit a strong norm of deference toward Congress across the entire history under review here, much higher even than the level that the president receives in national security and foreign policy matters. We have seen the number of Supreme Court cases challenging Congress increase gradually following the Civil War and Reconstruction, with a concomitant increase in the number of nullifications of Congress. However, the dominant trend across the Court's history remains one of supporting Congress, with exceptions primarily during the decades of the 1960s and the 1990s. We have also seen a decline in proportion of cases nullifying Congress during times of national crises, specifically the two world wars. Not only has the level of judicial review and nullification rates varied across chief justice courts, the ideological outcomes have produced a significant pattern of the Courts supporting primarily one ideological position or other, but not usually both. Some Courts such as the Taney Court, the Stone Court, and the Burger Court have shown particularly high levels of ideological consistency, followed by the Warren and Rehnquist Courts. We also saw an interesting pattern revealed when the ideological direction of the outcomes were divided according to whether the Court was acting to nullify or acting to uphold; when the Court does decide to go against the norm of deference it usually does so in a consisten ideological direction that is quite opposite from the direction of its votes to uphold congressional statutes. This seems to suggest that the Court rarely goes against its ideological preferences when nullifying Congress. Finally, we have seen that the Court treats issue areas before it somewhat differently, at least at the aggregate level. The Court has been most likely to nullify Congress on First Amendment and criminal procedure issues, followed by issues of judicial power and federalism. We also saw, that contrary to normative expectations, in the broad category of civil rights and civil liberties (criminal procedure, First Amendment, civil rights and due process issue areas) the Court has been much more likely to vote against rather than support the rights claimed. In this set of cases, the Court has also been much more likely to support judicial power, and to support federal power over state rights, and it has been more likely to vote in the liberal direction on economic issues. But when the analysis is limited to the rarer occasions when the Court nullifies Congress, then we find the Court more likely to support rights claims and more likely to support business interests and property rights.

The analyses of this chapter are descriptive only, and do not represent rigorous tests of many of the hypotheses and expectations I have discussed thus far. Although some of the descriptive analysis may give a preliminary answer, it must be kept in mind that these analyses do not control for a variety of other factors. Thus many of the questions we seek to answer are left open. Chapters Five will test many of the hypotheses in relation to the justices' behavior overtime in fully specified multivariate models. Chapter Three will present a descriptive analysis of the justices' votes prior to engaging in Chapter Five's multivariate analysis.

Notes

1. A briefer version of this chapter was published in *Judicature* (Keith 2007).
2. To conduct this search I sorted the dataset and culled out all observations that were coded where AUTHDEC1 and AUTHDEC2 were equal to one. This data sort pulls out all cases in which the Court engaged in judicial review at the national level. I then read each of these cases in order to identify the false positives that were selected, as the operationalization of the Spaeth variable does not distinguish the type or level of federal action was reviewed in the case. In this data set and my analysis I have deliberately chosen to use the calendar year rather than the Supreme Court's term as a point of reference, which follows Caldeira and McCrone. I made this choice because ultimately I am trying to identify trends overtime and to link these trends to events in U.S. history, particularly in regard to partisan politics in the Congress and presidency. Changes in Congress and the presidency coincide

almost perfectly with the calendar year for most of the history under study here. But since the Supreme Court's term begins in October and only represents three months of the calendar year it is rather problematic to say that those three months represent the entire year.

3. Since Spaeth's dataset covers the 1946 term rather than the calendar year 1946, his dataset extends back only to the last three months of 1946, so I read and coded the entire year of 1946 myself as part of my validity tests described below.

4. I begin the dataset in 1803 when the Marshall Court officially claims the power of judicial review. Of course, there was one previous case, *Hylton v. United States* (1796) in which the Court could be said to have considered the constitutionality of a congressional statute, under Spaeth's definition. Justice Chase seems to duck the need to determine constitutionality with his assertion that the tax on carriages is not a direct tax, and along with this assertion, he finds it "unnecessary, at this time ... to determine, whether this court, constitutionally possesses the power to declare an act of Congress void" and additionally he states that in not "giving an opinion, at this time, whether this court has jurisdiction to decide that any law made by Congress contrary to the Constitution of the US is void." Clearly, some scholars would disagree with this assessment, and I admit it was a tough call. McCloskey (1994) includes this case in his development of the Court subtly laying the groundwork to claim formally the power of judicial review, and ultimately judicial sovereignty (16–34). And Schwartz (1993) concludes that even though Chase stated that he did not even consider whether the Court had review jurisdiction, the justices considered the constitutional claim and that the consideration indicated that the justices believed they possessed the review power. Epstein and Walker (2006) go even farther and argue that the Court reviewed the constitutionality of the act and upheld it (68). Ultimately I decided that I must follow the decision rule described in this chapter, and to do so based on the language of the opinion, as the rule dictates. And I believe based on the language of the decision the call would have to be in favor of leaving the case out, and trust my colleagues to understand the difficulty of the call in this particular case.

5. The key word searches included such phrases as unconstitutional and Congress, Congress and constitutional or constitution, Congress and power, act and constitution/constitutional or unconstitutional, statute(s) unconstitutional or constitutional/constitution, Congress and competent, violation and congress/act, (in)valid and Congress, (in)valid and act, act and violate, statute and infamous, act and infamous, constitutionality, infringe or abridge and amendment.

6. I would like to note here that unlike Howard and Segal (2004) I cannot say that this dataset represents all of the instances in which the Supreme Court had *opportunity* to review the constitutionality of congressional action, because I am unable to examine briefs before the Court across this two-century period. But, as Howard and Segal note, the Supreme Court does not appear to engage in review *sua sponte*,

so it is likely that this set of decisions very nearly represents the Court's opportunities to review as well.

7. *Stuart v. Laird* (1803) is not included in the dataset here because Paterson's opinion avoided the constitutional issues and ruled on narrow and technical grounds. As Geyh (2006) notes the Court's "short timid opinion … failed to even acknowledge that the issue of the repeal's constitutionality was before the Court" (54).

8. I realize that including 1937 in this period overlaps with the prior period, but I decided to go with the slight overlap in order to be able to compare periods with McCloskey's delineation.

9. Spaeth's coding is as follows: In the context of issues pertaining to criminal procedure, civil rights, First Amendment, due process, privacy, and attorneys, liberal decisions are pro-person accused or convicted of crime, or denied a jury trial pro-civil liberties or civil rights claimant, pro-indigent, pro-Indian, pro-affirmative action, pro-neutrality in religion cases, pro-female in abortion, pro-underdog, anti-government in the context of due process, except for takings clause cases where a pro-government, an anti-owner vote is considered liberal except in criminal forfeiture cases, pro-attorney and pro-disclosure in 537 issues except for employment and student records. Conservative votes are the reverse of above. In the context of issues pertaining to unions and economic activity, a liberal vote is pro-union except in union antitrust, pro-competition, anti-business, anti-employer, pro-competition, pro-liability, pro-injured person, pro-indigent, pro-small business vis-à-vis large business, pro-debtor, pro-bankrupt, pro-Indian, pro-environmental protection, pro-economic underdog, pro-consumer, pro-accountability in governmental corruption, anti-union member or employee vis-à-vis union, anti-union in union anti-trust, and pro-trial in arbitration. Conservative votes are the reverse of above. In the context of issues pertaining to judicial power, a liberal vote is pro-exercise of judicial power and a conservative vote is the reverse. In the context of issues pertaining to federalism, a liberal vote is pro-federal power or anti-state, and a conservative vote is the reverse. In the context of issues pertaining to federal taxation, a liberal vote is pro-United States and a conservative vote is pro-taxpayer. Interstate relations and miscellaneous issues are coded missing on this dimension.

10. This determination is not meant as a criticism of Spaeth's delineation for the Supreme Court Database; I have no reason to believe that Spaeth himself would argue that his delineation is appropriate backwards in time for the entire history of the Court.

11. In the analysis in Chapters Three and Four, I will try to control for whether the decisions were considered to be landmark or major decisions.

12. I expect that some of the difference here is due to the fact that in this study the authors coded liberalism as Spaeth does rather than the modified version here.

13. As above, I expect that most of the difference here is due to the fact that in this study the author's coded liberalism as Spaeth does rather than the modified version here.

14. However, the Court's level of liberalism was only in the mid-thirties on criminal procedure cases.

15. Another way to look at issue area would be based simply on the constitutional provision at issue. In congressional review case the Interstate Commerce Clause is the most contested constitutional clause: 132 of the cases (31 percent). The First Amendment is the second most prevalent constitutional provision: 78 cases (18.3 percent). The taxation clauses are only slightly below the First Amendment in numbers: 76 cases (17.8 percent). Three constitutional provisions appear in the 4 percent to 5 percent range: the Tenth Amendment (22 cases, 5.2 percent), the Fourteenth Amendment (18 cases, 4.2 percent), and the delegation of powers and separation of powers provisions (17 cases, 4 percent). The naturalization clause is close behind these three clauses with 16 cases (3.8 percent). The Sixteenth Amendment is the key legal provision in 16 cases (3.1 percent). The remaining seven provisions represent less than 3 percent of the cases: the bill of attainder provision (9 cases, 2.1 percent), the necessary and proper clause (9 cases, 2.1 percent), the District of Columbia clause (8 cases, 1.9 percent), the Thirteenth Amendment (7 cases, 1.6 percent), and the coin money clause (6 cases, 1.4 percent). And at 5 cases (1.2 percent) are: the Eleventh Amendment, the governance of the armed forces clause, and the postal powers clause.

16. These patterns are flipped when applying the Spaeth delineation.

References

Ackerman, Bruce. 1991. *We The People Foundations*. Cambridge: Harvard University Press.

Ackermann, L.W. H. 1989. "Constitutional Protection of Human Rights: Judicial Review." *Columbia Human Rights Law Review* 21(1): 59–71.

Caldiera, Gregory A., and Donald J. McCrone. 1982. "Of Time and Judicial Activism: A Study of the U.S. Supreme Court, 1800–1973." In *Supreme Court Activism and Restraint*, eds. Stephen C. Halpern, and Charles M. Lamb. Lexington, MA: Lexington Books.

Chowdhury, Subrata Roy. 1989. *Rule of Law in a State of Emergency.* New York: St. Martin's Press.

Danelski, David J. 1989. "The Influence of the Chief Justice in the Decisional Process of the Supreme Court." In *American Court Systems*, eds. Sheldon Goldman and Austin Sarat. New York: Longman.

Epstein, Lee, Jeffrey A. Segal, Harold J. Spaeth, and Thomas G. Walker. 2003. *The Supreme Court Compendium*. Washington, DC: Congressional Quarterly Press.

Geyh, Charles Gardner. 2006. *When Courts and Congress Collide: The Struggle for Control of America's Judicial System.* Ann Arbor: University of Michigan Press.

Glennon, Michael J. 1984. "The Use of Custom in Resolving Separation of Powers Disputes." *Boston University Law Review* 64: 109–48.

Goldman, Sheldon. 1966. "Voting Behavior of the United States Courts of Appeals, 1961–1964. *American Political Science Review* 60: 374–84.

Goldman, Sheldon. 1975. "Voting Behavior of the United States Courts of Appeals Revisited." *American Political Science Review* 69: 491–506.

Howard, Robert M. and Jeffrey A. Segal. 2004. "A Preference for Deference? The Supreme Court and Judicial Review." *Political Research Quarterly* 57(1): 131–43

International Commission of Jurists. 1983. *States of Emergency: Their Impact on Human Rights.* Geneva: International Commission of Jurists.

Keck, Thomas. 2004. *The Most Activist Supreme Court in History: The Road to Modern Judicial Conservatism.* Chicago: University of Chicago Press.

Keck, Thomas. 2007. "Party, Policy, or Duty: Why Does the Supreme Court Invalidate Federal Statutes?" *American Political Science Review* 101: 321–39.

Keith, Linda Camp. 2007. "The United States Supreme Court and Judicial Review of Congress: 1803–2001." *Judicature* (January/February 2007) 90: 1–14.

Keith, Linda Camp and Ayo Ogundele. 2007. "Legal Systems and Constitutionalism in Sub-Saharan Africa: An Empirical Examination of Colonial Influences on Human Rights." Human Rights Quarterly 29(4): 1065–1097.

Keith, Linda Camp, Tate C. Neal, and Steven C. Poe. 2007. "Is the Law a Mere Parchment Barrier to Human Rights Abuse?" Unpublished manuscript.

King, Kimi and James Meernik. 1999. "The Supreme Court and the Powers of the Executive: The Adjudication of Foreign Policy." *Political Research Quarterly* 52: 801–24.

Ladd, Everett Carll, Jr. 1970. *American Political Parties: Social Change and Political Response.* New York: Norton Press.

Lamb, Charles., 1982. "A Preference for Difference?" *Political Research Quarterly* 57: 131–43.

Lanier, Drew Noble., 2003. *Of Time and Judicial Behavior: United Supreme Court Agenda-Setting and Decision-Making, 1888–1997.* London: Susquehanna University Press.

Lindquist, Stephanie A., and Rorie Spill Solberg. 2007. "Judicial Review by the Burger and Rehnquist Courts: Explaining Justices' Responses to Constitutional Challenges." *Political Research Quarterly* 60: 71–90.

McCloskey, Robert. G., 1994. *The American Supreme Court.* Chicago: University of Chicago Press.

Ogundele, Ayo and Linda Camp Keith. 2006. "The Supreme Court, 1801–1887: An Empirical Overview." Paper presented at the annual meeting of the Southern Political Science Association, Jan. 3–6, New Orleans, La.

Powe, Lucas A. Jr., 2000. *The Warren Court and American Politics.* Cambridge, MA: Belknap Press.

Rehnquist, William H., 1998. *All the Laws but One: Civil Liberties in Wartime.* Knopf: New York.

Reichley, James., 1992. *The Life of the Parties: A History of American Political Parties.* New York: The Free Press.

Savage, David G., 1992. *Turning Right: The Making of the Rehnquist Court.* New York: John Wiley and Sons.

Schwartz, Bernard. 1993. *A History of the Supreme Court.* New York: Oxford University Press.

Schwartz, Herman. 2002. *The Rehnquist Court: Judicial Activism on the Right.* New York: Hill and Wang.

Segal, Jeffrey A. and Harold J. Spaeth. 1993. *The Supreme Court and the Attitudinal Model.* Cambridge: Cambridge University Press.

Segal, Jeffrey A. and Harold J. Spaeth. 2002. *The Supreme Court and the Attitudinal Model Revisited.* Cambridge: Cambridge University Press.

Swisher, Carl b. 1974. *History of the Supreme Court of the United States, the Taney Period 1836–1864.* New York: Macmillan Publishing Co.

Wood, Sandra, Linda Camp Keith, Drew Lanier, and Ayo Ogundele. 1998. "The Supreme Court 1888–1940: An Empirical Overview." *Social Science History* 22: 204–24.

Yates, Jeff and Andrew Whitford. 1998. "Presidential Power and the United States Supreme Court." *Political Research Quarterly* 51: 539–50.

3

"Activist" or "Restraintist"? The Justices on the Bench

Introduction

Justices on the bench frequently have been praised as "restraintist" judges or maligned as "activist" judges. Critics typically argue that the justices have substituted their will or judgment for that of the democratically elected actors. In the context of the behavior under study here, justices who repeatedly overturn congressional statutes are frequently labeled and sometimes excoriated as judicial activists. Other scholars or commentators may praise the very same justices for exercising their judicial responsibility to defend the constitution against incursions by overreaching elected majorities, especially in regard to fundamental rights. Although I have noted through out the book, it is beyond the scope of this work to address the normative judgment inherent in these labels, I do make an empirical assessment of the individual justices' votes, examining the level of their support for congressional statutes under challenge or their willingness to overturn a congressional statute. I do not seek to examine the validity of such decisions, and thus as I discuss the justices' level of nullification or support of Congress, I try as much as possible to avoid the somewhat value-laden terms of "restraintist" and "activist;" however, these terms offer a convenient and short descriptor, such as in my title here, and often these justices are self-proclaimed restraintists or proponents of restraint or they been have categorized as such by legal scholars. I will, at times, in those cases refer the justices as such, but try to attribute the delineations to the justices or scholars making the claim. Certainly we will see justices who are much less restrained in their individual votes, relative to the norm of deference we saw in the previous chapter. In this chapter I also examine the emerging patterns of the justices' votes across various dimensions, including issue area and ideological preferences.

Even though I do not formally test the competing theories in this chapter, I will begin to test some initial theoretical expectations. The attitudinal model would predict that even if there is a norm of deference, we will find that the justices' votes will be affected by their individual policy preferences—that justices will typically overturn conservative laws or liberal laws but not both (Segal and Spaeth 1993, 2002). Thus we would expect to see strong patterns of liberalism and conservatism in the justices' votes. In these analyses we should be mindful that inferences are based on a dichotomous delineation of the ideological direction of the outcome of cases: the outcome is either conservative or liberal, according to a set of rules which I do believe are largely accepted by judicial behavioralists. Nonetheless, it is an oversimplification and does not take into consideration the degree of liberalism or conservatism of the outcome; it is a simple dichotomy. Although it seems somewhat justifiable to make ideological inferences from the patterns of strongly liberal votes in the exercise of judicial review by Douglas, for example, or from the patterns of strongly conservative votes by Antonin Scalia, it is harder to draw such distinctions from justices who exhibit mixed or moderate levels of ideology in their votes. Does such behavior represent an absence of influence from the justice's individual policy preferences or is it simply an indication of moderate ideology. In this descriptive level analysis I am not able to sort out such distinctions, but I will try to address them more rigorously in the next chapters. However, in this chapter I am able to draw some inferences from the justice's party affiliation and the appointing president's party affiliation, both of which have been strong predictors in Supreme Court justices' votes on the merit (e.g., Tate 1981; Tate and Handberg 1991; George and Epstein 1992). Though the descriptive analysis here does not test definitively the theoretical issues that concern us, it will provide a foundation upon which to build that analysis in the next chapters, and equally as important, the more detailed analysis will allow us to examine the individual justices' behavior systematically with depth that typically is missing in the quantitative work of judicial behavioralists published in refereed political science journals.

The Justices' Votes on the Constitutionality of Congressional Statutes

The research presented here focuses on the individual justice and their votes either to uphold or to nullify congressional action. I examine several dimensions of their behavior. First, I will present their overall patterns of deference to Congress. Next, I will analyze the ideological patterns of their congressional review votes, both in their overall votes and in distinguishing between votes to nullify and votes to uphold the congressional statute. Finally, I will analyze their votes across various key issue areas. Table 3.1 reports each justice's individual nullification rate: the percentage of votes in which the justice voted to nullify a congressional statute out of all the cases in which the justice had opportunity to either uphold or nullify congressional statutes.[1] Examining the full set of justices, I find an average nullification rate of 23.1 percent or put differently, the justices' mean support rate for Congress is 76.9 percent across the two-hundred-year period under study here. This is a somewhat lower level of deference than the Court's overall support rate of 83 percent uphold and 17 percentage nullification. It was to be expected that we would find a slightly lower support rate since here our votes include dissents and concurrence, not just the majority votes, and additionally since the overwhelming majority votes are to uphold Congress we would expect the dissenting votes to be overwhelmingly votes to nullify.

Ten justices earn nullification rates of zero and 4 justices earn 100 percent nullification rates, and thus would qualify statistically for the label "restraintist" or "activist" respectively. However, we must consider that 20 of the justices under study here participated in less than 10 cases each; 5 had only 1 vote and 9 had only 2 or 3 votes. Their small number of votes is too few to draw inferences with any level of confidence. It is also somewhat problematic, in terms of generalizations, as 14 of the 20 earned either 100 percent nullification or 100 percent uphold rates. In addition, each of those fourteen justices' served terms on the bench prior to the Court's consolidation of power following the Civil War. This fact is in itself an important indicator of court norms during a period in which the Supreme Court was rather cautiously building its power. Thus, we have a statistical weakness that results in part from a substantive and theoretically interesting phenomenon, so I chose to include them in the first table, but note that some caution might be in order in generalizing from these particular scores. I then disregard these justices in the analyses that follow this first section, satisfied to just note their presence here. These twenty justices include: Cushing (100 percent nullification, 1 vote), Paterson (100 percent, 1 vote), Chase (100 percent, 1 vote), Washington (33.3 percent, 1 vote), Moore (100 percent, 1 vote), Marshall (33.3 percent, 3 votes), Johnson (0 percent, 2 votes), Livingston (50 percent, 2 votes), Todd (0 percent, 2 votes), Duvall (0 percent, 2 votes), Story (0 percent, 2 votes), Thompson (0 percent, 2 votes), Baldwin (0 percent, 2 votes), Barbour (0 percent, 1 vote), McKinley (0 percent, 5 votes), Daniel (33.3 percent, 9 votes), Woodbury (0 percent, 3 votes),

Table 3.1 Individual Justice's Deference to Congress

	Number of Votes to Uphold Congress (Percentage of Votes)	Number of Votes to Nullify Congress (Percentage of Votes)	Total Number of Votes
Washington Appointments			
William Cushing (Feb. 1790–Sept. 1810)	0(0)	1(100)	1
William Paterson (March 1793–Sept. 1806)	0(0)	1(100)	1
Samuel Chase (Feb. 1796–June 1811)	0(0)	1(100)	1
Adams Appointments			
Bushrod Washington (Feb. 1799–Nov. 1829)	2(66.7)	1(33.3)	3
Alfred Moore (Apr. 1800–Jan. 1804)	0(0)	1(100)	1
John Marshall (Feb. 1801–July 1835)	2(66.7)	1(33.3)	3
Jefferson Appointments			
William Johnson (May 1804–Aug. 1834)	2(100)	0(0)	2
Brockholst Livingston (Jan. 1807–March 1823)	1(50.0)	1(50.0)	2
Thomas Todd (May 1807–Feb. 1826)	2(100)	0(0)	2
Madison Appointments			
Gabriel Duvall (Nov. 1811–Jan. 1835)	2(100)	0(0)	2
Joseph Story (Feb. 1812–Sept. 1845)	4(100)	0(0)	4
Monroe Appointment			
Smith Thompson (Sept. 1823–Dec. 1843)	2(100)	0(0)	2
Jackson Appointments			
John McLean (Jan. 1830–Apr. 1861)	10(90.9)	1(9.1)	11
Henry Baldwin (Jan. 1830–Apr. 1844)	2(100.0)	0(0)	2
James Wayne (Jan. 1835–July 1867)	15(83.3)	1(16.7)	18
Roger Taney (March 1836–Oct. 1864)	10(90.9)	1(9.1)	11
Philip Barbour(May 1836–Feb. 1841)	1(100.0)	0(0)	1
John Catron (May 1837–May 1865)	10(90.9)	1(9.1)	11
Van Buren Appointments			
John McKinley (Jan. 1838–July 1852)	5(100.0)	0(0)	5
Peter Daniel (Jan. 1842–May 1860)	6(66.7)	3(33.3)	9
Tyler Appointment			
Samuel Nelson (Feb. 1845–Nov. 1872)	25(73.5)	9(26.5)	34

	Number of Votes to Uphold Congress (Percentage of Votes)	Number of Votes to Nullify Congress (Percentage of Votes)	Total Number of Votes
Polk Appointments			
Levi Woodbury (Sept. 1845–Sept. 1851)	3(100.0)	0(0)	3
Robert Grier (Aug. 1846–Jan. 1870)	16(69.6)	7(30.4)	23
Benjamin Curtis (Oct. 1851–Sept. 1857)	6(100.0)	0(0)	6
Pierce Appointment			
John Campbell (Apr. 1853–Apr. 1861)	4(80.0)	1(20.0)	5
Buchanan Appointment			
Nathan Clifford (Jan. 1858–July 1881)	26(57.8)	19(42.2)	45
Lincoln Appointments			
Noah Swayne (Jan. 1862–Jan. 1881)	35(77.8)	10(22.2)	45
Samuel Miller (July 1861–Oct. 1890)	57(82.6)	12(17.4)	69
David Davis (Dec. 1862–March 1877)	20(69.0)	9(31.0)	29
Stephen Field (May 1863–Dec. 1897)	71(69.0)	32(31.0)	103
Salmon P. Chase (Dec. 1864–May 1873)	17(68.0)	8(32.0)	25
Grant Appointments			
William Strong (March 1870–Dec. 1880)	24(77.4)	7(22.6)	31
Joseph Bradley (March 1870–Jan. 1892)	50(83.3)	10(16.7)	60
Ward Hunt (Jan. 1873–Jan 1882)	17(85.0)	3(15.0)	20
Morrison Waite (March 1874–1888)	32(80.0)	8(20.0)	40
Hayes Appointments			
John Marshall Harlan (Dec. 1877–Oct. 1911)	146(86.0)	22(13.1)	168
William Woods (Jan. 1881–May 1887)	14(73.7)	5(26.3)	19
Stanley Matthews (May 1881–March 1889)	15(75.0)	5(25.0)	20
Arthur Appointments			
Horace Gray (Jan. 1882–Sept. 1902)	70(87.5)	10(12.5)	80
Samuel Blatchford (Apr. 1882–July 1893)	32(86.5)	5(13.5)	37
Cleveland Appointments			
Lucius C.Q. Lamar (Jan. 1888–Jan. 1893)	13(86.7)	2(13.3)	15
Melville Fuller (Oct. 1888–July 1910)	93(79.5)	24(20.5)	117
Harrison Appointments			
David Brewer (Jan. 1890–March 1910)	88(78.6)	24(21.4)	112
Henry Brown (Jan. 1891–May 1906)	77(91.7)	7(8.33)	84

Table 3.1 *(continued)*

	Number of Votes to Uphold Congress (Percentage of Votes)	Number of Votes to Nullify Congress (Percentage of Votes)	Total Number of Votes
George Shiras (Oct. 1892–Feb. 1903)	50(87.7)	7(12.2)	57
Howell Jackson (March 1893–Aug. 1805)	8(88.9)	1(11.1)	9
Cleveland II Appointments			
Edward White (March 1894–Dec. 1921)	179(85.2)	31(14.8)	210
Rufus Peckham (Jan. 1896–Oct. 1909)	61(72.6)	23(27.4)	84
McKinley Appointment			
Joseph McKenna (Jan. 1898–Jan. 1925)	191(86.0)	31(14.0)	222
T. Roosevelt Appointments			
Oliver Wendell Holmes (Dec. 1902–Jan. 1932)	231(91.3)	22(8.7)	253
William Day (March 1903–Dec. 1922)	143(84.6)	25(15.4)	169
William Moody (Dec. 1906–Nov. 1910)	16(88.9)	2(11.1)	18
Taft Appointments			
Horace Lurton (Jan. 1910–July 1914)	42(87.5)	6(12.5)	48
Charles Evan Hughes (Oct. 1910–June 1916) and Feb. 1930–June 1941)	162(88.5)	21(11.5)	183
Willis Van Devanter (Jan. 1911–July 1937)	214(80.8)	51(19.3)	265
Joseph Lamar (Jan. 1911–Jan. 1916)	54(88.5)	7(11.5)	61
Mahlon Pitney (March 1912–Dec. 1922)	86(82.7)	18(17.3)	104
Wilson Appointments			
James McReynolds (Oct. 1914–Jan. 1941)	176(72.4)	67(27.6)	243
Louis Brandeis (June 1916–Feb. 1939)	197(92.9)	15(7.1)	212
John Clarke (Oct. 1916–Sept. 1922)	51(89.5)	6(10.5)	57
Harding Appointments			
William Taft (July 1921–Feb. 1930)	60(83.3)	12(16.7)	72
George Sutherland (Oct. 1922–Jan. 1938)	105(76.1)	33(23.9)	138
Pierce Butler (Jan. 1923–Nov. 1939)	116(70.7)	48(29.3)	164
Edward Sanford (Feb. 1923–March 1930)	53(85.5)	9(14.5)	62
Coolidge Appointment			
Harlan Fiske Stone (March 1925–Apr. 1946)	169(89.5)	20(10.5)	189

	Number of Votes to Uphold Congress (Percentage of Votes)	Number of Votes to Nullify Congress (Percentage of Votes)	Total Number of Votes
Hoover Appointments			
Owen Roberts (June 1930–July 1945)	110(78.6)	30(21.4)	140
Benjamin Cardozo (March 1932–July 1938)	57(89.1)	7(10.9)	64
F. Roosevelt Appointments			
Hugo Black (Aug. 1937–Sept. 1971)	139(68.8)	63(31.2)	202
Stanley Reed (Jan. 1938–Feb. 1957)	108(95.6)	5(4.4)	113
Felix Frankfurter (Jan. 1939–Aug. 1962)	116(87.9)	12(12.1)	132
William Douglas (Apr. 1939–Nov. 1975)	121(57.9)	88(42.1)	209
Frank Murphy (Feb. 1940–July 1949)	50(83.3)	10(16.7)	60
James Byrnes (July 1941–Oct. 1942)	9(90)	1(10)	10
Robert Jackson (July 1941–Oct. 1954)	34(91.9)	3(8.1)	37
Wiley Rutledge (Feb. 1943–Sept. 1949)	34(82.9)	7(17.1)	41
Truman Appointments			
Harold Burton (Oct. 1945–Oct. 1958)	57(91.9)	5(8.1)	62
Fred Vinson (June 1946–Sept. 1953)	32(97.0)	1(3.0)	33
Tom Clark (Aug. 1949–June 1967)	70(81.4)	16(18.6)	86
Sherman Minton (Oct. 1949–Oct. 1956)	29(93.6)	2(6.5)	31
Eisenhower Appointments			
Earl Warren (Oct. 1953–June 1969)	46(60.5)	30(39.5)	76
John Marshall Harlan II (March 1955–Sept. 1971)	65(74.7)	22(25.3)	87
William Brennan (Oct. 1956–July 1990)	148(62.5)	89(37.6)	237
Charles Whittaker (March 1957–March 1962)	22(95.7)	1(4.3)	23
Potter Stewart (Oct. 1958–July 1981)	119(72.1)	46(27.9)	165
Kennedy Appointments			
Byron White (Apr. 1962–June 1993)	186(82.7)	39(17.3)	225
Arthur Goldberg (Oct. 1962–July 1965)	11(73.3)	4(26.7)	15
L. Johnson Appointments			
Abe Fortas (Oct. 1965–May 1969)	8(42.1)	11(57.9)	19
Thurgood Marshall (Oct. 1967–Oct. 1991)	119(63.0)	79(37.0)	189
Nixon Appointments			
Warren Burger (June 1969–June 1986)	136(87.2)	20(12.8)	156
Harry Blackmun (June 1970–Aug. 1994)	159(84.6)	29(15.4)	188

Table 3.1 *(continued)*

	Number of Votes to Uphold Congress (Percentage of Votes)	Number of Votes to Nullify Congress (Percentage of Votes)	Total Number of Votes
Lewis Powell (Jan. 1972–June 1987)	120(83.9)	23(16.1)	143
William Rehnquist (Jan. 1972–Sept. 2005)	171(78.8)	46(21.2)	217
Ford Appointment			
John Paul Stevens (Dec. 1975–)	134(75.7)	43(24.3)	177
Reagan Appointments			
Sandra Day O'Connor (Sept. 1981–Jan. 2006)	80(66.1)	41(33.8)	121
Antonin Scalia (Sept. 1986–)	47(59.5)	32(40.5)	79
Anthony Kennedy (Feb. 1988–)	44(62.0)	27(38.0)	71
Bush I Appointments			
David Souter (Oct. 1990–)	32(58.1)	23(41.8)	55
Clarence Thomas (Oct. 1991–)	26(51.0)	25(49.0)	51
Clinton Appointments			
Ruth Bader Ginsburg (Aug. 1993–)	25(56.8)	19(43.2)	44
Stephen Breyer (Aug. 1994–)	22(55.0)	18(45.0)	40
MEAN(SD)	76.9(21.0)	23.1(21.2)	

Curtis (9 percent, 6 votes), Campbell (0 percent, 5 votes), and Howell Jackson (11.1 percent, 9 votes).

If we disregard these twenty justices in the analysis, the resulting average nullification rate is 21.6, with average support of Congress being 78.3 percent. Eight justices earn nullification scores of approximately 40 percent or more. Abe Fortas earns the highest nullification rate by quite a large margin, voting to nullify Congress in 57.9 percent of his votes; he is the only justice who did not vote to defer to Congress at least half the time. The second highest nullification rate belongs to Clarence Thomas, who at 49 percent defers to Congress only slightly more than half the time. Only 3 of the 8 justices with scores of 40 percent or more serve prior to the Rehnquist Court: Buchanan appointee Nathan Clifford, an ardent Jeffersonian (42.2) and liberals William Douglas (42.1) and Abe Fortas (57.9), as mentioned above. In addition to Thomas, four of the current Supreme Court justices earn scores over 40 percent: Antonin Scalia (40.5), David Souter (41.8), Ruth Bader Ginsburg (43.2), and Stephen Breyer (45). It is interesting to note the presence of the two conservative justices, Scalia and Thomas, among the liberal justices, countering the long held popular conception that the so-called activist judges are liberal. This occurrence supports Sunstein's assertion that Rehnquist, Scalia, and Thomas have created a role reversal in which conservatives are as activist as liberals in past periods of the Court's history (2005), although here we must note that Rehnquist's score (21.2) is actually slightly lower than the mean nullification score. We might expect this difference due to his role of chief justice, since nullifying statutes promulgated by the elected branches of government may put the Court's legitimacy at risk if the power is exercised imprudently, and thus for institutional reasons, the chief justice may tend to be less likely to vote to strike congressional statutes. it is surprising that on average the chief justices have lower nullification rates than associate justices, an average of 17.9 compared to 21.4 percent. However, when we separate out Rehnquist's votes as chief justice from those when he was associate justice, we see he votes to nullify Congress at a much higher rate as chief justice (28.9 percent) than he did as associate justice (16.4 percent). Of course, these bivariate statistics cannot control for numerous other factors affecting Rehnquist's votes simultaneously so until we examine the behavior in multivariate models, our observations are still tentative. In the following chapters, I will test more rigorously the impact of role to see whether serving as chief justice does increase the probability of higher levels of deference, ceteris paribus.

Returning to the nullification rates in Table 3.1, we find fourteen justices who earn scores of ten percent or less, showing relatively high levels of deference to Congress. Fred Vinson earns the lowest score, voting to nullify Congress in only 3 percent of his votes, and is followed by Charles Whittaker, Potter Stewart and Stanley Reed, with scores 4.3, 4.3, and 4.4 scores, respectively. Other justices earning scores below 10 percent included: Sherman Minton (6.5), Louis Brandeis (7.1), Henry Brown (8.3), Oliver Wendell Holmes, Jr. (8.7), Harold Burton (8.1), Robert Jackson (8.1), John McLean (9.1), Roger Taney (9.1), John Catron (9.1) and John Byrnes (10). Vinson and Reed were both members of the Vinson Court bloc led by Felix Frankfurter (12.2) that "urged judicial restraint as the only criterion of constitutional adjudication" (Schwartz 1993, 255). Other members of the Vinson Court bloc included Robert Jackson (8.1). It is noteworthy that Whittaker, of whom it has been said, "may have been the least talented Justice appointed during this century" (Schwartz 1993, 271) was considerably more restraintist than his fellow Warren Court proponents of restraint, Frankfurter (12.2), Harlan (25.3), and Clark (18.6). And clearly, Stewart, who has been called the "'swing man' between the activist and restraint bloc" of the Warren Court (Schwartz

1993, 272) earns an even more restraintist score than the "restraint bloc." Burton and Minton, both of whom were strongly influenced by Frankfurter and highly deferential to him (Schwartz and Lesher 1983, 65–6), are more restraintist than their intellectual mentor. Examining the justices from the earlier courts that fall into this narrow set of highly deferential justices, we find the not too well-known Henry Brown and William Moody, who have been lumped into the group of "less than mediocre justices" who served on the Fuller Court and who have been virtually "buried in a shroud of anonymity" (Schwartz, 178). Taney and Catron the two remaining justices in this category, both obviously a part of the Taney Court, which as previous analysis of these cases has shown, was largely deferential to the national government until *Dred Scott.* It is not surprising that Catron, who maintained such close ties with the president as to be deemed inappropriate, even for that period of time, largely supported the national government. At this point, we do not know whether their votes to defer to Congress tended to reflect a strong ideological direction. I will address that question in the next section.

As we move beyond this narrow set of justices earning highly deferential nullification scores of less than ten percent, we find that prior to the Four Horsemen's consistent challenge of Roosevelt's New Deal programs there are only a few justices with nullification rates above twenty percent. Robert Grier, a well-known proponent of states' rights earns a nullification rate of 30.4 percent. Nathan Clifford, also an ardent Jeffersonian that favored state rights, earns an even higher nullification rate (42.2). Stephen Field's congressional nullification rate of 31.0 percent is somewhat surprising given his strong Hamiltonian views on national supremacy. Salmon P. Chase's nullification rate of 32 percent is in line with his fellow justices, Fields and Clifford, and is perhaps easier to explain when breaking down the ideological direction of the votes, as I will do in the next section. McCloskey's analysis of the Taney Court may give us some insight into these justices' higher than expected nullification rates; he posits that Marshall "succeeded in planting a judicial tradition of mentorship" and that justices who "began coming to the Court—men like Chase and Bradley and Field—felt authorized to help America decide what kind of nation it should be" (1994, 69). We will examine these ideological links in sections that follow.

Not surprisingly, three of the four Horsemen whose overall voting patterns have been perceived to be strongly driven by conservative political preferences, each earn nullification scores that are significantly higher than the overall average as well as that of their contemporaries on the bench: James McReynolds (27.6 percent), George Sutherland (23.9 percent), and Pierce Butler (29.3 percent); the exceptional fourth member of the Horsemen, Willis Van Devanter, earns a score that is just slightly lower than average at 19.3 percent. It is possible that Van Devanter's leadership role which he is argued to have shared with Chief Justice Taft (Danelski 1989), contributes to his lower nullification voting patterns. He may have been less willing to dissent, as chief justices in their leadership positions are. In fact, we find that he dissented less than the other three Horsemen. He dissents in only 13 of 265 votes (5 percent); whereas, the Sutherland dissented in 11 of 138 votes (8 percent), Butler in 11 of 138 votes (15 percent), and McReynolds in 41 of 243 votes (17 percent). We find only three additional justices that joined the bench prior to Chief Justice Warren who earn nullification scores of greater than 20 percent: Owen Roberts (21.4 percent) whose eventual switch to support Roosevelt's New Deal legislation is often attributed to saving the Court from further court-curbing plans of the president, and two eventual Warren Court liberals, Hugo Black (31.2 percent) and William Douglas (42.1 percent). After Warren joins the bench, it becomes abnormal for a justice to have a score *below* 20 percent, with only five justices earning such scores: Charles Whittaker (4.3 percent), who we have already mentioned, Byron White (17.3 percent), Warren Burger (12.8 percent), Harry Blackmun (15.4 percent), and Lewis Powell (16.1 percent). As mentioned above, Rehnquist earns a nullification rate around 20 percent (21.2 percent). With the exception of John Paul Stevens (24.3 percent), all of the current justices included in this study place in the top ten nullification rates: Anthony Kennedy ranks tenth with a score of 38 percent and Antonin Scalia ranks eighth with a score of 40.5 percent. David Souter ranks seventh with a score of 40.5 percent, Ruth Bader Ginsburg ranks fourth with a score of 43.2 percent, Breyer ranks third with a score of 45.0 percent, and Thomas ranks second with a score of 49.0 percent. We will examine the ideological implication of these scores in the following sections.

Table 3.2 presents summary scores of the ideological direction of the justices' votes. Column one in Table Two presents the percentage of votes that were supportive of the republican or conservative tradition and column two presents the percentage of votes that were supportive of the liberal tradition as delineated in Chapter Two.[2] Column three reports the difference between the justices' liberalism and conservatism scores, which is another way to gauge the magnitude of the justice's ideological patterns. The more moderate ideologically the justice's votes are the smaller the distance between his or her scores will be. Although this first set of analyses will consider the liberalism/conservatism patterns across the justices' votes generally, the subsequent analyses will break down the votes by issue areas, and examine the extent to which the justices' votes are pro-civil rights or pro-economic interests, and so forth. Before discussing Table 3.2, I need to return briefly to the issue of the ideological direction of federalism votes. Here,

Table 3.2 Ideological Direction of Votes: Percent Supporting Republican/Conservative and Liberal Traditions*

Appointing President and Justice (party affiliation at time of appointment in parenthesis)	Number of Votes in Republican/ Conservative Tradition (Percentage of Votes)	Number of Votes in Liberal Tradition (Percentage of Votes)	Distance between Support for Liberal and Republican/ Conservative Tradition	Total Number of Votes
Jackson (Dem)				
John McLean (Dem)[a]	6(54.5)	5(45.5)	9.1	11
James Wayne (Dem)	10(55.6)	8(44.4)	11.1	18
Roger Taney (Dem) [b]	8(72.7)	3(27.3)	45.5	11
John Catron (Dem)	8(72.7)	3(27.3)	45.5	11
Tyler (Dem)				
Samuel Nelson (Dem) [a]	22(64.7)	12(35.3)	29.4	34
Polk (Dem)				
Robert Grier (Dem)	12(52.2)	11(47.8)	4.3	23
Buchanan (Dem)				
Nathan Clifford (Dem)	16(35.6)	29(64.4)	28.9	45
Lincoln (Rep)				
Noah Swayne (Rep) [c]	22(48.9)	23(51.1)	2.2	45
Samuel Miller (Rep) [d]	34(50.7)	33(49.3)	1.5	67
David Davis (Rep) [d]	18(46.2)	21(53.8)	7.7	29
Stephen Field (Dem)	44(45.4)	53(54.6)	9.3	97
Salmon P. Chase (Rep) [d]	12(48.0)	13(52.0)	4.0	25
Grant (Rep)				
William Strong (Rep) [c]	15(48.4)	16(51.6)	3.2	31
Joseph Bradley (Rep) [d]	31(53.4)	27(46.6)	6.9	58
Ward Hunt (Rep) [c]	5(25.0)	15(75.0)	50.0	20
Morrison Waite (Rep) [d]	15(38.5)	24(61.5)	23.1	39
Hayes (Rep)				
John Marshall Harlan(Rep) [d]	80(49.7)	81(51.3)	1.6	161
William Woods (Rep) [c]	7(38.9)	11(61.1)	22.2	18
Garfield (Rep)				
Stanley Matthews (Rep) [c]	8(42.1)	11(57.9)	15.8	19
Arthur (Rep)				
Horace Gray (Rep)	38(51.4)	36(48.6)	2.7	74
Samuel Blatchford (Rep)	20(60.6)	13(39.4)	21.2	33

Appointing President and Justice (party affiliation at time of appointment in parenthesis)	Number of Votes in Republican/ Conservative Tradition (Percentage of Votes)	Number of Votes in Liberal Tradition (Percentage of Votes)	Distance between Support for Liberal and Republican/ Conservative Tradition	Total Number of Votes
Cleveland (Dem)				
Lucius C.Q. Lamar (Dem)	11(91.7)	1(8.3)	83.3	12
Melville Fuller (Dem)	58(52.3)	53(47.7)	4.5	111
Harrison (Rep)				
David Brewer (Rep)	48(44.9)	59(55.1)	10.3	107
Henry Brown (Rep)	37(46.8)	42(53.2)	6.3	79
George Shiras (Rep)	22(41.5)	31(58.5)	17.0	53
Cleveland II (Dem)				
Edward White (Dem)	113(56.5)	87(43.5)	13.0	200
Rufus Peckham (Dem)	27(32.9)	55(67.1)	34.1	82
McKinley (Rep)				
Joseph McKenna (Rep) c	117(55.2)	95(44.8)	10.4	212
T. Roosevelt (Rep)				
Oliver Wendell Holmes (Rep)	124(53.2)	109(46.8)	6.4	233
William Day (Rep)	91(65.5)	70(43.5)	13.0	161
William Moody (Rep)	12(66.7)	6(33.3)	33.3	18
Taft (Rep)				
Horace Lurton (Dem)	31(66.0)	16(34.0)	32.0	47
Charles Evan Hughes (Rep)	93(53.4)	81(46.6)	6.0	174
Willis Van Devanter (Rep)	119(50.0)	119(50.0)	0	238
Joseph Lamar (Dem)	39(65.0)	21(35.0)	30.0	60
Mahlon Pitney (Rep)	57(58.8)	40(41.2)	17.5	97
Wilson (Dem)				
James McReynolds (Dem)	99(45.8)	117(54.2)	8.3	216
Louis Brandeis (Rep)	85(45.7)	101(54.3)	8.6	186
John Clarke (Dem)	44(58.7)	31(41.3)	17.3	75
Harding (Rep)				
William Taft (Rep)	27(43.5)	35(56.5)	12.0	62
George Sutherland (Rep)	48(39.7)	73(60.3)	20.7	121
Pierce Butler (Dem)	63(43.4)	82(56.6)	13.1	145
Edward Sanford (Rep)	21(40.4)	39(51.6)	13.1	52

Table 3.2 *(continued)*

Appointing President and Justice (party affiliation at time of appointment in parenthesis)	Number of Votes in Republican/ Conservative Tradition (Percentage of Votes)	Number of Votes in Liberal Tradition (Percentage of Votes)	Distance between Support for Liberal and Republican/ Conservative Tradition	Total Number of Votes
Coolidge (Rep)				
Harlan Fiske Stone (Rep)	68(39.5)	104(60.5)	20.9	172
Hoover (Rep)				
Owen Roberts (Rep)	64(48.9)	67(51.1)	2.3	131
Benjamin Cardozo (Dem)	23(40.4)	34(59.6)	19.3	57
F. Roosevelt (Dem)				
Hugo Black (Dem)	37(18.9)	159(81.1)	62.2	196
Stanley Reed (Dem)	33(30.8)	74(69.2)	38.4	107
Felix Frankfurter (Ind)	49(38.9)	77(61.1)	22.2	126
William Douglas (Dem)	32(16.0)	172(84.3)	68.3	204
Frank Murphy (Dem)	10(17.5)	47(82.5)	65.0	57
Robert Jackson (Dem)	8(22.9)	27(77.1)	54.2	35
Wiley Rutledge (Dem)	8(20.0)	32(80.0)	78.0	40
Truman (Dem)				
Harold Burton (Rep)	28(47.5)	31(52.5)	5.0	59
Fred Vinson (Dem)	13(43.3)	17(56.7)	13.4	30
Tom Clark (Dem)	42(51.2)	40(48.8)	2.4	82
Sherman Minton (Dem)	19(65.5)	10(34.5)	31.0	29
Eisenhower (Rep)				
Earl Warren (Rep)	23(30.3)	53(69.7)	39.4	76
John Marshall Harlan II(Rep)	49(57.0)	37(43.0)	14.0	86
William Brennan (Dem)	64(27.6)	168(72.4)	44.8	232
Charles Whittaker (Rep)	13(56.5)	10(43.5)	13.0	23
Potter Stewart (Rep)	94(57.3)	70(42.7)	14.6	164
Kennedy (Dem)				
Byron White (Dem)	121(55.2)	98(44.8)	10.4	219
Arthur Goldberg (Dem)	4(26.7)	11(73.3)	46.6	15
L. Johnson (Dem)				
Abe Fortas (Dem)	3(15.8)	16(84.2)	68.4	19
Thurgood Marshall (Dem)	45(24.7)	137(75.3)	50.6	182

Appointing President and Justice (party affiliation at time of appointment in parenthesis)	Number of Votes in Republican/ Conservative Tradition (Percentage of Votes)	Number of Votes in Liberal Tradition (Percentage of Votes)	Distance between Support for Liberal and Republican/ Conservative Tradition	Total Number of Votes
Nixon (Rep)				
Warren Burger (Rep)	106(69.3)	47(30.7)	38.6	153
Harry Blackmun (Rep)	101(55.5)	81(45.5)	10.0	182
Lewis Powell (Dem)	90(64.3)	50(35.7)	28.6	140
William Rehnquist (Rep)	148(71.2)	60(28.8)	42.4	208
Ford (Rep)				
John Paul Stevens (Rep)	66(39.3)	102(60.7)	21.4	168
Reagan (Rep)				
Sandra Day O'Connor (Rep)	68(60.2)	45(39.8)	20.4	113
Antonin Scalia (Rep)	47(64.4)	26(35.6)	28.8	73
Anthony Kennedy (Rep)	38(57.6)	28(42.2)	15.4	66
Bush I (Rep)				
David Souter (Rep)	14(27.4)	37(72.6)	45.2	51
Clarence Thomas (Rep)	31(63.3)	18(36.7)	26.6	49
Clinton (Dem)				
Ruth Bader Ginsburg (Dem)	11(26.2)	31(73.8)	47.6	42
Stephen Breyer (Dem)	11(29.0)	27(71.0)	42.0	38
Mean (SD)	46.7(15.9)	51.9(15.2)	23.9(19.7)	

*The analysis includes only justices with at least ten votes. [a]Former Democratic-Republican; [b]Former Federalist; [c]Former Democrat; [d]Former Whig

I decide to deviate from the Spaeth delineation on the federalism issue and switch the coding of ideological direction on federalism votes for justices who joined the bench prior to Franklin Roosevelt's first judicial appointment, Hugo Black, taking the bench in 1937. Although this accommodation is not 100 percent satisfactory, I believe a summative measure of the individual justices' ideological patterns is justifiable, so long as we consider the limitations of the measure in drawing conclusions, and do not over rely on these summative labels as a mere convenience of analysis.[3]

The mean liberalism score is approximately 52 percent (51.9) with the mean conservatism score approximately 47 percent (46.7) and the average distance between the judge's liberalism and conservatism is 23.9 percent.[4] For the sake of clarity and consistency I will focus here on reporting the liberalism scores, as has been the norm of other studies of judicial behaviors (e.g., Tate 1981). The liberalism scores range from a high of 84.3 (Douglas) and 84.2 (Fortas) to lows of 8.3 (Lucius C.Q. Lamar) and 27.7 (Taney and Catron). If we consider judges in the moderate range to be those who would support conservative and liberal positions approximately equally, we would expect their liberalism and conservatism scores to approximate 50 percent, all things being equal. If we consider a moderate judge's score a bit more broadly, to fall within the range of 40 to 60 percent, we find slightly more than one-half (53.2 percent) of the justices consistently balance their votes between the two ideological positions.[5]

As we examine these ideological patterns of the justices' votes over time, we find patterns that largely fit with anecdotal and doctrinal expectations. Two of the lowest liberalism scores are earned by Jackson's appointees, Taney and Catron; while McLean and Wayne, Jackson's other two appointees included in the analyses here, earn relatively low liberalism scores of 45.5 and 44.4 percent respectively. These justices participated in a relatively small number of congressional review cases (only 11 decisions with the exception of Wayne with 18), over half of which dealt with federalism as the primary issue of the case. This finding fits with Goldman's assessment that the majority of the justices serving on the Taney Court were devoted to national supremacy and the rights of private property (1982, 108) and Schwartz's (1993) assertion that the Supreme Court under Taney "continued the essential thrust of constitutional development begun under Marshall and his colleagues" (74). Both McLean and Wayne were strong nationalists on the bench and were referred by fellow associate justice Curtis as "McLean & Wayne, who are the most high-toned Federalists on the bench" (Schwartz 98). The next seventeen justices to join the bench (which includes appointments from presidents Tyler through Arthur) predominantly earn scores in the moderate range with only two justices substantially outside the range:[6] Tyler-appointee Nelson (35.3) whose twenty-seven years on the bench was spent primarily on the Taney Court (all but eight years) and Grant-appointee Hunt (75 percent), who had replaced Nelson on the bench in 1872 but whose tenure was brief and marred by illness from a stroke he suffered in 1878 (Schwartz 162).[7]

Of the next 16 justices to join the bench (which covers appointees of presidents Cleveland through Taft), we find 5 justices that do not fall in the moderate range. As mentioned earlier, the lowest liberalism score (8.3) over the entire historical period here is earned by the Cleveland appointment of Lucius Q.C. Lamar, the Southern Democrat from Mississippi, who was the first Supreme Court justice who had served in the Confederate Army (Schwartz, 170). This conservative score fits with his tenure-length score (Ogundele and Keith 2006). Cleveland appointment Justice Peckham score of 67.1 conflicts with Schwartz' description of Peckham as "the exemplar of the conservative jurist early in this century" (179); however, this reference is primarily in relation to his laissez-faire opinions in economic decisions. In the last section, we will examine the votes by issue area, but we will find Peckham only to be conservative in civil rights and liberties cases. Of course, the congressional review cases are a non-representative, albeit important sample, of the justices' overall judicial behavior. Theodore Roosevelt-appointee Moody, one of the twelve highly deferential justices earning nullification rates of less than ten percent, has a liberalism score of 33.3 that fits within his conservative record on the bench, albeit at a somewhat higher degree. Not unexpectedly two Taft justices fall within this highly conservative range; Schwartz asserts that "Taft devoted more attention to the choice of Justices than any other president" (204). Lurton (34 percent) who has been described as a "mediocre judge who turned out to be a mediocre Justice," however, only served five years, joining the bench at the age of almost sixty-six, and is said to have contributed little to Supreme Court jurisprudence" (Schwartz 205). His conservatism score matches almost exactly his tenure length scores (Wood et al. 1998). Taft appointment Joseph Lamar also earns a highly conservative score of 35 percent, but his tenure was short as well (less than five terms) and of little note. His ideological score on congressional review cases also matches his tenure length score. Thus, we see a fairly strong ideological pattern even in these earlier Courts.

Interestingly, none of the appointees of Presidents Wilson, Harding, Coolidge or Hoover earns a score outside the moderate range. Most of the justices earn scores around 50 percent and are strongly within the moderate range. One point to keep in mind with these justices' scores is that they are the last of the justices' to have their votes considered conservative if pro-national government (on federalism issues) in the coding of liberalism here. If the shifting alignment on the federalism issue was more gradual than Ladd recognizes, it may be that these justices' votes were affected by the shift. However, if we examine the federalism votes of these justices, we find all of these Republican justices have strong levels of support for the national government: Brandeis (90.7), Sutherland (62.1), Sanford (91.7), Stone (91.7), and Roberts (80). However, the two Southern Democrats do have more states' rights supporting scores, McReynolds (52.4) and Butler (60.5), and Democrat Cardozo has a pro-national government record, with a score of 86.7. We will return to this issue and continue the ideological comparison of these justices across the full set of issues in the next section.

Not surprisingly, as we move over time to Franklin Roosevelt's appointees and into today's Court, we find justices consistently earning scores outside the moderate range—20 of the 32 justices. Fourteen justices earn scores higher than the 60 percent range. All but one of Roosevelt's appointees (Frankfurter, 61.1) fall into this category: Black (81.1), Reed (69.1), Douglas (84.3), Murphy (82.5), Jackson (77.1), and Rutledge (80). These scores are in line with the justices' general liberalism rates found by Tate (1981): Douglas (93.4 percent in civil rights and civil liberties cases and 82.1 in economic cases), Murphy (94.3 percent and 96.4, respectively) and Black (73.3 percent and 85.4, respectively) (357). Felix Frankfurter's score is the lowest at 61.1 percent. Interestingly, Frankfurter's scores here are substantially more liberal here than in Tate's analysis; Tate found Frankfurter's vote to be only 46.6 percent liberal in civil rights and liberties cases and even more conservative on economic issues at 21 percent liberalism. Again, the difference may be that this analysis examines both unanimous and nonunanimous decisions; whereas, Tate only examined only decisions in which the votes were split.

Not unexpectedly, Truman and Eisenhower's appointees' liberalism scores are substantially lower than FDR's appointees, with the exception of Eisenhower's two "mistakes": Earl Warren (69.7 percent) and William Brennan (72.4 percent). In comparison with Tate's (1981) analysis of the justices' liberalism on economic issues and civil rights and liberties, we find the justice's liberalism dampened here: Warren (79.1 on rights issues and 82 percent on economic issues) and Brennan (81.4 and 74.5, respectively). Sherman Minton achieves the lowest score, 34.5 percent, but he participates in a relatively small number of congressional review cases, only 29. The rest of Truman's appointees' scores are in the upper forties to mid-fifties (Burton 52.5 percent, Vinson 56.7 percent, and Clark 48.8 percent) and Eisenhower's other appointee's scores are in the low to mid-forties (John Marshall Harlan II, 43 percent, Charles Whittaker 43.5 percent, and Potter Stewart 42.7 percent). We generally find these justices' ideology to be moderated in this set of cases, compared to Tate's tenure length analysis: Burton (20.4 on rights cases and 30.3 on economic cases), Vinson (17.3 and 41.5), Clark (25.3 and 52.2), Harlan II (23.3 and 23.3), Whittaker (26.3 and 17.2), and Stewart (45.8 and 35.6).

Kennedy's appointees are split, one moderate conservative and one strong liberal: Byron White (44.8 percent) and Arthur Goldberg (73.3 percent). White's scores in Tate's analysis are roughly equivalent here (41.5 and 58.4), but Goldberg's congressional review votes are more moderate than his Tate scores on rights issues but not economic issues (89.2 and 66.0, respectively). Both LBJ appointees exhibit quite strong liberal voting patterns, consistent with their reputations: Abe Fortas (84.2 percent) and Thurgood Marshall (75.3 percent). As with Goldberg we find these high liberalism scores are more moderate than the Tate scores on rights issues but not economic issues (Fortas 84.3 and 67.6 and Marshall 84.2 and 67.5). Not unexpectedly, Nixon's appointees, with one exception, earn the lowest liberalism scores of all the justices, including Reagan's: Warren Burger (30.7 percent), Lewis Powell (35.7 percent), and William Rehnquist (28.8 percent). Harry Blackmun's score of 45.5 percent would be considered moderately conservative. As above, these justices' scores in the Tate analysis were generally more ideologically consistent than we find here in the congressional review cases: Burger (16.2 and 20), Powell (30.8 and 36.6), Rehnquist (4.5 and 15.6), and Blackmun (26.0 and 32.1). Ford's one appointment to the bench, John Paul Stevens, earns a moderate score, leaning toward the liberal side (60.7 percent). This score compares equally to *The Supreme Court Compendium's* assessment of Steven's liberalism across key issue areas. Reagan's appointees clearly fall within the conservative range, including the so-called moderates: Anthony Kennedy (42.2 percent), Antonin Scalia (35.6 percent) and Sandra Day O'Connor (39.8 percent). These scores also fit the *Compendium's* assessment of the justices, but they are somewhat moderated. The first Bush president's appointees are drastically split in their liberalism patterns: David Souter earns a solid liberalism score of 72.6 and Thomas earns the fourth lowest liberalism score, 36.7 percent. Thomas's congressional review scores are more moderate than his *Compendium* scores are generally; however, Souter's *Compendium* scores are more moderate than his congressional review scores. Clinton's two appointees earn, as expected, solid but not extreme liberal ideological scores: Ruth Bader Ginsburg (73.8 percent) and Stephen Breyer (71 percent). It is hard to compare Ginsburg and Breyer's scores with the *Compendium* scores because they both have much more variation in their scores across issue areas than the other justices, and because of their relatively small number of votes in the dataset at this point. Of course, these Clinton appointment's scores are substantially lower than the liberalism of the appointees of Franklin Roosevelt and Lyndon Johnson. Although the justices appointed to the bench in the twentieth-century have tended to show more consistently ideological voting patterns than we saw in the earlier periods, we actually see rather consistent evidence that the ideological nature of even these twentieth-century justices' votes are somewhat attenuated in congressional review cases, perhaps giving further evidence of an overriding norm to defer to Congress. We may see additional distinctions as we move into the next sections of analysis, which separates out the nullification votes and which examines the votes by key issue area or which.

Table 3.3 further continues the ideological analysis of the justices' votes, separating out the nullification votes from the justices' votes to uphold Congress. The

Table 3.3 Ideological Direction of Nullification and Uphold Votes Percent Supporting Republican/Conservative and Liberal Traditions

	Votes to Nullify: Number of Votes in Republican/ Conservative Tradition* (Percentage of Nullification Votes)	Votes to Nullify: Number of Votes in Liberal Tradition* (Percentage of Nullification Votes)	Votes to Uphold: Number of Votes in Republican/ Conservative Tradition* (Percentage of Uphold Votes)	Votes to Uphold: Number of Votes in Liberal Tradition* (Percentage of Uphold Votes)
John McLean	0(100)	1(100)	6(60)	4(40)
James Wayne	2(66.7)	1(33.3)	8(53.3)	7(46.7)
Roger Taney	1(100)	0(0)	7(70)	3(30)
John Catron	1(100)	0(0)	1(10)	9(90)
Samuel Nelson	6(66.7)	3(33.3)	16(64.0)	9(36.0)
Robert Grier	4(57.1)	3(42.9)	8(50)	8(50)
Nathan Clifford	6(31.6)	13(68.4)	10(38.5)	16(61.5)
Noah Swayne	5(71.5)	2(28.5)	17(48.5)	18(51.5)
Samuel Miller	6(50)	6(50)	28(56.0)	27(44.0)
David Davis	6(66.7)	3(33.3)	12(40)	18(60)
Stephen Field	13(40.6)	19(59.4)	31(47.7)	34(52.3)
Salmon P. Chase	3(37.5)	5(62.5)	9(52.9)	8(47.1)
William Strong	2(33.3)	4(66.7)	12(50)	12(50)
Joseph Bradley	6(60)	4(40)	16(33.3)	32(66.7)
Ward Hunt	0(0)	3(100)	5(29.4)	12(70.6)
Morrison Waite	3(37.5)	5(62.5)	12(38.7)	19(61.3)
John Marshall Harlan	8(36.6)	14(63.4)	72(51.8)	67(48.2)
William Woods	2(40)	3(60)	5(38.5)	8(61.5)
Stanley Matthews	2(40)	3(60)	6(42.9)	8(57.1)
Horace Gray	5(50)	5(50)	33(51.6)	31(48.4)
Samuel Blatchford	2(40)	3(60)	18(64.3)	10(35.7)
Lucius C.Q. Lamar	1(50)	1(50)	10(100)	0(0)
Melville Fuller	12(50)	12(50)	46(52.9)	41(47.1)
David Brewer	8(33.3)	16(66.7)	40(48.2)	43(51.8)
Henry Brown	3(42.9)	4(57.1)	34(47.2)	38(52.7)
George Shiras	3(42.9)	4(57.1)	19(41.3)	27(58.7)
Edward White	13(41.9)	18(58.1)	100(59.2)	69(40.8)
Rufus Peckham	9(39.1)	14(60.9)	23(39.0)	36(61.0)
Joseph McKenna	7(24.1)	22(75.8)	110(60.1)	73(39.9)

	Votes to Nullify: Number of Votes in Republican/ Conservative Tradition* (Percentage of Nullification Votes)	Votes to Nullify: Number of Votes in Liberal Tradition* (Percentage of Nullification Votes)	Votes to Uphold: Number of Votes in Republican/ Conservative Tradition* (Percentage of Uphold Votes)	Votes to Uphold: Number of Votes in Liberal Tradition* (Percentage of Uphold Votes)
Oliver Wendell Holmes	7(33.3)	14(66.7)	117(55.2)	95(44.8)
William Day	7(28.0)	18(72.0)	84(61.8)	52(38.2)
William Moody	1(50)	1(50)	11(68.7)	5(31.3)
Horace Lurton	2(33.3)	4(66.7)	29(70.7)	12(29.3)
Charles Evan Hughes	10(50)	10(50)	83(59.3)	71(46.1)
Willis Van Devanter	19(39.6)	29(60.4)	100(52.6)	90(47.4)
Joseph Lamar	3(42.9)	4(57.1)	36(67.9)	17(32.1)
Mahlon Pitney	6(33.3)	12(67.7)	51(64.6)	28(35.4)
James McReynolds	25(39.1)	39(60.9)	74(48.7)	78(51.3)
Louis Brandeis	4(30.8)	9(69.2)	81(46.8)	92(53.2)
John Clarke	29(48.3)	31(51.7)	15(100)	0(0)
William Taft	4(36.4)	7(63.6)	23(45.1)	28(54.9)
George Sutherland	14(46.7)	16(53.3)	34(37.4)	57(62.6)
Pierce Butler	24(52.2)	22(47.8)	39(39.4)	60(60.6)
Edward Sanford	3(42.9)	4(57.1)	18(40)	27(60)
Harlan Fiske Stone	6(35.3)	11(64.7)	62(40)	93(60)
Owen Roberts	17(58.6)	12(41.4)	47(46.1)	55(53.9)
Benjamin Cardozo	3(50)	3(50)	20(39.2)	31(60.8)
Hugo Black	8(13.1)	53(86.9)	29(21.5)	106(78.5)
Stanley Reed	2(40)	3(60)	31(30.4)	71(69.6)
Felix Frankfurter	7(50)	7(50)	42(37.5)	70(62.5)
William Douglas	10(11.5)	77(88.5)	22(18.8)	95(81.2)
Frank Murphy	6(66.7)	3(33.3)	4(8.3)	44(91.7)
Robert Jackson	0(0)	3(100)	8(25.0)	24(75.0)
Wiley Rutledge	1(14.3)	6(85.7)	7(21.2)	26(78.8)
Harold Burton	3(60)	2(40)	25(46.3)	29(53.7)
Fred Vinson	1(100)	0(0)	12(41.4)	17(58.6)
Tom Clark	6(37.5)	10(62.5)	36(54.6)	30(45.5)
Sherman Minton	2(100)	0(0)	17(63.0)	10(37.0)
Earl Warren	4(13.3)	26(86.7)	19(41.3)	27(58.7)
John Marshall Harlan II	9(40.9)	13(59.1)	40(62.5)	24(37.5)

Table 3.3 *(continued)*

	Votes to Nullify: Number of Votes in Republican/ Conservative Tradition* (Percentage of Nullification Votes)	Votes to Nullify: Number of Votes in Liberal Tradition* (Percentage of Nullification Votes)	Votes to Uphold: Number of Votes in Republican/ Conservative Tradition* (Percentage of Uphold Votes)	Votes to Uphold: Number of Votes in Liberal Tradition* (Percentage of Uphold Votes)
William Brennan	4(4.6)	83(95.4)	60(41.4)	85(58.6)
Charles Whittaker	0(0)	1(100)	13(59.1)	9(40.9)
Potter Stewart	11(24.4)	34(75.6)	83(69.8)	36(30.3)
Byron White	10(27.0)	27(73.0)	111(61.0)	71(39.0)
Arthur Goldberg	1(25.0)	3(75.0)	3(27.3)	8(72.7)
Abe Fortas	1(9.0)	10(90.9)	2(25.0)	6(75.0)
Thurgood Marshall	1(1.5)	67(98.5)	44(38.6)	70(61.4)
Warren Burger	6(33.3)	12(66.7)	100(74.1)	35(25.9)
Harry Blackmun	4(14.3)	24(85.7)	97(63.0)	57(37.0)
Lewis Powell	6(28.6)	15(71.4)	84(70.6)	35(29.1)
William Rehnquist	27(65.9)	14(34.2)	121(72.5)	46(27.5)
John Paul Stevens	4(10.3)	35(89.7)	62(48.1)	67(51.9)
Sandra Day O'Connor	23(60.5)	15(39.5)	45(60)	30(40)
Antonin Scalia	19(67.8)	0(32.2)	28(62.2)	17(37.8)
Anthony Kennedy	15(62.5)	9(37.5)	23(54.8)	19(45.2)
David Souter	4(20)	16(80)	10(32.3)	21(67.7)
Clarence Thomas	14(60.9)	9(39.1)	17(65.4)	9(34.6)
Ruth Bader Ginsburg	3(16.7)	15(83.3)	8(33.3)	16(67.7)
Stephen Breyer	4(25.0)	12(75.0)	7(31.8)	15(68.2)
MEAN (SD)	41.5(23.8)	57.3(23.7)	46.9(18.7)	50.3(17.0)

*The analysis includes only justices with at least ten votes.

mean conservatism and liberalism scores for the votes to uphold (46.9 and 50.3) are almost identical to overall means (46.7 and 51.9), which is not surprising given the preponderance of votes are to uphold Congress. Again, we see the means almost dead-center in the moderate range. The mean conservatism and liberalism scores in the nullification votes also fall in the moderate range, but show a higher overall liberal tendency, with the liberalism mean in nullification votes being 58.7, compared to 57.3 in the uphold votes, and the mean conservatism score when justices vote to nullify is being only 41.5, compared to 46.9 in the uphold votes.

As we look across the patterns in Table 3.3, we find nine justices that either only nullify in the conservative direction, striking liberal laws or that only nullify in the liberal direction, striking conservative laws. These extreme scores have to be considered with caution as the number of votes to nullify (mostly justices who cast only one or two votes to nullify) is perhaps too small to draw conclusions with any level of confidence. When we limit our attention to justices with a fuller set of votes, we do find more extremes in the justices' nullification votes, at least on the liberal end of the continuum. Here we find quite a few liberalism scores above Douglas' high of 84.3 from the overall vote analysis in Table 3.2: Black (86.9), Douglas (88.5), Rutledge (85.7), Warren (86.7), Brennan (95.4), Fortas (90.9), Marshall (98.5), Blackmun (85.7), and Stevens (89.7). Ginsburg and Souter are just below these scores at 83.3 and 80 respectively. In the other direction, when we eliminate the justices with less than ten votes to nullify, we see two nullification liberalism scores below thirty-five percent: Rehnquist (34.2) and Scalia (32.2). In examining all of the justices in Table 3.3 it is noteworthy that we find a several justices' whose level of liberalism when voting to nullify is quite different than their votes to uphold. Seven justices have rather extraordinary differences of fifty percent or more: McLean (60 percent difference: more liberal in nullifying than upholding), Catron (90 percent difference: more conservative in nullifying), LCQ Lamar (50 percent more liberal), Clarke (51.7 percent: more liberal) is, Murphy (58.4 percent: more conservative), Vinson (58.6 percent: more conservative), and Whittaker (59.1 percent: more liberal). Of these justices, Catron, McLean, Vinson, and Whittaker only voted to nullify in one case and Lamar only voted to nullify in two cases. Twelve other justices' scores differ between 30 and 50 percent on their level of liberal support in nullification votes and votes to uphold: Taney (30 percent: more conservative in nullifying), Lurton (37.4 percent: more liberal), Pitney (32.3 percent: more liberal), Clark (37 percent: more conservative), Brennan (36.8 percent: more liberal), Stewart (45.6 percent: more liberal), White (34.0 percent: more liberal), Marshall (37.1 percent: more liberal), Burger (40.8 percent: more liberal), Blackmun (48.7 percent: more liberal), Powell (42.3 percent: more liberal), and Stevens (37.8 percent: more liberal).

Eleven more justices earn differences in the twenty percent range, and of those justices all but three are more liberal in their votes to nullify than in their votes to uphold. Examining these thirty justices that have large differences between their nullification scores, we find that all but eight are more likely to nullify in the liberal direction than in support of conservative values. Over half of the justices have scores that are consistent ideologically, producing only small differences between their nullification and uphold ideology scores; less than ten or fifteen percent.

Overall, when we examine the justices' votes to nullify congressional statutes, we clearly find more evidence of extreme ideological patterns than in their votes to uphold, suggesting that when the justices do step outside the norm of deference, they are more likely to buck the norm to support their individual policy preferences than to vote against them. Thus, the attenuated levels of ideology we saw in the overall votes likely reflect the justices' votes to defer to Congress. The next step is to examine the variations across issue areas.

Although research on the U.S. Congress has suggested that ideology is primarily unidimentional (Poole and Rosenthal 1997), research on the U.S. Supreme Court has suggested that the justices' ideological behavior varies somewhat by legal issues. For example, Tate (1981) found that while there was a strong correlation between liberalism on civil rights and liberties cases with economic cases, many of the justices were significantly more or less liberal, depending upon the issue. Wood, Keith, Lanier and Ogundele (1998) found the same phenomenon in comparing liberalism on civil rights and liberties with economic liberalism and liberalism on judicial power issues. In 1993, Segal and Spaeth found considerable variation across some issue areas. For example, Burton who earns consistently strong conservative scores in all other issue areas, such 15 percent in due process cases and 31.8 percent in criminal procedure cases, earns quite a liberal score in federal taxation cases (76.2 percent). And Scalia who earns quite conservative scores across all other areas (20s and 30s) earns 60.5 percent in federalism cases and 69.6 percent in federal taxation cases. In order to test for this possibility, I next break down the justices' congressional review votes by the major issue areas that have been significant enough across the Court's agenda to provide a large enough body of votes to analyze with a sufficient level of confidence. Only justices with ten or more votes on each particular issue area are included in the analysis.

These analyses are reported in Table 3.4 and include the following issue areas: civil rights and civil liberties (36.6 percent of the congressional review cases), federalism (17.6 percent of the congressional review cases), economic issues (23.6 percent of the congressional review cases), and taxation (11.5 percent of the congressional review cases).[8] To facilitate the analysis I have chosen to present the issue area scores by individual justice in a single table rather than issue by issue tables, making it easier to see a particular justice's voting behavior in a single look, rather than flipping from table to table. The tradeoff for that advantage is that the single table becomes somewhat lengthy. Here, though, I am able to write more descriptively meaningful labels in terms of what the justice was supporting in their votes: such as, for or against the rights (and liberties) claims, for or against the federal government's claim (as opposed to the state rights claim), or whether the

Table 3.4 Ideological Direction of Vote by Issue Area

	Votes to Uphold		Votes to Nullify		N	Percentage Ideological Support	
	Against Rights & Fed. Gov't Claims or Pro-Business	For Rights & Fed. Gov't Claims or Anti-Business	Against Rights & Fed. Gov't Claims or Pro-Business	For Rights & Fed. Gov't Claims or Anti-Business		% Against Rights & Fed. Gov't Claims or Pro-Business	% For Rights & Fed. Gov't Claims or Anti-Business
Samuel Nelson							
Federalism	1	12	2	0	15	20.0	80.0
Robert Grier							
Federalism	1	7	3	0	11	36.4	63.6
Nathan Clifford							
Federalism	2	6	7	0	15	60.0	40.0
Noah Swayne							
Federalism	2	11	2	0	15	26.7	73.3
Samuel Miller							
Federalism	2	16	3	0	21	23.8	76.2
David Davis							
Federalism	1	9	1	0	11	18.2	81.8
Stephen Field							
Civil Rights/Liberties	15	3	4	7	29	65.5	34.5
Federalism	2	15	9	0	26	42.3	57.7
Federal Taxation	0	10	3	0	13	23.1	76.9
Salmon P. Chase							
Federalism	1	6	4	0	11	45.4	54.6

Table 3.4 (continued)

	Votes to Uphold		Votes to Nullify		N	Percentage Ideological Support	
	Against Rights & Fed. Gov't Claims or Pro-Business	For Rights & Fed. Gov't Claims or Anti-Business	Against Rights & Fed. Gov't Claims or Pro-Business	For Rights & Fed. Gov't Claims or Anti-Business		% Against Rights & Fed. Gov't Claims or Pro-Business	% For Rights & Fed. Gov't Claims or Anti-Business
Joseph Bradley							
Federalism	1	12	2	0	15	20.0	80.0
John Marshall Harlan							
Civil Rights/Liberties	31	11	2	7	51	64.7	35.3
Federalism	3	32	4	0	39	17.9	82.1
Economic Activity	8	22	2	0	32	31.3	68.7
Taxation	1	20	3	0	24	16.7	83.3
Horace Gray							
Civil Rights/Liberties	17	3	2	4	26	73.1	26.9
Federalism	0	15	1	0	16	6.3	93.7
Taxation	0	11	1	0	12	8.3	91.7
Samuel Blatchford							
Civil Rights/Liberties	11	2	1	2	16	75.0	25.0
Melville Fuller							
Civil Rights/Liberties	22	4	2	5	33	72.7	27.3
Federalism	0	17	6	0	23	26.1	73.9
Economic Activity	6	19	3	0	28	32.1	67.9
Taxation	1	13	5	0	19	31.6	68.4

David Brewer							
Civil Rights/Liberties	18	3	2	8	31	64.5	35.5
Federalism	0	15	7	0	22	31.8	68.2
Economic Activity	2	12	0	0	14	14.3	85.7
Taxation	0	16	4	0	20	20.0	80.0
Henry Brown							
Civil Rights/Liberties	19	4	1	2	26	76.9	23.1
Federalism	0	11	2	0	13	15.4	84.6
Economic Activity	3	13	1	0	17	23.5	76.5
Taxation Cases	1	17	1	0	19	10.5	89.5
George Shiras							
Civil Rights/Liberties	8	2	0	3	13	61.5	38.5
Economic Activity	2	7	1	0	10	30.0	70.0
Taxation	0	11	2	0	13	15.4	84.6
Edward White							
Civil Rights/Liberties	41	7	3	5	56	78.5	21.5
Federalism	3	46	7	0	56	17.9	82.1
Economic Activity	12	29	11	12	64	35.9	64.1
Taxation	1	25	5	3	34	17.6	82.4
Rufus Peckham							
Civil Rights/Liberties	11	4	2	6	23	56.5	43.5
Federalism	0	7	7	0	14	50.0	50.0
Economic Activity	2	10	1	0	13	23.1	76.9
Taxation	0	12	5	0	17	29.4	70.6

Table 3.4 *(continued)*

	Votes to Uphold		Votes to Nullify		N	Percentage Ideological Support	
	Against Rights & Fed. Gov't Claims or Pro-Business	For Rights & Fed. Gov't Claims or Anti-Business	Against Rights & Fed. Gov't Claims or Pro-Business	For Rights & Fed. Gov't Claims or Anti-Business		% Against Rights & Fed. Gov't Claims or Pro-Business	% For Rights & Fed. Gov't Claims or Anti-Business
Joseph McKenna							
Civil Rights/Liberties	41	9	2	4	56	76.8	23.2
Federalism	3	52	10	0	65	20.0	80.0
Economic Activity	4	17	0	0	21	19.1	80.9
Taxation	2	30	4	3	39	15.4	84.6
Oliver Wendell Holmes							
Civil Rights/Liberties	38	12	3	3	56	73.2	26.8
Federalism	1	64	3	0	68	5.9	94.1
Economic Activity	11	27	3	0	41	34.2	65.8
Taxation	2	51	1	4	58	5.2	94.8
William Day							
Civil Rights/Liberties	34	7	2	2	45	80.0	20.0
Federalism	1	40	10	0	51	21.6	78.4
Economic Activity	10	18	4	0	32	43.8	56.2
Taxation	0	24	0	3	27	0	100.0
Horace Lurton							
Civil Rights/Liberties	8	1	1	0	10	90.0	10.0

Charles Evan Hughes

Civil Rights/Liberties	21	5	2	0	28	82.1	17.9
Federalism	1	54	4	0	59	8.5	91.5
Economic Activity	5	27	4	0	36	25.0	75.0
Taxation	0	35	4	3	42	9.5	90.5

Willis Van Devanter

Civil Rights/Liberties	36	5	2	3	46	82.6	17.4
Federalism	1	52	18	0	71	26.8	73.2
Economic Activity	7	28	5	0	40	30.0	70.0
Taxation	1	53	12	3	69	18.8	81.2

Joseph Lamar

Civil Rights/Liberties	12	1	2	0	15	93.3	6.7
Economic Activity	4	6	1	0	11	45.5	55.5
Federalism	2	20	1	0	23	13.0	87.0
Taxation	0	8	0	2	10	0	100.0

Mahlon Pitney

Civil Rights/Liberties	22	4	1	1	28	82.1	17.9
Economic Activity	6	8	2	1	17	47.1	52.9
Federalism	1	23	6	2	32	21.9	78.1
Taxation	0	15	1	3	19	5.3	94.7

James McReynolds

Civil Rights/Liberties	29	3	1	5	38	79.0	21.0
Federalism	1	33	29	0	63	47.6	52.4

Table 3.4 *(continued)*

	Votes to Uphold		Votes to Nullify		N	Percentage Ideological Support	
	Against Rights & Fed. Gov't Claims or Pro-Business	For Rights & Fed. Gov't Claims or Anti-Business	Against Rights & Fed. Gov't Claims or Pro-Business	For Rights & Fed. Gov't Claims or Anti-Business		% Against Rights & Fed. Gov't Claims or Pro-Business	% For Rights & Fed. Gov't Claims or Anti-Business
Economic Activity	6	27	7	0	40	32.5	67.5
Taxation	2	43	16	2	63	28.6	71.4
Louis Brandeis							
Civil Rights/Liberties	21	8	1	0	30	73.3	26.7
Federalism	0	49	5	0	54	9.3	90.7
Economic Activity	3	23	2	0	28	17.9	82.1
Taxation	2	58	1	2	63	4.8	95.2
John Clarke							
Civil Rights/Liberties	12	2	0	2	16	75.0	25.0
Federalism	1	13	3	0	17	23.5	76.5
William Taft							
Federalism	0	16	3	0	19	15.8	84.2
Taxation	0	20	4	1	25	16.0	84.0
George Sutherland							
Civil Rights/Liberties	11	0	1	1	13	92.3	7.7
Federalism	0	18	11	0	29	37.9	62.1
Economic Activity	0	17	2	0	19	10.5	91.5
Taxation	1	37	11	1	50	24.0	76.0

Pierce Butler

Civil Rights/Liberties	11	2	1	2	16	75.0	25.0
Federalism	0	23	15	0	38	39.5	60.5
Economic Activity	0	21	6	0	27	22.2	77.8
Taxation	1	34	17	1	53	34.0	66.0

Edward Sanford

Federalism	0	11	1	0	12	8.3	91.7
Taxation	1	18	3	1	23	17.4	82.6

Harlan Fiske Stone

Civil Rights/Liberties	13	5	2	2	22	68.1	31.9
Federalism	0	44	4	0	48	8.3	91.7
Economic Activity	1	32	3	0	36	11.1	88.9
Taxation	0	52	1	2	55	1.8	98.2

Owen Roberts

Civil Rights/Liberties	10	4	1	2	17	64.7	35.3
Federalism	0	32	8	0	40	20.0	80.0
Economic Activity	1	19	10	0	30	36.7	63.3
Taxation	0	29	6	0	35	17.1	82.9

Benjamin Cardozo

Federalism	0	13	2	0	15	13.3	86.7
Economic Activity	0	10	2	0	12	16.7	83.3
Taxation	0	19	0	0	19	0	100.0

Hugo Black

Civil Rights/Liberties	22	23	4	52	101	25.7	74.3

Table 3.4 *(continued)*

	Votes to Uphold		Votes to Nullify		N	Percentage Ideological Support	
	Against Rights & Fed. Gov't Claims or Pro-Business	For Rights & Fed. Gov't Claims or Anti-Business	Against Rights & Fed. Gov't Claims or Pro-Business	For Rights & Fed. Gov't Claims or Anti-Business		% Against Rights & Fed. Gov't Claims or Pro-Business	% For Rights & Fed. Gov't Claims or Anti-Business
Federalism	2	28	0	0	30	6.7	93.3
Economic Activity	1	35	3	1	40	10.0	90.0
Taxation	1	14	0	0	15	6.7	93.3
Stanley Reed							
Civil Rights/Liberties	26	5	1	3	35	77.1	22.9
Federalism	1	24	0	0	25	4.0	96.0
Economic Activity	1	28	1	0	30	6.7	93.3
Taxation	1	10	0	0	11	9.1	90.9
Felix Frankfurter							
Civil Rights/Liberties	35	10	2	7	54	68.5	31.5
Federalism	1	21	0	0	22	4.6	95.4
Economic Activity	2	26	4	0	32	18.8	81.2
Taxation	1	10	0	0	11	9.1	90.9
William O. Douglas							
Civil Rights/Liberties	17	30	3	74	124	16.1	83.9
Federalism	1	21	0	0	22	4.5	95.5
Economic Activity	1	29	5	1	36	16.7	83.3
Taxation	1	9	0	0	10	10.0	90.0

Frank Murphy							
Civil Rights/Liberties	1	4	4	3	12	41.7	58.3
Federalism	1	17	0	0	18	5.6	94.4
Economic Activity	1	15	2	0	18	16.7	83.3
Wiley Rutledge							
Civil Rights/Liberties	5	2	1	6	14	42.8	57.1
Economic Activity	1	13	0	0	14	7.1	92.9
Harold Burton							
Civil Rights/Liberties	25	2	2	2	31	87.1	12.9
Economic Activity	0	14	1	0	15	6.7	93.3
Fred Vinson							
Civil Rights/Liberties	12	1	1	0	14	92.9	7.1
Tom Clark							
Civil Rights/Liberties	34	6	6	10	56	71.4	28.6
Economic Activity	1	10	0	0	11	9.1	90.9
Sherman Minton							
Civil Rights/Liberties	16	0	1	0	17	100.0	0
Earl Warren							
Civil Rights/Liberties	19	13	2	26	60	35.0	65.0
John Marshall Harlan II							
Civil Rights/Liberties	38	10	7	13	68	66.2	33.8
William Brennan							
Civil Rights/Liberties	54	37	1	74	166	33.1	67.9
Federalism	0	10	1	0	11	9.1	90.9

Table 3.4 *(continued)*

	Votes to Uphold		Votes to Nullify		N	Percentage Ideological Support	
	Against Rights & Fed. Gov't Claims or Pro-Business	For Rights & Fed. Gov't Claims or Anti-Business	Against Rights & Fed. Gov't Claims or Pro-Business	For Rights & Fed. Gov't Claims or Anti-Business		% Against Rights & Fed. Gov't Claims or Pro-Business	% For Rights & Fed. Gov't Claims or Anti-Business
Economic Activity	3	24	2	4	33	15.5	84.5
Charles Whittaker							
Civil Rights/Liberties	13	4	0	1	18	72.2	27.8
Potter Stewart							
Civil Rights/Liberties	74	22	4	33	133	58.6	41.4
Economic Activity	5	6	5	0	16	62.5	37.5
Byron White							
Civil Rights/Liberties	96	25	9	25	155	67.7	32.3
Federalism	0	11	0	0	11	0	100.0
Economic Activity	8	22	1	1	32	28.3	71.9
Arthur Goldberg							
Civil Rights/Liberties	3	5	0	3	11	27.3	72.7
Abe Fortas							
Civil Rights/Liberties	2	4	1	10	17	17.6	82.4
Thurgood Marshall							
Civil Rights/Liberties	39	32	1	59	130	30.8	69.2
Economic Activity	3	19	0	3	25	12.0	88.0
Warren Burger							
Civil Rights/Liberties	86	11	3	11	111	80.2	19.8

Economic Activity	5	15	0	1	21	23.8	76.2
Harry Blackmun						
Civil Rights/Liberties	85	16	3	19	123	71.5	28.5
Economic Activity	7	21	0	2	30	23.3	76.7
Lewis Powell						
Civil Rights/Liberties	74	11	2	12	99	76.8	23.2
Economic Activity	4	13	1	2	20	25.0	75.0
William Rehnquist						
Civil Rights/Liberties	106	11	9	12	138	83.3	16.7
Federalism	1	6	10	0	17	64.7	35.3
Economic Activity	8	19	4	0	31	38.7	61.3
John Paul Stevens						
Civil Rights/Liberties	55	19	2	30	106	53.8	46.2
Federalism	0	16	0	0	16	0	100.0
Economic Activity	5	20	1	1	27	22.2	77.8
Sandra Day O'Connor						
Civil Rights/Liberties	37	9	6	13	65	66.2	33.8
Federalism	1	3	11	0	15	80.0	20.0
Economic Activity	5	11	2	1	19	36.8	63.2
Antonin Scalia						
Civil Rights/Liberties	24	4	6	9	43	69.8	30.2
Federalism	0	4	8	0	12	66.7	33.3
Economic Activity	3	7	2	0	12	41.7	58.3

Table 3.4 *(continued)*

	Votes to Uphold		Votes to Nullify		N	Percentage Ideological Support	
	Against Rights & Fed. Gov't Claims or Pro-Business	For Rights & Fed. Gov't Claims or Anti-Business	Against Rights & Fed. Gov't Claims or Pro-Business	For Rights & Fed. Gov't Claims or Anti-Business		% Against Rights & Fed. Gov't Claims or Pro-Business	% For Rights & Fed. Gov't Claims or Anti-Business
Anthony Kennedy							
Civil Rights/Liberties	21	7	3	8	39	61.5	38.5
Federalism	0	2	8	0	10	80.0	20.0
Economic Activity	2	6	2	0	10	40.0	60.0
David Souter							
Civil Rights/Liberties	9	9	0	15	33	27.3	72.7
Clarence Thomas							
Civil Rights/Liberties	14	4	4	9	31	58.1	41.9
Ruth Bader Ginsburg							
Civil Rights/Liberties	8	6	1	13	28	32.1	67.9
Stephen Breyer							
Civil Rights/Liberties	7	6	1	11	25	32.0	68.0
Means for Civil Rights/Lib Cases						61.5	38.5
Means for Federalism Cases						24.9	75.1
Means for Economic Issue Cases						26.4	73.6
Means for Taxation Cases						13.7	86.3

*Analysis includes only justices which had voted in ten or more cases in the issue.

vote for pro- or anti-business. In this issue–based analysis, it will be easier to avoid the problem of the switching labels of liberal or conservative on the federalism issue and simply refer to the level of support for the national government or states' rights position. The issue areas in which the justices cast sufficient votes to analyze varies over time with federalism and national taxation issues too thin for many of the later court justices and civil rights and liberties issues too thin for many of the earlier court justices.

The mean support scores are reported by issue area at the bottom of Table 3.4. Overall, across the congressional review cases, we see the justices are least supportive of rights and liberties claims. The justices support the rights claims on average 38.5 percent. This finding runs counter to normative expectations. As Howard and Segal point out, "it is clear that the dominant viewpoint is for the judiciary to restrain from overturning laws passed by the democratic majority *unless necessary to protect fundamental rights or suspect classes*" (emphasis added) (132). Yet here we find that rights claims are the least likely to be supported by the justices' votes in the exercise of judicial review. The finding runs counter to expectations of international human rights proponents (e.g., Becker 1970; International Commission of Jurists 1983; Rosenn 1987; Ackerman 1989; Chowdury 1989; Garro 1993; Stotzky 1993; Larkins 1996); however, the finding fits with those I and my co-authors have found in regard to judicial review and human rights globally. We have found that judicial review is associated with curbing human rights not protecting them (Keith 2004; Keith, Tate and Poe 2007; Keith and Ogundele 2007). Here, if we examine the justices' pro-rights scores across time, we find that it is not until Black joins the bench that we see a single justice support even a slim majority of the rights and liberties claims in the congressional review cases. Scores on civil rights and liberties run from no observed liberalism (Minton) to 83.9 percent (Douglas). With the exception of one vote, Minton's votes in this area were exercised only in deference to Congress, upholding the congressional statutes which went against rights claims. Douglas's high liberalism score is derived from votes in the opposite pattern from Minton, primarily voting to challenge Congress and nullify legislation that curbed civil rights and liberties (60 percent). There are very few justices, only six, that fit within the moderate range defined above (between 40 and 60 percent): Peckham (43.5 percent), Rutledge (57.1 percent), Murphy (58.3 percent), Stewart (41.4 percent), Stevens (46.2 percent), and Thomas (41.9 percent). Interestingly, there are only ten justices with scores over 60 percent, qualifying as a liberal here: Black (74.3 percent), Douglas (83.9 percent), Warren (65 percent), Brennan (67.9 percent), Goldberg (72.7 percent), Fortas (82.4 percent), Marshall (69.2 percent), Souter (72.7 percent), Ginsburg (67.9 percent), and Breyer (68.0 percent), all of whom are expected liberals on rights-based issues.

Another observation we can make from these data is that only twelve justices voted to support civil rights and liberties claim in more than half their votes, and not surprisingly there are no justices with such levels of support for rights claims prior to FDR's appointments joining the bench. Concomitantly we find that there are eleven justices with scores below 20 percent, including Chief Justices Burger and Vinson, and an additional sixteen justices with scores only in the twenties. Taken as a whole, there is strong evidence that the overwhelming majority of the justices do not exercise the power of judicial review to protect minority rights but rather appear to vote in such ways that either legitimize the legislature's diminishment of such rights or overturn legislative attempts to provide or protect such rights.

The justices are most supportive of the federal government's taxation claims; a mean support score of 86.3 percent across the justices, followed by a mean score of 82.4 supporting economic regulation. Interestingly, in this issue area, which represents over 14 percent of the cases under study here, no justice earns a score under 60 percent on the taxation issue, with many scores placing in the 90 percent range. In fact, all but six of the justices have scores over 80 percent. Clearly, the justices overwhelming support the national taxation legislature processed by Congress; however, when they do vote to nullify, it is almost always in the conservative direction, with a pro-taxpayer vote.[9] This issue was however only a significant component of these cases until 1945, tapering off to less than a case or two a decade. For example, no justice after Murphy had ten more or votes on federal taxation cases, my cut-off point for the analysis.

The second highest level of support is for the national government over the states in federalism issues, an average score of 75.1 percent for national power over states' rights claims. Federalism is the second most prevalent issue area in these cases, approximately one-fifth of the cases. In this table, unlike the analyses above, I am able to deal with liberalism in regard to federalism as an issue by itself, rather than as aggregated component of liberalism; therefore, here I simply report the level of support each justice has shown for the federal government in states' rights challenges. I do not make the modification for the ideological change in the mid-1930s because in this analysis it seems more meaningful to say that on average the justices' votes have supported the national government over three quarters of the time, than to say that on average have been 75.1 percent liberal on federalism cases, given that liberalism on this issues changes direction in the mid-1930s. When we examine the federalism scores for the justices from Black forward scores supporting the federal government can be considered liberal and for the justice prior to Black, scores supporting the federal government can be considered conservative. Thus, our early justices who are earning scores in the 80s and 90s in supporting the national government are arguably earning conservative scores. Support for national power ranges from 100 percent

(Stevens and White) to 20 percent (Kennedy and O'Connor, the Court's so-called moderates). Both Stevens and White's scores are due to 100 percent support of the congressional statutes under challenge. Neither justice votes to challenge Congress in this rather small subset of cases. Kennedy and O'Connor's pattern is nearly the complete opposite, with the justices almost completely voting to nullify Congress in the conservative direction—O'Connor casts only four votes in this area to uphold Congress and Kennedy only two. We only see five justices whose votes fall in the mid-level support for the national government, 40 to 60 percent: Clifford (40 percent), Field (57.7 percent), Chase (54.6 percent), Peckham (60 percent), and McReynolds (52.4 percent). Those scores are generally in the range of the justices' overall ideological patterns, controlling for ideological direction on federalism (Wood, Keith, Lanier, and Ogundele 1998; Ogundele and Keith 2006). Many of the justices earn scores over 90 percent: Gray (93.7 percent), Holmes (94.1 percent), Hughes (91.5 percent), Brandeis (90.7 percent), Sanford (91.7 percent), Stone (91.7 percent), Black (93.3 percent), Reed (96 percent), Frankfurter (95.4 percent), Douglas (95.5 percent), Murphy (94.4 percent), Brennan (90.9 percent), White (100 percent), and Stevens (100 percent). The first third of these justices would be considered quite conservative in their support of the federal government and the latter two-thirds would be considered quite liberal. Interestingly, the only four justices earn strongly states' rights scores are recent or current states rights proponents on the court: Rehnquist (35.3 percent), O'Connor (20 percent), Scalia (33.3 percent), and Kennedy (20 percent).[10] We must remember the Court has generally voted to support strong national government over state powers, in 84.3 percent of these cases (Keith 2007). In the overwhelming majority of these cases, the Court deferred to Congress, upholding congressional statutes that enhanced national power 83.3 percent of the time and nullifying a law that enhanced national power only 15.5 percent of the time. In part, this pattern is a dimension of the Court's overall pattern of deference to Congress, but may also reflect the Court's position as a national institution itself that makes it more protective of national power vis-à-vis state power.

The third highest liberalism scores are found in cases where the primary issue area was economic activity, an area that represents about 23.6 percent of the congressional review cases. The mean liberalism score is 73.6 percent with justices primarily voting to uphold liberal economic legislation coming from Congress. For example, in *Skinner* v. *Mid-American Pipeline* (1989) the Rehnquist Court unanimously upholds Section 7005 of the Consolidated Omnibus Budget Reconciliation Act of 1985 which directs the United States Secretary of Transportation to establish a system of user fees to cover the costs of administering programs under the Natural Gas Pipeline Safety Act of 1968 and the Hazardous Liquid Pipeline Safety Act of 1979. Scores range from Stewart's 37.5 to Burton's

93.3. Burton, who was said to be "fully appreciative of his modest abilities [was] most deferential toward [Frankfurter,] the former professor," and here we see his liberalism score to be quite within Frankfurter's range (81.2), along with Clark (90.9), another of Truman's appointees of whom were said to usually fall in the Frankfurter camp (Schwartz 1993, 255). A significant pattern emerges in this issue area—while the justices are largely voting to uphold liberal economic legislation—when the justices do go against the norm of deferring to Congress, we see that the votes consistently nullifying liberal legislation. For example, James McReynolds votes to uphold economically liberal laws 27 times, compared to upholding conservative laws 6 times, but then when he votes to nullify congressional statutes we see him vote to nullify a liberal law seven times; however, at no time does he nullify an economically conservative law. This pattern holds up even with liberals such as Douglas who votes to uphold 29 economically liberal laws compared to 1 conservative law, but then when he votes to nullify he votes against liberal laws five times and against conservative laws only once. There are only a couple of exceptions to the pattern—Thurgood Marshall, Brennan, and Blackmun—who vote to overturn conservative laws more than with liberal laws.

Conclusions

With this important initial examination of the justices' congressional review votes we have been able to observe several significant patterns across the justices' votes, examining as much as space limitations would allow each justices' particular behavior on the bench. First, we find that even though the justices on average are highly deferential to Congress, we are able to identify significant numbers of justices who depart from the norm. We find, among the justices who are most willing to challenge Congress, both liberals and conservatives, and both Democrats and Republicans. We find that after Warren joins the bench very few justices have extremely deferential scores, and in addition, we find that all of the recent justices on the bench (excluding Roberts and Alito who are not included in this work) place within the top thirteen nullification rates.

When we examine the ideological dimension of these votes, we find several significant patterns as well. First, we find that the majority of the justices' votes fall in the moderate range, with only small proportions of the justices earning scores that could be considered consistently liberal or conservative. However, this finding also has a time-related caveat, in that as we move into the appointees of Franklin Roosevelt and beyond, the moderate tendency disappears rather quickly. Overall, the ideological dimension of the justices' votes in congressional review cases tends to be moderated, in comparison to reports of the liberalism scores based on the justices' decisions across their tenure. In addition, we find that when we separate out the justices' votes to nullify from those to uphold the statute, the nullification votes were more extreme ideologically. However, it is interesting to note that the movement in ideology was in the liberal direction. In fact when we examine justices with large differences in their uphold votes and votes to nullify, we find that the difference was primarily with justices being more liberal in their nullifying votes than in their votes to uphold Congress.

When we examine the votes across issues, again, we find several important trends as well. We find that on average, the justices were much less likely to support civil rights and civil liberties claims, despite the claim that judicial review is most legitimately exercised in protection of rights-based claims. In addition, we find the justices were much more likely to support national government claims over states' rights claims and against tax-payer claims. We also find that justices on average were much more likely to vote against business claims in favor of government regulation.

I believe the analyses here are an important first look at the individual justices' behavior, and these initial analyses present initial theoretical insights, especially about the effect of the justices' political preferences. However, such simple descriptive analysis must lead to the important next step, the examination of the votes in controlled explanatory models which can assess the justices' votes in light of the competing theories in judicial behavior. Chapters Four and Five presents such analysis.

Notes

1. Each concurrence and dissent was read to determine the justices' votes on the constitutional question under review.
2. Justices who cast less than ten votes were excluded from the analysis since our level of confidence based on such a small N would be quite low; thus the analysis begins with Jackson's appointees to the bench, since the earlier justices did not have sufficient numbers of votes.
3. The author will make available to any reader the analysis and results with the federalism variable delineated along the original Spaeth coding upon request.
4. Analysis conducted with the federalism scores coded along the original Spaeth delineation with no switch direction resulted in a much higher liberalism score (mean 67 percent) and lower conservatism score (37 percent) with an average distance of 33 percent. And following that delineation only one-fifth of the justices'

votes fell within the moderate range when judging ideological distance scores, compared to one-half with the adjusted coding. I believe the more moderate average across the entire two-hundred-year period would more closely reflect scholarly expectations. The difference should add to our confidence in the modification of the measure as I have done here.

5. Another way to statistically identify ideological extremism is the departure of the justice's vote from the mean liberalism score (51.9 percent) which would lead us to consider a justice to be exhibit extreme ideology if he or she scores either one standard deviation or more below the mean (36.7 percent) or one standard deviation or more above the mean (67.1 percent). In order to be fully justifiable we would need to calculate a weighted average, since the justices votes vary substantially in numbers, but this would introduce the problem in changes in the Court's control of its agenda. Instead, I have chosen to stay with the more simple delineation.

6. These moderate scores fit the justices' overall moderate scores they earn in their full set of votes (Ogundele and Keith 2006).

7. Waite and Woods are slightly on the liberal side with scores of approximately 61 percent and Blatchford would round up to 40 percent.

8. Civil rights and liberties include three and one-half of Spaeth's issue areas: criminal procedure, civil rights, First Amendment, and non-economic due process. Economic activity includes Spaeth's economic activity issue area plus economic due process cases (mostly taking clause cases). Spaeth's economic activity includes anti-trust, mergers, bankruptcy, liability, securities, land claims, patents, copyrights and so forth. Cases under the interstate commerce clause are coded as federalism cases under Spaeth's delineation.

9. Goldman's (1966) study of the U.S. Courts of Appeals found that of all issues he examined in the context of liberalism, the liberal position (same delineation as Spaeth followed) on fiscal issues, which were largely taxation and eminent domain cases, did not seem to align other categories of liberal positions. He notes the similarity in his finding with those of Schubert (1965) in *The Judicial Mind* in which the author noted that the justices' rankings on fiscal issues were different from economic and civil liberties.

10. Thomas, Ginsburg, and Breyer lacked enough federalism votes in this dataset to be included in the federalism analysis.

References

Ackermann, L.W. H. 1989. "Constitutional Protection of Human Rights: Judicial Review." *Columbia Human Rights Law Review* 21(1): 59–71.

Becker, Theodore. 1970. *Comparative Judicial Politics*. Landham, MD: University Press of America.

Chowdhury, Subrata Roy. 1989. *Rule of Law in a State of Emergency.* New York: St. Martin's Press.

Danelski, David J. 1989. "The Influence of the Chief Justice in the Decisional Process of the Supreme Court." In *American Court Systems*, eds. Sheldon Goldman and Austin Sarat. New York: Longman.

Garro, Alejandro. 1993. "Nine Years to Democracy in Argentina: Partial Failure or Qualified Success?" *Columbia Journal of Transnational Law* 31: 1–102.

George, Tracey E. and Lee Epstein. 1992. "On the Nature of Supreme Court Decision Making." *American Political Science Review* 86(3): 323–37.

Goldman, Sheldon. 1966. "Voting Behavior of the United States Courts of Appeals, 1961–1964." *American Political Science Review* 60: 374–84.

Goldman, Sheldon. 1982. *Constitutional Law and Supreme Court Decision-Making: Cases and Essays.* New York: Harper & Row.

Howard, Robert M. and Jeffrey A. Segal. 2004. "A Preference for Deference? The Supreme Court and Judicial Review." *Political Research Quarterly* 57(1): 131–43.

International Commission of Jurists. 1983. *States of Emergency: Their Impact on Human Rights.* Geneva: International Commission of Jurists.

Keith, Linda Camp. 2004. "National Constitutions and Human Rights Protection": Regional Differences and Colonial Influences." In *The Systematic Study of Human Rights*, eds. Sabine Carey and Steven C. Poe, Ashgate Publishing.

Keith, Linda Camp. 2007. "The United States Supreme Court and Judicial Review of Congress: 1803–2001." *Judicature* (January/February 2007) 90: 1–14.

Keith, Linda Camp and Ayo Ogundele. 2007. "Legal Systems and Constitutionalism in Sub-Saharan Africa: An Empirical Examination of Colonial Influences on Human Rights." *Human Rights Quarterly* 29(4):1065–1097.

Keith, Linda Camp, Tate C. Neal, and Steven C. Poe. 2007. "Is the Law a Mere Parchment Barrier to Human Rights Abuse?" Unpublished manuscript.

Larkins, Christopher M. 1996. "Judicial Independence and Democratization: A Theoretical and Conceptual Analysis." *American Journal of Comparative Law* 44: 605–26.

McCloskey, Robert. G. 1994. *The American Supreme Court.* Chicago: University of Chicago Press.

Ogundele, Ayo and Linda Camp Keith. 2006. "The Supreme Court, 1801–1887: An Empirical Overview." Paper presented at the annual meeting of the Southern Political Science Association, January 3–6, New Orleans, LA.

Poole, Keith T. and Howard Rosenthal. 1997. *Congress: A Political-Economic History of Roll-Call Voting.* New York: Oxford Press.

Rosenn, Keith S. 1987. "The Protection of Judicial Independence in Latin America." *University of Miami Inter-American Law Review* 19: 1–35.

Schubert, Glendon. 1965. *The Judicial Mind.* Evanston: Northwestern University Press.

Schwartz, Bernard. 1993. *A History of the Supreme Court.* New York: Oxford University Press.

Schwartz, Bernard and Steven Lesher. 1983. *Inside the Warren Court: 1953–1969*. New York: Doubleday.

Segal, Jeffrey A. and Harold J. Spaeth. 1993. *The Supreme Court and the Attitudinal Model*. Cambridge: Cambridge University Press.

Segal, Jeffrey A. and Harold J. Spaeth. 2002. *The Supreme Court and the Attitudinal Model Revisited*. Cambridge: Cambridge University Press.

Solberg, Rorie Spill, and Stephanie Lindquist. 2006. "Activism, Ideology, and Federalism: Judicial Behavior in Constitutional Challenges Before the Rehnquist Court, 1986–2000." *Journal of Empirical Legal Studies* 3: 237–61.

Stotzky, Irwin P. 1993. "The Tradition of Constitutional Adjudication." In *Transitions to Democracy in Latin America: The Role of the Judiciary*, ed. Irwin P. Stotzky. Boulder, CO: Westview.

Tate C. Neal. 1981. "Personal Attribute Models of the Voting Behavior of U.S. Supreme Court Justices: Liberalism in Civil Liberties and Economic Decisions, 1946–1978." *American Political Science Review* 75: 355–67.

Tate C. Neal and Roger Handberg. 1991. "Time Building and Theory Building in Personal Attribute Models of Supreme Court Voting Behavior, 1916–1988." *American Journal of Political Science* 35: 460–80.

Wood, Sandra, Linda Camp Keith, Drew Lanier, and Ayo Ogundele. 1998. "The Supreme Court 1888–1940: An Empirical Overview." *Social Science History* 22: 204–24.

Majoritarian Issues: An Initial Exploration

Introduction

As we saw in Chapter One, a significant body of quantitative research has examined empirically majoritarian issues that arise out of the U.S. Supreme Court's exercise of its power of judicial review. In this chapter I will review briefly the key literature that was presented in the first chapter, and then in the following sections I will present the testable hypotheses that may be derived from these works in regard to various dimensions of the majoritarian issue and, where appropriate, test the hypotheses with the data under study here. Early evidence presented by Dahl (1957, 1967) suggested that the Supreme Court's exercise of judicial review was not counter-majoritarian nor did it represent a significant exercise of judicial power; however, subsequent data and analysis demonstrated that this initial assessment was inaccurate, especially as the time horizon lengthened; Casper (1976) found that the Court did exercise this power in a manner that was more counter-majoritarian and more influential than Dahl had concluded. Scholarly evidence also suggested that the Court was not likely to perform this counter–majoritarian role over long periods of time but rather only during a transitional period in party realignments (Funston 1975). Recent scholars, such as Graber (1993), have argued that the Court has exercised this power "only when the dominant national coalition is unable or unwilling to settle some public dispute;" therefore, the Court's exercise of this power stems from the *lack* of a popular majority and not due to the Court acting *against* a political majority (36), or as Whittington (2005) has claimed, the Court's exercise of this power frequently has been an act of "friendly" judicial review that has enforced the current regime's attempts to overcome entrenched obstructions in obtaining its policy goals through the legislative process. Both Graber and Whittington find support for their arguments in their case studies across a small set of issue areas; however, it is difficult to test in a rigorous systematic manner these theoretical arguments that the Court's judicial review decisions are in response to the legislative obstruction and coalition failures that permeate the current legislative process. Friedman and Harvey (2003) also challenge the assumption that just because the Court is nullifying congressional statutes it naturally follows that the sitting Congress "disagrees with what the Court is doing" (125), and they observe that despite the high level of nullification and rhetorical response of some political actors to the Court's actions, Congress generally has acquiesced to the Court's rulings and has not taken action against the Court, which they take to suggest "congressional contentment with the situation" (128). Ultimately they argue that the Court may not be acting in a counter-majoritarian manner, because the current elected branch may actually support the Court's nullification of a congressional statute, presumably passed by previous Congresses. They eventually find that the Court is more likely to strike congressional action when facing a "friendly" Congress—which provides at least some indirect support for Whittington's arguments.

Other scholars make more specific arguments to explain why it is that the Court is not frequently out of sync with the majoritarian branches. Ferejohn (1999) holds that the Court's jurisprudence is not out of line with the preferences of the elected branches for long periods of time due to the stability of the system which keeps elected officials in office for fairly long periods of time, while at the same time ensuring a fairly stable set of justices on the bench, whose professional norms of stability and predictability "work to make doctrine evolve quite slowly in most areas of the law" (382–83). He identifies five periods of history in which the United States has experienced stable political rule where the makeup of the Court has tended to "come into alignment with the dominant political configuration" and four periods of imbalance in which a decisive electoral shift leaves the Court out of alignment and suddenly vulnerable to attempts to alter its jurisprudence (383). Geyh (2006) argues that Congress largely has been acquiescent to the Court, giving it oversight of the Constitution, through a gradual establishment of customary judicial independence, which became increasingly entrenched toward the end of the nineteenth century. He notes, as many of these authors do, that despite the variety of tools at Congress' disposal that would enable it to act significantly against an unfavorable decision, Congress has either historically declined to use the tool or only rarely used their powers to respond to a case, especially in contemporary times. Geyh identifies five periods when Congress curbed or attempted to rein in the Court, but his lengthy analysis of each period and the intervening calm lead him to conclude that "although the level of criticism across the cycles may have been comparably shrill, the political branches' responses to such criticism diminished over time" (80). He ultimately concludes that each cycle became less extreme, came to comparatively little, or was less destructive to customary judicial independence than it appeared (80–81). He argues that the restraint shown by Congress towards the Court in most contexts has been reciprocated in turn by the Court in three ways: (1) the Court has developed conflict-avoidance doctrines to sidestep retaliation; (2) the Court has acquiesced when hostility reached its peak; and (3) the Court has exercised its powers of self-government deferentially. Geyh's historical analyses leads him to conclude that when the Court's "occasional genuflections to the legislature are reexamined in tandem with the evolution of independence norms in Congress, a more nuanced explanation emerges, in which the Courts' occasional, short-term displays of deference, offered in a spirit of comity, have promoted long-term congressional acceptance of customary judicial independence" (224). Rather than perceiving the Court's exercise of judicial review as being counter-majoritarian in respect to Congress, Geyh seems to perceive the judiciary acting overtime within the norms that Congress itself has established and to which largely adheres. As we saw in Chapter One Pickerill's (2005) research seems to support both Geyh and Whittington, as well as Friedman and Harvey, in that he finds the overwhelming congressional response to nullification decisions is to modify the legislation in a manner that complies with or makes concessions to the Court's constitutional holding but that still preserves the statutory policy in some form (162). Ultimately, Pickerill concludes that the only congressional responses that truly amount to challenges of the Court's constitutional holdings were congressional responses to the responses to *Oregon v. Mitchell and INS v. Chadha* (167).

A final majoritarian issue that frequently is overlooked particularly by those concerned with the counter-majoritarian nature of judicial review is the role of judicial review as a check against tyranny of the majority. When we look to the constitutional founders, such as Madison and Hamilton, and early commentators, such as Alexis de Tocqueville, we see strong arguments in favor of this counter-majoritarian role. James Madison, in defense of the bill of rights, argued that judges, when faced with individual rights constitutionally incorporated into a bill of rights would consider themselves as guardians of these rights and would thus serve as an impenetrable bulwark against encroachment upon these rights by the legislative and executive branches (1789, 439). Danelski notes that in claiming the power of judicial review in *Marbury v. Madison* (1803), Chief Justice John

Marshall in effect argued that "the very essence of civil liberty" was recourse to the courts to ensure their protection (1992, 22). Over time, the U.S. Supreme Court and students of the Court have continued to accept this link between judicial review and the protection of rights as historical fact across several periods of time. Danelski concludes that "a strong argument can also be made for the proposition that in the late eighteenth century the principle purpose of judicial review in the United States was also the protection of individual rights" (21). In 1911, Justice Horace Lurton posited that the course of American history "supports the contention that the exercise of judicial review is an obligation of the judiciary as a guarantor of liberty" (as cited in Slotnick 1987, 20). And more specifically, in 1938 Justice Stone, speaking for the Court in the *Carolene Products* footnote penned the preferred freedoms doctrine setting forth the special status of rights and freedom in constitutional challenges stating that the Court will assume "legislation constitutional unless it facially abridges a provision of the Bill of Rights, restricts access to normal political processes or reflects prejudices against discrete and insular minorities." McCloskey asserts that the concern reflected in the "more exacting judicial scrutiny" standards of the *Carolene Products* has actually "been the tradition running back to Marshall and beyond, that the Court has the power and duty to right wrongs, to translate its moral convictions into constitutional limitations" (1994, 129). Although some normative theorists and empirical researchers see judicial review as a largely antidemocratic exercise, we find a special exception made in regard to this negative assessment—when the power is exercised in protection of individual rights; Howard and Segal (2004) conclude that "the dominant viewpoint is for a judiciary to restrain from overturning laws passed by the democratic majority unless necessary to protect fundamental freedoms or suspect classes" (132). Keck (2002) suggests that "the very mission of an independent Supreme Court [has] come to be identified—in the minds of ordinary citizens and the justices themselves—with the enforcement of rights-based limits on political action" and "for the justices to abandon this role would be to call into question the very justification for their office" (135).

Despite these scholarly and popular expectations, we certainly have strong anecdotal historical evidence that the power of judicial review has been used to curb rather than protect rights. Obvious examples would be *Dred Scott, Plessy,* and *Korematsu*—decisions in which, as Sherry (1998) reminds us, it is now the dissenters whom we admire rather than the justices in the majority. As I mentioned in Chapter Three, international human rights proponents have also expected this rights-protective role for the judiciary and the power of constitutional or judicial review (e.g., Becker 1970; International Commission of Jurists 1983; Caine 1988;

Ackerman 1989; Chowdury 1989; Garro 1993; Stotzky 1993; Larkins 1996); however, in regard to human rights practices globally, scholars thus far have found that judicial review is associated with curbing human rights not protecting them (Keith 2004; Keith and Ogundele 2007; Keith, Tate, and Poe 2007). As we saw in Chapters Two and Three, the U.S. Supreme Court's historical exercise of judicial review overall has tended to go against rather than support rights-based claims, at least in its review of congressional statutes.[1] I will further explore this relationship in the analysis presented here and in Chapter Four as well.

Hypotheses and Initial Tests of the Early Counter-Majoritarian Studies

Dahl (1957, 1967) examined the 85 instances in which the Court overturned congressional statutes between 1789 and 1965. He reported that in more than half of the 85 decisions, the nullified statutes were voided at least four years after they were passed; meaning that the enacting Congress would have gone through two election cycles and thus presumably would no longer have constituted the same lawmaking majority. He concluded that the Court was not challenging a current law-making majority in these cases. To determine the influence of the Court's action, he analyzed the historical impact of the decisions in which laws were declared unconstitutional within four years after passage, presumably the portion of cases that could be counter-majoritarian under his delineation. He found only fifteen cases which he could classify (by some undisclosed criteria) as major policy, and ultimately he concluded that this small set of decisions were then usually reversed, either by congressional amendments or legislation or by the Court reversing itself. He considered this evidence in conjunction with his finding that most presidents have been able on average to make a new appointment to the Court every two years and are, thereby, able to change the ideological majority of the Court in a relatively short time. As a result, he concluded that the Court does not have significant policy influence, because it had been unable to hold out against the national majority or the other branches of the government for long, and in only a few important cases has it been able to thwart or delay the national will. Casper (1976) updated Dahl's original analysis and reached a different conclusion. Casper discovered that the Court had become more activist in the years 1958–1974, but reading his data we can see the Court still followed somewhat the pattern Dahl had found, since only one-fifth of its nullification decisions reversed congressional statutes that had been passed within the preceding four years. But

Casper also argued that Dahl's assessment of the counter-majoritarian nature ignored laws older than four years when struck, which was especially important given Congress' longer tenure in office, and it ignored the larger body of struck state statutes. In terms of the long-term policy significance, Casper pointed out that only one case, *Oregon v. Mitchell*, was reversed by Congress (with the Twenty-Sixth Amendment). The other twenty-seven decisions striking federal statutes were left to stand.

Since the data I have collected encompasses both the decisions in which the Court upheld and nullified congressional statutes, and encompasses the Court's history until 2001, we have a broader and deeper set of data to analyze. In this set of congressional review cases the ages of the statutes under review range from 1 year to 150 years. The oldest congressional statute under review was the Act of July 6, 1798 (the Enemy Alien Act) which was 150 years old when upheld by the Supreme Court in *Ludecke v. Watkins* (1948) where the Court noted that "the Act is almost as old as the Constitution, and it would savor of doctrinaire audacity now to find the statute offensive to some emanation of the Bill of Rights," and second oldest was the Fort Laramie Treaty of 1868, which was 112 years old when upheld by the Supreme Court in *United Nations v. Sioux Nation of Indians et al.* (1980).[2] On average, though, the age of the statute at review was approximately 12.3 years old. Statutes that were ultimately nullified by the Court were on average only four-fifths of one year younger (11.7 years) than those which the Court eventually upheld (12.5 years). Table 4.1 reports the ages of the statutes in groupings of four years, except for the last two rows in which the dispersion of the small number of statutes was too broad to merit multiple groupings. Approximately one third (32.3 percent) of the statutes are four or fewer years old and over one half (56 percent) of the statutes are eight or fewer years old. And almost three-fourths (70.2 percent) of the statutes are twelve years old or less, leaving over one-fourth that range from thirteen to over hundred years. Table 4.2 reports the ages of the nullified statutes in the same age delineation as Table 4.1. Here one sees almost identical patterns: 33.1 percent of the statutes are four years old or less, 56 percent are 8 or fewer-years old, and 71.0 percent of the statutes are 12 or fewer-years old. The oldest statutes to be nullified are 61 to 65 years old. Dahl had found that at least half of the nullified statutes were at least four years old; here at least two-thirds are more than four years old. Casper found that at least one-fifth of the nullified statutes had been passed within the last four years. Here the number is slightly more at one-third. Dahl's main point was that since the majority of the laws that were overturned were at least four years old, then the Court was not acting counter to a current majority, given that two elections would have changed the makeup of

Table 4.1 Age of Statutes Under Review

1–4 years	281
5–8 years	206
9–12 years	124
13–16 years	71
17–20 years	43
21–24 years	27
25–28 years	23
29–32 years	12
33–36 years	20
37–40 years	13
41–44 years	12
45–48 years	6
49–52 years	7
52–56 years	9
57–60 years	4
61–64 years	2
65–68 years	1
69–72 years	1
73–77 years	3
95–150 years	5
Total	870

the sitting Congress. In this fuller analysis we find that all but 281 statutes would be promulgated by congresses of at least two terms previously, but on the other hand as Casper pointed out members of Congress are serving longer terms than they were in the early years Dahl analyzed, and as we find here, 56 percent of the statutes that are nullified were promulgated within eight years of the time they are nullified.[3]

Dahl's assertion that the Court was only thwarting Congress in a few important cases is not fully supported in this analysis; sixty-three (41.5 percent) of the cases which nullify a statute are considered major or landmark cases, in that they appear in either list of major decisions: *The New York Times* or *Congressional Quarterly*, as reported in *The Supreme Court Compendium* (Epstein, Segal, Spaeth, and Walker 2003).[4] Interestingly, only 95 (12.8 percent) of the decisions that upheld congressional statutes are considered to be major decisions, which may suggest in part that

Table 4.2 Age of Statutes Nullified

1–4 years	49
5–8 years	34
9–12 years	22
13–16 years	15
17–20 years	8
21–24 years	2
25–28 years	1
29–32 years	0
33–36 years	6
37–40 years	4
41–44 years	1
45–48 years	0
49–52 years	1
52–56 years	2
57–60 years	1
61–64 years	1
65–68 years	1
69–72 years	0
73–77 years	0
95–150	0
Total	148

the very act of nullifying Congress makes a case fit the undisclosed criteria of these lists of major Court decisions. The Court's stamp of legitimacy on congressional action can have a significant historical impact as well, such as did *Korematsu* and the several Espionage Act cases in 1920. Even so, as whole only seventeen percent of the congressional review cases make into one of these lists of salient cases. In regard to Casper's final assertion against Dahl's conclusions, that only one of the nullification cases had been overturned subsequently by Congress, there has been no amendment overturning Court decisions since Casper wrote, leaving the total at only four cases, which have been overturned by Congress. And as we saw in Chapter One, Geyh's recent work has found that Congress is largely acquiescent to the Court, and when it does respond to Court decisions it does so primarily to modify the law to conform to the Court's constitutional jurisprudence. On the whole we find that the counter-majoritarian pattern of these decisions fits somewhere in between Dahl and Casper, with the Court somewhat more counter-majoritarian than Dahl found but certainly less so than Casper asserted.

Although Dahl and Casper's analysis and their conclusions rested on an examination of the Court's behavior as a single period of time, Funston (1975) distinguished the circumstances under which the Court acted. He argued that the Court was not likely to perform a counter-majoritarian role, nullifying congressional statutes, over the long periods of stable party systems he identifies, but that rather the Court was only likely to do so during a transitional period of party realignments in which the Court is suddenly out of sync with the political majority in power until the nomination process slowly brings onto bench justices whose political preferences are aligned with this new political majority. Funston evaluated all instances in which the Court overturned congressional statutes, comparing the number of nullifications across the two different types of periods, in addition to evaluating the number of decisions in which the Court declared legislation unconstitutional within four years of its promulgation. He found that in critical years the Court had a significantly higher average number of nullification cases per year (.66) compared to noncritical periods (.54), and he also found that in critical periods, the Court struck a higher average number of statutes that were four or fewer years old in critical periods (.50) than in noncritical periods. Thus, he finds the Court exercising a counter-majoritarian more strongly in these briefer critical periods than in the predominant stable party systems. I replicate Funston's bivariate analysis here; with the added rigor of being able to test the hypothesis more appropriately using the percentage of statutes under review that nullified in the periods rather than the mere number of nullifications, which does not control for the opportunities before the Court at the time.

Funston identifies five party systems and four realignment phases or critical periods, which he calculates to precede each party system by eight years (based on Chambers and Burnham 1967). The party system periods and realignment phases include the Jefferson Republic (1800–1820), realignment phase 1820–1827, the Jacksonian Democracy 1828–1852, realignment phase 1852–1859, Radical Republican 1860–1888, realignment phase 1888–1895, McKinley Republican 1896–1928, realignment phase 1928–1935, and New Deal Democracy 1936–? (803). I extrapolate the phases forward, assuming that the 1960 reelection brought in the New Frontier Democracy (Nardulli 1995) and that the 1994 elections marked an ideological realignment (Abramowitz and Saunders 1998), and therefore following Funston's delineation I designate 1952–1059 and 1986–1993 as the eight-year critical periods to the realignments. During periods considered to be critical years, the Supreme Court reviewed 188 cases which represent 21 percent of the cases here; within those cases in which the Court had opportunity to nullify Congress, it did so only in 15.4 percent of the cases. During periods considered non-critical or party system years the Court reviewed 708 cases (79 percent of the review cases) and nullified statutes in 17.4 percent of the cases, an increase of 2 points *above* the critical period score. Funston had calculated an index that was the ratio of years within each type of period divided by the number of cases nullifying Congress, which would be the equivalent number of nullifications per year. He calculated a .66 index for critical periods compared to .54 in stable periods. Even we when follow this weaker measurement that lacks a control for the number of review cases and we can still find a higher level of nullification in the non-critical periods than in the critical periods; .82 compared to .60. These contra-findings do not hold up, though, as we examine the nullification rates based on statute age, testing whether, as Funston found, the Court overturns more statutes within four years of enactment during critical periods than non-critical. In considering those statutes passed within four years of review we can see a nullification rate of 27.3 percent in critical periods and 14.5 in non-critical periods which does then clearly supports Funston's finding. In both critical and non-critical periods the proportion of cases under review that are four years old or less represent about one third of the cases, the same proportion as the full set of cases. Taken as a whole, these analyses indicate that Funston's findings do not uphold over time or as we control for the opportunity to nullify with one exception, in regard to the age of the statutes being nullified where we do find evidence of more counter-majoritarian nature among the critical years. These hypotheses were also tested in the preliminary exploratory multivariate models in Chapter Five and there was no evidence to support the hypotheses.

Majoritarian Hypotheses from Recent Empirical Studies

More recent scholarship on judicial review published by law professors or by political scientists in strategic approach-related law review articles makes arguments similar to Funston's arguments, but without any apparent awareness of his work, explaining why it is that the Court is not frequently out of sync with the majoritarian branches. Ferejohn (1999) holds that the Court's constitutional jurisprudence is not out of line with the preferences of the elected branches for long periods of time due to the stability of the political system which keeps elected officials in office for fairly long periods of time, while at the same time ensuring a fairly stable set of justices on the bench, who possess professional norms of stability and predictability that "work to make doctrine evolve quite slowly in most areas of the law" (382–83). As noted above he also identifies five periods of history—those in which we have experienced this stable political rule, which he posits to be characterized by a dominant majority party or by divided government, in which he believes the makeup of the Court has tended to "come into alignment with the dominant political configuration" and also four periods of imbalance in which a decisive electoral shift leaves the Court out of alignment and suddenly vulnerable to attempts to alter its jurisprudence (383). The stable periods of a dominant majority party are the Democrats (1828–1860 and 1932–1968) and the Republicans (1898–1930) and divided government (1876–1896 and 1968–1994). The periods of imbalance occurred following Jefferson's first election in 1800, during the post Civil War period, during the early years of the New Deal period, and following the 1994 congressional elections. Although most of Ferejohn's analysis is focused on explaining Congress' respect for judicial independence and to some extent explaining constraints upon the Court's voting behavior, it has a direct relationship to the majoritarian issue since he is suggesting that during these stable periods the Court would be acting in sync with the *sitting* majority but not during periods of imbalance. During imbalance, the Court is counter-majoritarian but during stable periods the Court would be engaged in "friendly" judicial review as both Whittington and Friedman and Harvey hypothesized, but based on Ferejohn we would also expect that decisions to uphold statutes would be ideologically consistent with the sitting Congress, not just the nullification decisions, although we might expect the nullifications, that go against the norm of deference, to be even more ideologically consistent with Congress.

Analysis of these cases demonstrates that in stable years the Court nullifies at a rate of 14.8 percent compared to the periods of imbalance where the rate rises to 35.4 percent. The rates are identical if we separate the stable periods that had dominant party control and the stable periods with divided government. Table 4.3 presents the Supreme Court's liberalism in these cases by the periods as delineated by Ferejohn. The left-hand side of the table reports the data for the periods identified by Ferejohn as stable and the right-hand side reports those identified as periods of imbalance. The ideological direction of the votes is based on Spaeth's delineation described in the preceding chapters, with federalism modified as in the analyses of previous chapters. We would expect here that periods under Democratic control, as delineated by Reichley, would be more liberal than periods under the control of parties in the Republican tradition. Examining the stable periods we find two of the four periods in which the ideological direction of the Court's outcomes appears

Table 4.3 Liberalism of Supreme Court Votes by Periods of Stability and Periods of Imbalance*

Stable		Expectation	Imbalance		Expectation
1828–1860	Mostly DEMOCRAT with one WHIG Controlled Congress	Mostly Liberal	1800–1828	DEMOCRAT-REPUBLICAN	Liberal
Overall	27%		Overall	33%	
Null	0%		Null	100%	
1876–1896	MIX REPUBLICAN and DEMOCRAT	Moderate	1860–76	REPUBLICAN	Conservative
Overall	50%		Overall	41%	
Null	64%		Null	44%	
1898–1930	REPUBLICAN	Conservative	1930–32	REPUBLICAN	Conservative
Overall	49%		Overall	67%	
Null	71%		Null	0%	
1932–68	DEMOCRAT	Liberal	1994–2001	Mostly REPUBLICAN Controlled Congress	Mostly Conservative
Overall	71%		Overall	40%	
Null	63%		Null	48%	
1968–1994	Mostly DEMOCRAT Controlled Congress	Liberal			
Overall	42%				
Null	83%				

*Dates here are divided by the election periods as designated by Ferejohn, but in the analysis I took in account that Congress does not take office until January or March of the preceding year and thus adjusted the periods including the actual dates of the congressional session.

to be aligned with policy preferences of the sitting government, as we might expect under Ferejohn's hypothesis. The Court is moderately liberal in the overall outcomes of the cases in the 1932–1968 period and moderate in the overall outcomes in the 1876–1896 period; however, in the 1828–1860 period the Court produced quite conservative outcomes in these decisions. In the 1898–1930 period the Court is moderate, not conservative, in its overall outcomes, and in the 1968–1994 period the Court's outcomes are moderately conservative. If we limit the analysis to include only the nullification votes, the ideological fit actually worsens, except for the 1968–1994 period. When we examine the periods of imbalance in which we would expect the Court to be voting in a direction that is less ideologically consistent with the sitting government than in stable periods, we find the ideological match to be about the same as with the set of stable party years. In two of the periods the Court's ideological direction in reviewing Congress does fit the ideological direction of the sitting government; in the 1860–1876 period the Court produces moderately conservative outcomes and in the 1994–2001 period the Court produces conservative outcomes; however, in the 1800–1828 period the Court is rather conservative and in the 1930–1932 period the Court is moderately liberal. Furthermore, we see in these periods of imbalance, the direction of the nullifications matches the ideological direction of the sitting government for all four periods. These data would suggest that overall Ferejohn's hypothesis is not supported; the court does not seem to be more in alignment with popularly elected branches during stable periods than periods of imbalance. Additionally, tests of the periods of stability and imbalance did not perform as expected in preliminary exploratory multivariate models in Chapter Five.

Whereas Ferejohn argues that the Court will use its power of judicial review consistently with the policy preferences of the sitting Congress in periods of party balance, in which Congress may be better positioned to curb its constitutional decisions or with whom the Court's policy preferences may be aligned, Friedman and Harvey (2003), ultimately argue that the Court is generally more likely to nullify congressional statutes when facing an ideologically congenial sitting Congress, presumably without regard to periods of stability or critical elections. More succinctly, they argue the fact that the Rehnquist Court at present is unusually active in striking congressional statutes could be a clear signal that the conservative Court faces an ideologically congenial sitting Congress, which may not be all that displeased that the Court is striking liberal legislative. They note that the conservative Rehnquist Court did not begin to actively nullify congressional statutes until a conservative Congress was elected in 1994, even though there has been a conservative majority on the bench, disposed to strike liberal legislation, in place since 1986 (125). Although their arguments in regard to the strategic approach are more nuanced, and will be addressed more fully in Chapter Five, their argument which relates to the majoritarian question that we are interested in here would be that at least during some periods, such as the post-1994 Rehnquist Court, the Court is not engaging in behavior that counters the policy preferences of the *current* majority in review decisions.[5] It remains of course an empirical question as to how often this happy alignment occurs between the reviewing Court and the sitting Congress. The data under study here allow me to make an initial examination of this question. First, we can examine the overall ideological match between the policy direction of the Court's opinion and that of Congress, at least to the extent that political party serves as a surrogate for these preferences.

Following Reichley, I separate the congressional years into those controlled by parties in the Republican tradition, those in the Democrat tradition, and those in which party control of Congress was divided. As above, in terms of ideological consistency or a satisfied Congress, we would expect to see in those periods in which Congress is controlled by a party of the Democrat tradition, the Court's review decisions would be more liberal, and in those periods during which Congress is controlled by a party of the Republican tradition would be more conservative, and the decisions during divided government would be mixed–or moderate on average. The results merely reflect the historical average moderation in ideological outcomes that we saw in these decisions in Chapter Two: during periods of Democratic control of Congress the review decisions were 55.3 percent liberal, during periods of Republican control of Congress the review decisions were 50.1 percent liberal, and during periods of divided control of Congress the review decisions were 49.7 percent liberal. If we limit the analysis to nullification outcomes only, we do find that the Court is more likely to overturn conservative statutes during periods when Congress is controlled by Democrats (70.8 percent liberal outcome); however, during periods of Republican control, the Court still votes in the moderate range, nullifying both liberal and conservative statutes (57.1 percent liberal outcome), and in periods of divided government the Court is more likely to nullify conservative statutes than liberal ones (71.4 percent liberal outcome). It appears that Republicans in Congress, whether in majority control or sharing control with Democrats in divided government, are not as likely to be happy with the Court's review decisions. These data reveal that no matter what party is sitting in Congress, the Court tends to exercise the power of judicial review in a moderate ideological direction, on average, despite significant periodic deviation. However, when the Court uses this power to nullify Congress, its more conflictual dimension, it does appear to be more consistent with the policy direction of Congress but only that of sitting liberal congresses, but not conservative congresses. Of course, attitudinalists would argue that crucial distinction in whether the Court's decisions align with the sitting Congress is simply a matter of who is sitting on the bench and the values or preferences they bring to the bench. In Chapter Five, I will control for these factors simultaneously as well as their interactions. For now, from the perspective of the counter-majoritarian issue, we have seen another piece of evidence that the Court is only somewhat counter-majoritarian, in terms of reflecting the general policy direction of the sitting Congress. Overall, in terms of the counter majoritarian question, it appears that the Court is fairly majoritarian, except in the context of the sitting Congress. As I noted above, the one area in which even the strongest critics of judicial review agree that the Court might be justified in exercising this extra–democratic power to nullify Congress is in protecting fundamental freedoms or suspect classes. I turn next to that dimension of the power.

The Court as Protector against "Tyranny of the Majority" Hypothesis

As we discussed above, the power of judicial review has long been associated with the premise that the Court stands as a guarantor of rights, protecting political minorities' fundamental freedoms from incursions of the majority elected branches of government. This assumption has informed bilateral and multilateral efforts at establishing rule of law systems in newly independent or newly democratizing states across the globe. However, as I mentioned above, thus far, the empirical evidence suggests that our optimism in this judicial check is misplaced; the power of judicial review is much more likely to be associated with rights abuses than with their protection. Scholars and aid-grantors continue to seek a better understanding of the circumstances under which judicial review is exercised to benefit rights, rather than to curb them. The United States Supreme Court, with its two-hundred-year history of exercising this power, offers perhaps the best case study available to examine the longitudinal exercise of this potential check. We saw in Chapter Two, that cases involving civil rights and civil liberties claims make up almost forty percent of the Court's congressional review cases, which suggests, not surprisingly, the Court has become, at least over time, a forum for such rights claims. And we saw that the Court had a higher nullification rate in most of the rights issue areas than in the other issue areas before the Court. However, we also saw in Chapter Three that of all claims before the Court, the justices were least likely to vote in favor of rights claims in these congressional review cases. Tables 4.4 and 4.5 summarize the Court's outcomes in these decisions, but here I have separated the four different components of the broad civil rights and civil liberties category, following Spaeth's delineation. Although support of the rights claims has been low overall (30.7 percent), the level of support has varied across issue areas

Table 4.4 Support of Rights Claim by Issue Area

	Percent that Supported the Rights Claim	Percent that Went Against the Rights Claim
Criminal Procedure	27.6	72.3
Civil Rights	33.9	66.1
First Amendment	33.0	67.0
Non-economic Due Process	21.2	78.8
Total	30.7	69.3

Table 4.5 Support of Rights Claims in Nullification Votes and Votes to Uphold by Issue Area

	Votes to Nullify Statutes		Votes to Uphold Statutes	
	Percent that Supported the Rights Claim	Percent that Went Against the Rights Claim	Percent that Supported the Rights Claim	Percent that Went Against the Rights Claim
Criminal Procedure	95.5	5.0	9.5	90.5
Civil Rights	70.4	29.6	23.4	76.6
First Amendment	84.6	15.4	13.2	86.8
Non-economic Due Process	67.3	33.3	16.7	83.3
Total	81.6	18.4	16.2	83.8

within the broader civil rights and civil liberties category. The Court has been most likely to support civil rights, followed by First Amendment rights (33.9 and 33.0 percent, respectively) and least likely to support due process claims, followed by rights claims of criminal defendants (21.2 and 27.6 percent, respectively). Spaeth's due process category, when economic due process cases are removed, includes a mixture of civil liberties due process issues along with due process in a criminal procedure context as well. Thus, it is not surprising that these areas of civil liberties receive the lowest level of support. Even the staunch liberals on the bench such as Douglas, Warren, Brennan, and Marshall have tended to support criminal defendants rights at much lower level. The same pattern holds for liberals on the bench today. Interestingly, though, as Ferejohn points out, it is the area of the Court's federal jurisprudence, along with the rights of third world immigrants, that has been unpopular with *both* sides of the aisle in Congress, not just the right.

Even though we see that historically the exercise power of judicial review has overwhelmingly gone against rights claims, we can see in Table 4.5 that in the relatively small percentage of times when the Court has challenged Congress on rights issues (76 out of 342 cases) it has done so overwhelmingly to protect rights. This level of support has varied across the four issue areas in this dimension as well, albeit with some notable differences. The Court is much less likely to nullify Congress to support civil rights (70.4 percent) and due process (67.3 percent) than it is to nullify Congress in support of criminal procedure (95.5 percent) and First Amendment (84.6 percent) claims. Thus criminal rights have the highest level of support in the votes to nullify and the lowest level of support in the votes to uphold (only 9.5 percent). The low number in part reflects the fact that, as Epstein and Knight (1998) note, it is typically a given that congressional statutes go against the rights of the accused, and coupled with the Court's norm of deference we see an extremely high percentage of votes to uphold that do not support the criminal defendant's rights (150).

We would expect that the Supreme Court's level of support for rights claims may have increased following Stone's *Carolene Products* footnote in 1938 that set forth the preferred freedoms doctrine in constitutional challenges, as described above. Table 4.6 divides the rights-related decisions into those that were decided before and those that were decided after the *Carolene* footnote. First, we can see a substantial increase in the overall support rate of rights claims, going from 19.4 percent prior to the *Carolene Products* footnote to 35.4 percent after the proclamation of the preferred freedoms doctrine. We find almost no difference

Table 4.6 Support of Rights Claim by Issue Area (Before and After the *Carolene* Footnote)

	Percent that Supported the Rights Claim	Percent that Went Against the Rights Claim
Prior to the *Carolene* Footnote		
Criminal Procedure	26.2	73.8
Civil Rights	17.7	82.3
First Amendment	0.0	100.0
Non-economic Due Process	20.0	80.0
Total	19.4	80.6
Following the *Carolene* Footnote		
Criminal Procedure	28.6	71.7
Civil Rights	40.2	59.8
First Amendment	37.8	62.2
Non-economic Due Process	22.2	77.8
Total	35.4	64.6

in the rate of support for due process claims—a 2.2 point increase or the rate of support in criminal procedure claims—a 2.4 point increase. However, in civil rights and First Amendment claims where we would expect a stronger impact, we do find a substantial increase in each—a 37.8 point increase in support of First Amendment claims and a 22.5 point increase in support of civil rights claims. In the post-*Carolene* era we clearly see an improvement in the rate of support for rights claims, but the level is still far below even a minimal majority support for rights claims.

Table 4.7 further delineates the votes in those that uphold and those that nullify Congress. Here we are able to observe even more of an effect from the *Carolene Products* footnote. First, before the *Carolene Products* case, we find that the Court nullified statutes that both protected and curbed rights at fairly even rate; 47.4 percent that went against rights claims and 52.6 that supported rights claims. The pattern following the footnote, not surprisingly more closely matches the full time period, but at a more extreme level, with 91.2 percent of the nullifications

Table 4.7 Support of Rights Claims in Nullification Votes and Votes to Uphold by Issue Area (Before and After the *Carolene* Footnote)

	Votes to Nullify Statutes		Votes to Uphold Statutes	
	Percent that Supported the Rights Claim	Percent that Went Against the Rights Claim	Percent that Supported the Rights Claim	Percent that Went Against the Rights Claim
Prior to the *Carolene* Footnote				
Criminal Procedure	90.0	10.0	6.3	93.7
Civil Rights	12.5	87.5	19.2	80.8
First Amendmentt	0.0	100.0	0.0	100.0
Non-economic Due Process	20.0	80.0	20.0	80.0
Total	52.6	47.4	11.9	88.1
Following the *Carolene* Footnote				
Criminal Procedure	100.0	0.0	11.9	88.1
Civil Rights	94.7	5.3	25.0	75.0
First Amendment	88.0	12.0	15.8	84.2
Non-economic Due Process	66.7	33.3	13.3	86.7
Total	91.2	8.8	18.0	82.0

supporting rights claims. The uphold rate of support for rights claims is 82 percent which is approximately six points less than the rate before the footnote. We see the least amount of change in the criminal procedure area, which again has not been as closely linked to the preferred freedoms doctrine. We see the biggest difference in the use of nullifications to support First Amendment claims which have been strongly linked to the preferred freedoms doctrines by liberal justices on the bench, followed by the civil rights. It is interesting to observe that prior to the footnote, nullifications were used overwhelmingly against rights claims, with the exception of criminal procedure, and thus the moderated average reflects the effect of the one significant outlier, the criminal procedure issue area. Overall we are still left with the conclusion that the Court has exercised the power of judicial review in such a manner that rights claims were diminished or ignored, even if it has primarily voted to uphold rights when it chooses to go against the norm of deference to nullify. Interestingly, we find here the level of support for civil rights by the Court (the branch of government most frequently argued to be a check against tyranny of majority) is only slightly better than the level of rights protection promulgated by the public itself through venues of direct democracy, when there are the fewest filters and presumably the greatest opportunity for a self-interested majority to defeat the rights of the minority. Gamble (1997) found that the public, when directly voting on civil rights as a policy issue on the ballot in either initiatives or referenda (during the period of 1959–1993), voted either to repeal or to limit minority rights at a rate of 78 percent, compared to the Court here voting against the rights claims, at a rate of 69.3.

Conclusions

What can we conclude about the majoritarian nature of the exercise of judicial review by the Supreme Court? At least in regard to its exercise of this power in congressional review cases, it is somewhat more majoritarian than counter-majoritarian, along multiple dimensions, than is frequently asserted by those concerned about the undemocratic nature of this power. The overwhelming majority of statutes under review are older than four years old, which would seem to represent a somewhat different enacting Congress than the current sitting Congress. In addition, only one-third of the cases that nullified a statute were statutes four or less years old; however, if we broaden the time frame to include the equivalent two additional election cycles, we find slightly over half of the nullified statutes to be eight years or less. Thus use of the power to nullify statutes appears to be somewhat counter-majoritarian; but not as much as we might expect. In terms of their significance in the development of constitutional jurisprudence, only a small percentage of the review cases are considered to be landmark decisions, particularly those upholding congressional statutes. In addition, much less than half of even the nullification cases are considered to be landmark cases as distinguished here. Overall, it seems that Dahl's assessment is more accurate than Casper's. In addition, it appears that most of Funston's assertions do not hold when the analysis is extended to include the full exercise of review of Congress and extended in time; the Court is *more* likely to nullify in the longer stable periods not the briefer periods of transitions. However, Funston's other significant assertion does hold in the extended analysis; the Court is more likely to strike younger laws in critical years, laws which presumably are more likely to be passed by sitting majorities in Congress. Additionally, the analysis found Court in its review decisions, whether nullifying or upholding, is not acting consistently in the general policy direction of the sitting Congress, unless the sitting Congress is controlled at least in part by Democrats. As we will see in Chapter Five, this finding is in part a function of the justices' policy preferences. Continuing with the analysis of Chapter Two, we also saw that in regard to the final majoritarian issue, the Court largely acts in a majoritarian role, not as the bulwark against intrusions against minority rights by the political majority. Instead, we find that the Court has exercised the power to review congressional legislation in way that has produced outcomes that diminish or ignore rights claims, even though it has primarily voted to uphold rights when going against the norm of deference to nullify congressional action. As I concluded above, the level of support for civil rights by the Court, the branch of government claimed to be the guarantor of rights, is only slightly better than the rights protection promoted in forums of direct democracy, when a self-interested majority has to defeat the rights of the minority. Ultimately we are left to conclude that the concern about or conversely the optimism for the Court's counter-majoritarian exercise of this power, at least, in regard to Congress, may be somewhat overstated.

Notes

1. This remains an empirical question in regard to its review of state statutes.
2. For most cases the date of the statute was reported in the opinion, but in the other cases the date of the statute was determined using LEXIS or the Legal Information Institute's U.S. Code Collection. If the statute was amended, revised, or recodified at a later date, I continued to use the original date the statute was enacted unless it was the amendment or the revision that was under review. For twenty six of the 896 cases I was not able to determine the age of the statute.

3. For example in the 1997–1998 members in both the House and the Senate had served ten years on average, with 47 percent of the House and 36 percent of the Senate having served twelve years or more.

4. This delineation follows Brenner and Arrington (2002) and Arrington and Brenner (2004).

5. I will address their fuller arguments in Chapter Five when we examine and test the strategic approach. While their analysis does confirm their hypothesis in regard to the Rehnquist Court, my results do not find an impact from the consistency between the justices' policy preferences and the sitting Congress' policy preference. Rather it is consistency with the enacting Congress' policy preference that makes a difference. I discuss these results as well as some of the limitations in my measures, in Chapter Five.

References

Abramowitz, Alan I. and Kyle L. Saunders. 1998. "Ideological Realignment in the U.S. Electorate." *Journal of Politics* 60: 634–52.

Ackermann, L.W. H. 1989. "Constitutional Protection of Human Rights: Judicial Review." *Columbia Human Rights Law Review* 21 (1): 59–71.

Arrington, Theodore S. and Saul Brenner. 2004. "Strategic Voting for Damage Control on the Supreme Court." *Political Research Quarterly* 57: 565–73.

Becker, Theodore. 1970. *Comparative Judicial Politics.* Landham, MD: University Press of America.

Brenner, Saul and Theodore S. Arrington. 2002. "Measuring Salience on the Supreme Court: A Research Note." *Jurimetrics* 43: 99–113.

Caine, Burton. "The Influence Abroad of the United States Constitution on Judicial Review and a Bill of Rights: Introduction." 1988. *Temple International and Comparative Law Journal* 2: 59–78.

Casper, Jonathan D. 1976. "The Supreme Court and National Policy Making." *American Political Science Review* 70: 50–63.

Chambers, William Nesbit and Walter Dean Burnham. 1967. *The American Party Systems: States of Political Development.* New York: Oxford Press.

Chowdhury, Subrata Roy. 1989. *Rule of Law in a State of Emergency.* New York: St. Martin's Press.

Dahl, Robert A. 1957. "Decision-Making in a Democracy: The Supreme Court as a National Policy Maker." *Journal of Public Law* 6: 279–95.

Dahl, Robert A. 1967. *Pluralist Democracy in the United States.* Chicago: Rand McNally & Company.

Danelski, David J. 1992. "Documenting the Establishment of Judicial Review: Japan and the United States." In *Comparative Judicial Review and Public Policy,* eds. Donald W. Jackson and Tate C. Neal. Westport, CT: Greenwood.

De Tocqueville, Alexis. 1966. *Democracy in America*, ed. J.P. Mayer. New York: Harper and Row.

Epstein, Lee and Jack Knight. 1998. *The Choices Judges Make.* Washington, DC: Congressional Quarterly Press.

Epstein, Lee, Jeffrey A. Segal, Harold J. Spaeth, and Thomas G. Walker. 2003. *The Supreme Court Compendium.* Washington, DC: Congressional Quarterly Press.

Ferejohn, John. 1999. "Independent Judges, Dependent Judiciary: Explaining Judicial Independence." Southern California Law Review 72: 353–84.

Friedman, Barry and Anna Harvey. 2003. "Electing the Supreme Court." *Indiana Law Journal* 78: 123–39.

Funston, Richard. 1975. "The Supreme Court and Critical Elections." *American Political Science Review* 69: 795–811.

Gamble, Barbara S. 1997. "Putting Civil Rights to a Popular Vote." *American Journal of Political Science* 41: 245–69.

Garro, Alejandro. 1993. "Nine Years to Democracy in Argentina: Partial Failure or Qualified Success?" *Columbia Journal of Transnational Law* 31: 1–102.

Geyh, Charles Gardner. 2006. *When Courts and Congress Collide: The Struggle for Control of America's Judicial System.* Ann Arbor: University of Michigan Press.

Graber, Mark A. 1993. "'The Non-Majoritarian Difficulty' Legislative Deference to the Judiciary." *Studies in American Political Development* 7: 35–73.

Howard, Robert M. and Jeffrey A. Segal. 2004. "A Preference for Deference? The Supreme Court and Judicial Review." *Political Research Quarterly* 57(1): 131–43.

International Commission of Jurists. 1983. *States of Emergency: Their Impact on Human Rights.* Geneva: International Commission of Jurists.

Keck, Thomas. 2002. "Activism and Restraint on the Rehnquist Court: Timing, Sequence, and Conjuncture in Constitutional Development." *Polity* 35: 121–52.

Keith, Linda Camp. 2004. "National Constitutions and Human Rights Protection": Regional Differences and Colonial Influences." In *The Systematic Study of Human Rights*, eds. Sabine Carey and Steven C. Poe. Ashgate Publishing.

Keith, Linda Camp and Ayo Ogundele. 2007. "Legal Systems and Constitutionalism in Sub-Saharan Africa: An Empirical Examination of Colonial Influences on Human Rights." Human Rights Quarterly (forthcoming November 2007).

Keith, Linda Camp, C. Neal Tate, and Steven C. Poe. 2007. "Is the Law a Mere Parchment Barrier to Human Rights Abuse?" Unpublished manuscript.

Larkins, Christopher M. 1996. "Judicial Independence and Democratization: A Theoretical and Conceptual Analysis." *American Journal of Comparative Law* 44: 605–26.

Madison, James. 1789. "Federalist No, 48." In Kurland and Lerner, eds., The Founder's Constitution. http://press-pubs.uchicago.edu/founders/documents/v1ch10s15.html.

McCloskey, Robert. G. 1994. *The American Supreme Court.* Chicago: University of Chicago Press.

Nardulli, Peter F. 1995. "The Concept of a Critical Realignment, Electoral Behavior, and Political Change." *American Political Science Review* 89: 10–22.

Pickerill, J. Mitchell. 2005. "Congressional Responses to Judicial Review." In *Congress and the Constitution,* eds. Neal Devins and Keith E. Whittington. Durham: Duke University Press.

Reichley, James. 1992. *The Life of the Parties: A History of American Political Parties.* New York: The Free Press.

Sherry, Suzanna. 1998. "Independent Judges and Independent Justice." *Law & Contemporary Problems* 61: 15–20.

Slotnick, Elliot E. 1987. "The Place of Judicial Review in the American Tradition: The Emergence of an Eclectic Power." *Judicature* 71(2): 68–79.

Stotzky, Irwin P. 1993. "The Tradition of Constitutional Adjudication." In *Transitions to Democracy in Latin America: The Role of the Judiciary,* ed. Irwin P. Stotzky. Boulder, CO: Westview.

Whittington, Keith. 2005. "'Interpose Your Friendly Hand': Political Supports for the Exercise of Judicial Review by the United States Supreme Court." *American Political Science Review* 99: 583–96.

5

The Decision to Nullify or Uphold: Exploratory and Explanatory Models of Individual Justices' Judicial Review Votes

In this chapter I will examine the various factors that influence the justices' individual voting behavior in the congressional review cases in the context of the two dominant categories of theories in behavioralist research on the U.S. Supreme Court. These two preference-based theories can be broadly delineated as (1) social-psychological theories that focus on the justices' ideological attitudes and (2) economic theories that focus on the justices' strategic interactions within their institutional contexts (Epstein, Hoekstra, Segal, and Spaeth 1998, 802). These theories were presented in Chapter One along with an examination of the status of empirical research relative to the theories and the behavior under study here. In this chapter I will first identify the testable hypotheses that we can derive from these theories and that are appropriate for examination within the boundaries of this work. Then, I will present the operationalization of variables and data issues, particularly in regard to measuring the justices' policy preferences over a two-hundred-year period. During this process I will present some preliminary exploratory analysis and engage in preliminary model testing as we move toward building an integrated explanatory model. This step-process should facilitate building as fully and correctly specified and yet as parsimonious a model as possible and it should also enhance the clarity and depth of the presentation of the data and the statistical findings. Finally, I will estimate models for shorter historic periods to determine whether some of the explanations are time-bound.

Theoretical Expectations and Hypotheses

The Attitudinal Model

The attitudinal model generally posits that "the Supreme Court decides disputes in light of the facts of the case vis-à-vis the ideological attitudes and values of the justices" (Segal and Spaeth 1993, 65). In other words, as Segal and Spaeth explain, Rehnquist voted the way he did because he was extremely conservative, and conversely Thurgood Marshall voted the way he did because he was extremely liberal (65). Supreme Court justices are perceived to be goal-oriented actors who want case outcomes, and ultimately the law, to reflect as closely as possible their particular policy preferences, and the justices are assumed generally to be able to vote their individual policy preferences because "they lack electoral or political accountability, ambition for higher office, and comprise a court of last resort that controls its own jurisdiction" (69). As we saw in Chapter One, measures of judicial attitudes have proven to be good predictors of the justices' votes in economic cases and, particularly in civil rights and liberties cases, the two main issue areas before the Court in the last half century (Segal and Cover 1989; Segal, Epstein, Cameron, and Spaeth 1995). More importantly, for this study, surrogate measures for the justices' ideology, such as partisan identification and appointing president, have also been used successfully to explain the justices' votes in these key issue areas, extending back to the earlier part of the last century in at least one of the studies (Tate 1981; Tate and Handberg 1991; George and Epstein 1992). As we examine the Supreme Court's review of congressional statutes, the attitudinal model would predict, in the most simple terms, that a justice would vote to uphold those statutes that are consistent with his or her policy preferences and conversely would vote to strike those statutes that are inconsistent with his or her policy preferences. Large-N studies such as Howard and Segal (2004) and Lindquist and Solberg (2007) have found evidence to support this prediction, which gives us our first hypothesis,

> **Hypothesis 1**: A Supreme Court justice's vote on the constitutionality of a congressional statute will be influenced by the consistency between the policy direction of the statute and the justice's ideological preferences.

Much of the long-standing criticism of the Court's exercise of judicial review has come from the Right, by conservative political actors, scholars, or commentators, such as Meese (1985) and Bork (1990) who associate judicial activism with liberalism, particularly rights-based claims, and much of the discourse in this conflict centers on debates over originalism or original understanding in opposition to the living constitution approaches of the Warren Court. The attitudinal model seems to assume that *all* justices, regardless of the direction of their ideological preferences, would be more likely to support statutes that are consistent with their policy preferences than those which are not, and yet liberalism as defined by some judicial scholars such as Spaeth and Goldman is to some extent linked to the support of judicial authority. Goldman (1966, 1975) hypothesizes that a liberal justice is more likely to be an activist, in that he or she will be more likely to find federal jurisdiction in a case. Empirically, Goldman's study of the U.S. Circuit Courts of Appeals does find evidence of an association between this alleged dimension of liberalism and other dimensions of liberalism, and he does find evidence that Democrats are more activist than are Republicans. Spaeth's U.S. Supreme Court database considers a decision based on judicial power issues to be a liberal outcome if the decision is pro-judicial power, and the codebook goes as far to say "pro-activism." Thus, there appears be some expectation that liberal justices are more activist, even if there is not a strong theoretical justification put forth. Indeed, Keck (2007) asserts that Spaeth's assessment of pro-judicial authority votes as liberal outcomes is "far from obvious" (334), and he cautions that it is often hard to disentangle judicial power issues from the substantive issues with which they are intermingled.

Empirical studies of judge's self-reported ideology and role orientations have produced somewhat mixed results, but overall there has been consistent evidence of a correlation between liberalism and a more activist orientation, at least in regard to certain types of litigants or issue areas (Glick and Vines 1969; Wold 1974; Howard 1977; Scheb, Ungs, and Hayes 1989).[1] Recent large-N studies have supported the liberal "activist" link, with Howard and Segal's (2004) ten-year analysis finding that conservative justices were less likely than liberal ones to grant a request to vote to strike, and Solberg and Lindquist's (2006) finding that liberals on the Rehnquist Court were more likely to be activist in striking down laws than were conservatives, generally. Lindquist and Solberg's (2007) more extensive analysis of the Burger and Rehnquist Courts produced mixed results, with liberal ideology being associated with votes to strike challenged statutes in the Burger Court but not in the Rehnquist Court. The latter result appears to fit with Keck's (2007) analysis of Rehnquist Court nullification votes. He finds that most nullification decisions are formed by mixed coalitions of liberals and conservatives—for almost two-thirds of all the congressional nullification decisions in that period. However, as we saw in Chapter 2, Keck (2002) notes that the Rehnquist Court has been the least deferential court in American history and has developed "its own style of conservative judicial activism" (122), and he argues that three of the conservatives on the Court (Scalia and

Thomas, and Rehnquist, perhaps to a somewhat lesser extent) have "simply abandoned restraint in order to promote their own preferences wherever possible" and "to constitutionalize their New Right commitments," which seems to suggest a strong conservative link to judicial activism; however, the other conservatives, "Kennedy and O'Connor, in contrast, have generally supported judicial activism in defense of both liberal and conservative ends" (141). Overall, then we have somewhat substantial empirical evidence that links liberalism with some forms of "activism" defined broadly, and specifically in regard to Supreme Court nullification votes and in regard to judicial review votes generally.

> ***Hypothesis 2***: A liberal Supreme Court justice is more likely to vote to nullify a congressional statute than a conservative justice.

I will discuss the issues of operationalization of these hypotheses after presenting the hypotheses derived from the strategic approach and the control hypotheses.

Strategic and Institutional Influences

As discussed in Chapter One, the attitudinal model assumes that the Supreme Court justices are primarily seekers of legal policy who are largely unconstrained by the political system in voting their individual ideological attitudes (Rhode and Spaeth 1976; Segal and Spaeth 1993; Segal and Spaeth 2002). Although the strategic account of judicial behavior, derived in part from the early work of Walter Murphy (1964) and more formally from the rational choice model, also assumes the justices to be primarily seekers of legal policy; the justices however are not perceived to be unconstrained actors, but rather they are seen as "strategic actors who realize that their ability to achieve their goals depends on a consideration of the preferences of other actors, the choices they expect others to make, and the institutional context in which they act" (Epstein and Knight 1998, 10). The justices may be constrained by external institutional features such as the separation of powers system (Marks 1988) or by internal institutional constraints such as formal rules or informal norms that limit the justices' choices (Epstein and Knight 1998; Maltzman, Wahlbeck, and Spriggs 2000).

Separation of powers models argue that other political actors, Congress especially, possess a variety of tools to curb the Court's rulings, particularly in statutory interpretation cases, and therefore, the justices must act strategically to defuse potential negative consequences (e.g., Ferejohn and Shipan 1990; Eskridge

1991; Spiller and Gely 1992; Hansford and Damore 2000). Indeed, Ignagni and Meernik (1994) found that Congress reacted to the Supreme Court's nullification of congressional statutes in almost thirty percent of the instances (19 out of 65). However, in only 68 percent (13 of the 19 attempts) was the legislation passed into law, which means Congress was only successful in its reaction in 19 percent (13 out of 65) of its attempts. More importantly, as we saw in Chapters One and Three, Pickerill's (2005) research demonstrated that the overwhelming congressional response to the Court's congressional nullification decisions has been to modify the legislation in a manner that complies with or that makes concessions to the Court's constitutional holding while still preserving the statutory policy in some form (162). Ultimately, Pickerill concludes that the only congressional responses that truly amount to challenges of the Court's constitutional holdings were those in response to *Oregon v. Mitchell* and *INS v. Chadha* (167). Most proponents of the strategic approach argue that the justices will be less constrained, and therefore less strategic, in their votes in constitutional cases where Congress has infrequently overturned the Court's decisions (Eskridge 1991; Epstein and Knight 1998). Even though Epstein and Knight expect that the justices will thus be "less attentive to the preferences and likely actions of other actors in constitutional disputes than statutory cases," they argue that we should not expect the Court to ignore completely the inter-branch constraint in constitutional cases for three reasons: the other branches have some level of power to alter constitutional policy of the Court and they possess other weapons to punish justices, such as holding salaries constant or removing jurisdiction, and they can refuse to implement constitutional decisions (142–44). Indeed, Epstein and Knight find some evidence of this effect in their analysis of the justices' papers, discovering that the justices actually discussed the preferences of other actors in approximately 46 percent of the constitutional cases; while not as prevalent as in nonconstitutional cases (approximately 70 percent), it is still close to half of the cases.[2] Other scholars such as Ferejohn, Rosenbluth, and Shipan (2004) argue that constraints on the justice will vary by political circumstances, arguing specifically that during periods of political fragmentation the Court will have more space to take independent action against the other branches, and thus the Court would be more likely to act against the other branches during periods of divided government than unified government (7).

Although the strategic approach has strong theoretical appeal, empirical evidence to support the separation of powers model has been rather weak thus far (e.g., Eskridge 1991; Hansford and Damore 2000; Spriggs and Hansford 2001; Segal and Spaeth 2002; Bergera, Richman, and Spiller 2003). Most relevant here is the fact that several recent large-N studies of the Court's exercise of constitutional review have found either no observable evidence of strategic influences or only very limited influence (Howard and Segal 2004; Sala and Spriggs 2004; Segal and Westerland 2005). Howard and Segal examined the impact of a constrained political environment (unified governance of the other two branches); specifically, they examined the votes of conservative and moderate justices, testing the hypotheses that these justices would be more deferential to Congress when facing a unified liberal Congress and presidency that could more easily overrule any court nullification than they would be in periods of divided control. Their bivariate analysis produced no evidence of the strategic action, Ferejohn et al. (2004) would have predicted. Two other studies have found some evidence of a strategic effect or cross-institutional influences. Whereas Friedman and Harvey (2003) found that there is no evidence of the Court being sensitive to the ideological congruence of the enacting Congress as the attitudinal model would predict, they did find instead that the Court is sensitive to the ideological distance from the sitting Congress, meaning that the Court is more likely to strike congressional action when facing a friendly Congress. Similarly, Lindquist and Solberg (2007) did find some cross-institutional influence in that the Court was less likely to nullify statutes when the ideological direction of the law more closely matched the ideological direction of the sitting Congress. Thus we are presented with three testable hypotheses that are appropriate for analysis in this large-N case-based analysis for which there is mixed evidence of support thus far.

> ***Hypothesis 3***: A Supreme Court justice will be less likely to vote to nullify a congressional statute the greater the level of party unification there is among the sitting government (Congress and the president).

> ***Hypothesis 4***: A Supreme Court justice will be less likely vote to nullify a congressional statute when there is ideological congruence between the justice and the sitting Congress.

> ***Hypothesis 5***: A Supreme Court justice will be less likely vote to nullify a congressional statute when there is ideological consistency between the direction of the statute and the sitting Congress.

When Ignagni and Meernik (1992) examined factors that increased the likelihood of congressional attempts to reverse Court nullification decisions, they found that Congress was less likely to act against the Court the older the congressional legislation was. They concluded that "Congress is slightly less attached to legislation when the members are unfamiliar with or feel no allegiance to or that has become irrelevant with the passage of time" (366). Thus, the Court itself may feel freer to vote against a congressional statute the more remote in time its passage is from the current Congress. Sala and Spriggs (2004) found some empirical evidence of such an effect in their study, although Lindquist and Solberg did not. The Court itself suggests that there is some truth to this hypothesis. When the Supreme Court in *Ludecke v. Watkins* (1948) upheld the Act of July 6, 1798 (the Enemy Alien Act) that was 150 years old at that time, it noted that "the Act is almost as old as the Constitution, and it would savor of doctrinaire audacity now to find the statute offensive to some emanation of the Bill of Rights." Overall, it seems the literature and historical evidence justifies this hypothesis,

> **Hypothesis 6**: A Supreme Court justice will be less likely vote to nullify a congressional statute as the statute ages over time.

Moving on to the executive branch, a significant body of research has consistently demonstrated the unparalleled influence of the solicitor general on the Supreme Court's decisions to grant certiorari, and to a lesser extent, on its decisions on the merit (Tanenhaus et al. 1963; Ulmer 1972; Caldeira and Wright 1988; Segal 1988; Pacelle 2003), earning the solicitor general the title, "the tenth justice" (Caplan 1987). However, McGuire (1998) cautioned that there was not any empirical foundation that solicitor general brings a distinctive and influential reputation, and McGuire's analysis of decisions on the merits demonstrated that once the analysis controls for the litigation experience of all lawyers before the Supreme Court, the special status of the solicitor general disappears (510, 516). He concludes that at least on decisions on the merit the solicitor general is not the tenth justice (506). In relation to constitutional review decisions on the merit, however, Lindquist and Solberg (2007) and Howard and Segal (2004) found evidence of the solicitor general's influence on the justices' votes, but the influence was conditioned somewhat upon their ideology and the perceptions of the solicitor general's ideology. Even though some of the decisions in these cases predate the creation of the solicitor general's office in 1870, the hypothesis is a valid expectation for the period of time that the office has existed.

> **Hypothesis 7**: After 1870 we should find that the greater the level of participation by the solicitor general, the less likely a Supreme Court justice will be to vote to strike a congressional statute.

Historically, we have seen strong evidence that during times of war the Supreme Court has tended to give much greater deference to presidential and congressional action, especially in reference to civil liberties. In regard to congressional incursions against the exercise of freedom of speech, Holmes wrote that "when a nation is at war many things that might be said in a time of peace are such a hindrance to its effort that their utterance will not be endured so long as men fight."[3] Certainly in each of the major wars, we have seen the Supreme Court confer its legitimacy to presidential and congressional action that severely curbed civil rights and civil liberties. The Court's decisions to sustain the constitutionality of the Espionage Act of 1917 and Roosevelt's Executive Order 9066 are but two examples. In the context of the Civil War, we saw that while the Supreme Court does eventually challenge the president's use of military trials on civilians, as McCloskey notes, it is not until 1866, "when the fighting was over, and the judges felt that a back-ward slap at the wartime military trials was now in order" (71). These events led McCloskey to predict that "judicial review is to be weakest during grave national emergencies" (135), and even Chief Justice Rehnquist (2001) in his book *All the Laws but One* asserts that "there is some truth to the maxim *Inter arma silent leges*" (221). Empirically, we saw in the descriptive analysis of Chapter Two that the Court had lower nullification rates during its three major wars, and thus my next hypothesis is,

> **Hypothesis 8**: A Supreme Court justice will be less likely to vote to nul-
> lify a congressional statute during the Civil War, World
> War I, and World War II.

Political scientists have long studied the role of the chief justice's leadership, assuming that the chief justice has a particular opportunity for leadership or to exert special influence on the other justices because of his prerogatives and responsibilities such as presiding over the conference, where he presents his case first, presiding over oral arguments and assigning opinions when he is in the majority (Danelski 1989, 486). These studies have largely focused on the chief justice's influence in the certiorari process, in conference, in the assignment of opinions, and in achieving unanimity (Danelski 1989; Danelski and Danelski 1989; Wood, Keith, Lanier, and Ogundele 2000) and more recently in regard to the demise of consensus on the Court (Walker, Epstein, and Dixon 1988; Haynie 1992; Epstein, Segal, and Spaeth 2001). Scholars such as Lanier and Wood (2001), Wood, Keith, Lanier, and Ogundele (1998, 2000), Wahlbeck, Spriggs, and Maltzman (1999) have also argued that the chief justice "may circumscribe (though not entirely suppress) his own individual preferences in favor of institutional objectives, such as decisional unanimity and institutional legitimacy" (Hurwitz and Stefko 2004, 124). Certainly, the exercise of judicial review to nullify statutes promulgated by the elected branches of government may put the Court's legitimacy at risk if the power is exercised imprudently, and thus for institutional reasons, the chief justice may tend to be less likely to vote to strike congressional statutes and may try to persuade the Court as well. Thus far, none of the large-N studies have examined the role of the chief justice on the exercise of power of judicial review; however, Caldeira and McCrone did identify strong patterns of nullification under the White and Taft courts and under the Warren and Burger courts. Whereas Caldeira and McCrone's work predated the Rehnquist Court, the conservative court has been criticized for its activism as well. The descriptive analysis in Chapter Two supports these previous results, identifying strong patterns of judicial nullification under five chief justices whose courts heard thirty or more judicial review cases: Rehnquist (34 percent), Warren (30 percent), Waite (23 percent), Taft (18 percent), and Burger (15.5 percent). Obviously, such results, though, do not control for a variety of factors that would influence such outcomes. Thus, we are left with two hypotheses in regard to the chief justice. First, the chief justice himself may vote differently than the associate justices due to his higher concern for institutional legitimacy. Second, justices serving under certain chief justices will be more likely to vote to nullify a congressional statute, *ceteris paribus*. And though it is difficult to predict from a purely theoretical perspective the chief justices under which we would expect to see a higher level of nullifications, the historical and empirical evidence of Chapter Two does predict that the levels will be higher under Rehnquist, Warren, Waite, Taft, and Burger. I chose to take a more rigorous approach and test the impact of each of the chief justices, and I test them at the higher two-tailed test of statistical significance.

> **Hypothesis 9**: A chief justice will be less likely to vote to strike a congressional statute than will be an associate justice.[4]

> **Hypothesis 10**: A justice's vote to nullify or uphold a congressional statute will be influenced by the chief justice he or she is serving under.

A final institutional constraint I seek to control for is the level of the Court's discretion to control its agenda. Prior to Congress passing the Judiciary Act of 1925, which is argued to have "changed the Court's docket from one of obligation to one of discretion" (Walker, Epstein, and Dixon 1988, 364), the Court was often obligated to hear cases that were legally unimportant, frivolous, or that involved well-settled areas of law of the Supreme Court. The very fact that the set of cases under study here is limited to those in which the justices consider the constitutionality of congressional action makes it somewhat unlikely to fit within the above category of cases; I do control for the possibility that this obligation could potentially increase the probability of the justices voting to uphold congressional statutes in the period prior to 1925. In addition, Lindquist and Solberg (2007) found some evidence to suggest that the repeal in 1988 of the section of Public Law 86-3 which required "direct appeals to the Supreme Court from decisions invalidating Acts of Congress" (28 U.S.C. Section 1252) may be responsible for the Rehnquist Court reviewing fewer federal laws than the Burger Court but nullifying more of them than did the Burger Court (79–80)—the assumption being that the constitutional challenges before the Rehnquist Court might have more merit, thus increasing the odds of nullification. However, they note that it would be unlikely for the Court to deny certiorari in congressional review cases, regardless. Still, it seems statistically and theoretically prudent to control for such possible effects. Thus, we have two additional hypotheses.

> ***Hypothesis 11***: The passage of the Judiciary Act of 1925 will increase the probability of a Supreme Court justice voting to nullify a congressional statute.

> ***Hypothesis 12***: The repeal of Section 1252 in 1988 will further increase the probability of a Supreme Court justice voting to nullify a congressional statute.

Issue Areas and Policy Direction of the Statute

Finally, there is another potential influence we should examine in regard to the justices' votes in these cases: the key issue area of the case under review. This dimension crosscuts the theoretical approaches; so, I have chosen to delay its presentation until after the other hypotheses. The attitudinal model assumes that "sets of these cases that form around similar objects and situations will correlate with one another to form issue areas (e.g., criminal procedure, First Amendment freedoms, judicial power, federalism) in which an interrelated set of attitudes—that is, a value—will explain the justices' behavior" (Rohde and Spaeth 1976, 69). Whereas empirical research has shown that the justices' votes do cluster within issue area (Schubert 1965; Goldman 1966, 1975), the level of success in predicting votes has varied somewhat across issue area, with greater success demonstrated in explaining civil rights and civil liberties votes than in economic, federalism, or judicial power issues (Tate 1981; Segal and Cover 1989; Tate and Handberg 1991; Segal and Spaeth 1993; Segal Epstein, Cameron, and Spaeth 1995; Wood et al.

1998, 2000). Empirical studies have also shown that the Court's level of defer-ence to the president has varied by issue area (Yates and Whitford 1998; King and Meernik 1999) and they have shown that the justices' deference to Congress is conditioned upon the issue area at stake in the case; Lindquist and Solberg (2007) found that the Court was more likely to strike a congressional statute in a decision that raised a civil rights and liberties issue. In earlier chapters we also saw empirically the justices' level of deference vary by issue area. I believe that there are four issue area-related hypotheses that may be derived either from attitudinal expectations or from strategic and institutional expectations.

From a strategic perspective, we would expect that the Court would be con-cerned with its institutional powers and might be more protective against congres-sional incursions into the judiciary's independence or power, and thus it would be more likely to strike statutes that challenged or curbed judicial authority and less likely to strike those that enhanced or supported judicial power. Keck (2007) suggests that this possibility is likely an inherent institutional proclivity not unique to the judiciary; he cites Publius, "Having connected 'the interest of the man … with the constitutional rights of the place,' the framers assumed that judges would defend judicial authority just as surely as presidents would defend executive author-ity" (336). In Chapter Two we saw that the Court tended to have quite strong support for judicial power in these decisions; in decisions to uphold congressional statutes, 76.7 percent were in support of judicial power and in decisions to nullify 83.3 percent were in support of judicial power. Thus, on balance, we should expect to find that the Court might be more unlikely to uphold a statute that potentially weakens the power of the judiciary, and conversely more likely to uphold a statute that supports the judiciary as an institution.

> **Hypothesis 13**: A Supreme Court justice will be less likely to vote to strike a statute that is supportive of exercise of judicial power.

The Court, as a federal institution itself, might also be protective of general federal power relative to the state power. Comparativists argue that judges as part of the state will be sensitive toward the interests of the political branches of the state (Shapiro 1981; Larkins 1996). Perhaps more strategically, the Court might also per-ceive that Congress would be more interested in protecting a statute that enhanced the national government's power over the states' power, and thus Congress would be more likely to engage in Court-curbing attempts in response to nullifications of these statutes than others. This prediction would run counter to the attitudinal model which would predict (based on our discussion of federalism and liberalism in Chapter Two) that prior to 1935 conservative justices would be more likely to support national supremacy and liberal justices would be more likely to support national supremacy after 1935 than would conservatives but not vice versa. Instead we would see justices, regardless of their ideology, more likely to support laws that enhanced national power vis-à-vis state power. King and Meernik (1999) found the Court was more deferential to presidential action in cases involving issues of national supremacy over states rights, and Howard and Segal (2004) found that the justices were much more likely to give greater latitude to the federal government than the state governments, including O'Connor, a purportedly strong states' rights advocate (137). Lindquist and Solberg (2007) found that during the Burger Court the justices were more likely to vote to strike a state statute than a federal one, and Solberg and Lindquist (2006) found that even the Rehnquist Court struck state statutes at a higher rate than federal statutes. None of these studies, however, examine specifically cases in which the key issue itself was federalism.

Hypothesis 14: A Supreme Court justice will be less likely to vote to strike a statute that is supportive of federal power.

In addition, a third issue area seems likely to have a strong institutional link, as well as an attitudinal one: civil rights and civil liberties for which the Court is often held to be the guarantor. In Chapter Four we examined expectations of the constitutional founders and the arguments that judicial review will or should serve as an important check against tyranny of majority. We saw similar expectations by many scholars and justices such as Justice Stone, the father of the preferred freedoms doctrine, and Justice Lurton, who posited that the course of American history "supports the contention that the exercise of judicial review is an obligation of the judiciary as a guarantor of liberty" (as cited in Slotnick 1987, 70). We also saw some level of optimism among human rights proponents who argued for constitutionally enumerated rights protected by an independent judiciary armed with the power of judicial review. But, despite this optimism we saw strong anecdotal historical evidence that the power of judicial review has been used to curb rather than protect rights. The analyses of the previous chapters have demonstrated empirically that skepticism might be more justified, as has global analysis. Keith, Tate, and Poe (2007) find that judicial review not only fails to demonstrate a negative impact on human rights but in fact exhibits a positive relationship with repression that appears to support "the view that judges are political actors who possess the same values and pursue the same public goals as other state actors." Interestingly, studies of Supreme Court deference to the president have shown that the Court is less deferential to the president in civil liberties cases than in other policy areas such as war powers and foreign relations; however, as best as I can tell from their operationalization, King and Meernik (1999) do not control for the direction of the decision, and thus we do not with certainty know whether the action that was challenged was supportive of civil rights and liberties or prohibiting them. Lindquist and Solberg (2007) argue that because rights claims are often examined under the strictest level of scrutiny, "more statutes challenged as violations of citizens' liberties will fail to pass constitutional muster, even before a more conservative Supreme Court" (76), and while they do find that the Court is more likely to nullify a statute in cases involving a civil rights and liberties issue, it is not clear to me in my reading of their operationalization of this variable, that they actually control for whether the challenged statute supported or curbed civil liberties and rights. As neither the theoretical nor empirical evidence outside this dataset is conclusive, I decided to test this issue as alternative hypotheses using the stricter two-tailed test of significance. It is possible that this hypothesis is time-bound as well. I will discuss this possibility and test for it in the historical-periods models that follow in subsequent sections.

> ***Hypothesis 14a***: A Supreme Court justice will be more likely to vote to strike a statute that is supportive of civil rights and civil liberties.

> ***Hypothesis 14b***: A Supreme Court justice will be less likely to vote to strike a statute that is supportive of civil rights and civil liberties.

Finally, there is an issue area in which the strategic model would lead us to suspect that the Supreme Court would be more likely to strike than uphold—statutes that protect criminal defendant's rights, an area of rights in which neither party in Congress is likely to support. Epstein and Knight (1998) note that it is a given that Congress goes against criminal defendant's rights (150), and Ferejohn (1999) points out that it is the area of the Court's federal jurisprudence, along with the rights of third-world immigrants, that has been unpopular with both sides of the aisle in Congress, not just those on the right. Thus it appears likely that regardless of the party sitting in Congress, the Court would not have support for a pro-criminal defendant position. From an attitudinal perspective, studies such as Goldman (1966 and 1975) have found correlation between criminal defendants' rights and other dimensions of liberalism, but empirically if we examined the liberalism scores published in *The Supreme Court Compendium*, even the staunch liberals such as Douglas, Warren, Brennan, and Marshall have tended to support criminal defendants rights at much lower level than other civil liberties or issues

(Epstein, Walker, Segal, and Spaeth 2002). The same pattern holds for liberals on the bench today.

> **Hypothesis 15**: A Supreme Court justice will be more likely to vote to strike a statute that is supportive of criminal defendant's rights.

Data and Methods

Dependent Variable: Justices Votes to Nullify or Uphold Congressional Statute

For the analyses in this chapter the dependent variable is the justice's individual vote to uphold or nullify the congressional statute under review. Concurrences and dissents were read to determine the actual direction of the justice's vote in regard to the constitutional issue. Votes to nullify are coded 1 and votes to uphold are coded 0. The data collection process is described in Chapter 2.

Independent Variables: Justice's Policy Preferences and Personal Attributes

Judicial behavioralists face a difficult task in measuring judges' attitudes or political preferences directly. As Tate and Handberg (1991) noted, serious data limitations make it "prohibitively difficult or impossible to operationalize key variables (e.g., policy values and role perceptions) that are thought to be the most proximate causes of individual judicial decision making" (460). As we discussed in Chapter One, early Supreme Court studies *inferred* the presence of attitudes from patterns of the justices' votes, but it has proven quite difficult to create measures independent of the behavior we seek to explain. Segal and Cover (1989), and later Segal, Epstein, Cameron, and Spaeth (1995) developed measures based on the statements from editorials in the nation's leading newspapers in regard to Supreme Court nominees' attitudes toward civil rights and liberties and economic issues. For the purposes of this study, these measures would be difficult to extend backward in time, especially to cover the entire history of the Court, and would be difficult to create in regard to less salient issue areas before the court. Other measures have been employed by political scientists, such as the justices' tenure-length liberalism scores or the Martin Quinn ideology scores, but again these scores are not independent measures of the justices' behavior and the measures are not possible to construct at this point for the entire two-hundred-year history of the Court. Therefore, like many judicial behavioralists, I must seek to find an appropriate surrogate measure for the justices' policy preferences, one that is available for the full set of justices and the full set of years under study, and one that is fully independent of the behavior I seek to explain.

Scholars such as Tate (1981) and Tate and Handberg (1991) have argued that some of the justices' personal attributes can be "useful surrogates" for hard-to-measure attitudes. The use of personal attributes or personal background characteristics had been criticized because, as Tate notes, they "are only indirect causes of judicial decision making" and "a variety of important attitudinal variables intervene," and "it is these intervening variables that should account for most of the variation in decision behavior;" however, he along with Ulmer (1973, 627) argued that critics risked premature closure by rejecting the use of attributes to explain Supreme Court behavior (355). Furthermore, surrogate measures for the justices' ideology, particularly partisan identification and appointing president, have also been used successfully to explain the Supreme Court justices' votes in these key issue areas, extending back to the earlier part of the last century in at least one study (Tate 1981; Aliotta 1988; Tate and Handberg 1991; George and Epstein 1992; Yates and Whitford 1999). Studies of lower court justices have found the same effect across a wide variety of legal issues (e.g., Gottschall 1986; Carp et al. 1993). Gryski, Main, and Dixon (1986) theorized that shared personal attributes or background characteristics "reflect similar socialization processes and life experiences, which in turn produce similar attitudes and ultimately behavior (votes)" (528). Tate and Handberg noted that the justices' personal attributes are seen by scholars as "revealing 'the kinds of personal experiences and exposure the judges have had during their lives' that serve as 'indicators or clues about life experiences and judges perspectives toward cases'" (460), and in their analysis they found that political, social cleavages, family origins, and career socialization variables were highly successful in explaining the justices' behavior across the seventy-two years they studied, going back to 1916. However, they did find differences in the attributes' effect on voting in economic cases from that in civil rights and liberties cases. Political influences were strongly evident in both sets of cases, but in regard to the economic cases, political and career influences operated to near exclusion of cleavage and family origin influences. In the civil rights and liberties cases, they found evidence of all four types of influence.

In the discussion and the analysis that follows I will examine personal attributes that could potentially serve as surrogates for policy preferences, the socialization factors that likely contributed to the justices' formation of policy preferences, or their role orientation on the bench. Following the discussion of the influences and their operationalization, I will test the various attributes in initial exploratory models to determine which are most appropriate to include in the full-time-period model. In the second half of the chapter, when I examine the models by time period and by issue area, I will return to the issue of which attributes appear to be most appropriate.

Political Factors

The simplest indication that political party is an appropriate surrogate of the justices' policy preferences, beyond its previously demonstrated ability as a predictor of the justices' votes, is that the fact that presidents typically appoint justices to bench that share their party affiliation; of the justices under study here, only ten were appointed by presidents of a different party. The justice's party identification has demonstrated its strength as a surrogate for policy preferences in numerous Supreme Court and lower court studies (Nagel 1961; Schmidhauser 1961; Goldman 1966, 1975; Adamany 1969; Tate 1981; Songer and Davis 1990; Tate and Handberg 1991; George and Epstein 1992; Yates and Whitford 1999). Most studies have consistently shown that justices from the Democrat Party were more likely to be liberal than Republican justices on civil rights and liberties, economic or labor issues, and criminal issues. In 1999, Yates and Whitford found that Democratic justices were more likely to be deferential to the president. Tate and Sittiwong (1989) also found that political party in Canada predicts conservatism and liberalism, but they found that the appointing prime minister did not have as much effect as the appointing president did in the United States. It is my expectation that party affiliation of the justice will serve well as a surrogate for the justices' policy preferences in the decisions as well. Here, I set up the party variable specifically as *Democratic Party Identification* since the direction of the second hypothesis is that liberal justices will be more likely to nullify.[5]

Democrat Party Identification

This variable is measured as Democrat (1) and non-Democrat (0). As I mentioned above, since the data cover 201 years, party identification is not as easy to measure consistently as it would be the twentieth century. Here I follow Reichley's (1992) delineation that I discussed in Chapters One and Two, which also fits Tate and Handberg's (1991): Jeffersonian Republicans, National Republicans, Jacksonian Democrats, and Democrats are classified as Democrats and the Federalists, Whigs, American "Know Nothings," Republicans, and Liberal Republicans have been classified as non-Democrats. The data are gathered from *The Supreme Court Compendium* (Epstein et al. 2003).

Cleavages

The second attributes area Tate and Handberg examined was the "principle cleavages" that scholars, such as Lipset and Rokkan (1967), had identified as having "shaped the development of partisan politics in Western industrialized nations: *social class, religion, urban/rural, center/periphery* differences" (464). In the interest of creating a parsimonious model, and under the constraint of data availability, I chose four of the most successful attributes measures utilized by Tate and Handberg.

Center-Periphery (Southern Region)

Tate and Handberg focused solely on the regional dimension of center-periphery cleavages as the language distinction did not apply to any of the justices and the ethnicity distinction applied to only one justice. They argued that the regional distinctions in the United States have been noteworthy in regard to civil rights and liberties and economic issues. They expected that justices from southern and border-states would be more conservative than those from non-southern regions. They found this expectation to be true in regard to civil rights and liberties but not economic issues. Songer and Davis (1990) examination of Court of Appeals judges found that region was significant only in civil rights cases where southern judges of both parties were more conservative than northern judges before, but not after, 1969. Thus the time dimension may be a significant source of variation in the effects of some personal attributes. I will test for this possibility in the time-periods model. Tate and Sittiwong report that their Canadian study shows regional cleavages to be important in other cultures (Quebecois/non-Quebecois in Canada) as has been shown in the United States (south/non-south). The expectation here would be that if region is a significant cleavage that produces ideological differences along the liberal and conservative continuum, then a non-southern justice would be more likely to nullify a congressional statute than a southern, in keeping with hypothesis number two.

I created two dichotomous variables, one based on the justice's place of birth and one based on the justice's childhood location to capture Tate and Handberg's regional distinctions. An initial analysis demonstrated that the variable based on childhood location performed better than the one based on place of birth. The measures were too highly correlated to use in the same model, so I selected to continue with the childhood location delineation. Following Tate and Handberg the variables were coded with justices whose childhood was is in the south coded as 1 (this included South Carolina, Mississippi, Florida, Alabama, Georgia, Louisiana, Texas, Virginia, Arkansas, North Carolina, and Tennessee), and those from border-states coded as 1 (this included Delaware, Kentucky, Maryland, Missouri, and West Virginia), and 0 = Non-southern states (all other states). The data are gathered from *The Supreme Court Compendium* (Epstein et al. 2003).

Childhood Surroundings (Urban)

Tate and Handberg posited that "the growth of industrialism and of cities brought different attitudes concerning the legitimacy of governmental involvement in the economy and society" and that these different attitudes align with the distinction between rural and urban, and agricultural and industrial ways of life (468). Justices with rural upbringings were expected to be more traditional in their values, and thus were expected to be more conservative. Here I have hypothesized that liberal justices would be more likely to nullify than conservative justices, which fits with the idea that these justices would be accepting of the traditional norm of judicial restraint. It may be that the impact of this particular dimension of socialization has changed over time. I will test for this possible in the time-period models. This dichotomous variable distinguishes the justice's childhood surroundings, particularly distinguishing between urban, coded as 1 and rural, small town or village, and small city coded as 0. The data are gathered from *The Supreme Court Compendium* (Epstein et al. 2003).[6]

Childhood Social Status

Tate and Handberg hypothesized that social class origins would have an impact on economics liberalism as well as support for civil rights and liberties. They argued that people of high social status would not be expected to extend their sympathies to economic underdogs. This hypothesis fits well with McCloskey's conclusion that the Court's commitment to the cause of property rights was due to the bench being "composed of judges who were inevitably drawn largely from the ranks of the 'haves'" (69). Tate and Handberg expected however that people of higher social status would be more supportive of some types of civil rights and liberties based on studies of political tolerance but the opposite has been shown in economic issues. In the end, the attribute did not test well in either model. They note however that for the period they were studying, there was little variation in childhood or adult social status among the justices. Brudney, Schiavoni, and Merritt (1999) found that judges who attended elite undergraduate universities were significantly more likely to reject labor union claims; in fact, they found this factor to be the strongest explanatory factor in their analyses. They contend that this effect mirrors that found in most social science work which consistently demonstrates attendance of an elite university to be an indicator of more privileged economic circumstances. In addition, they argue that judges with blue collar backgrounds "may have in the aggregate been socialized to support the underdog or to be sympathetically inclined toward unions" (90). Although this variable has proven to be somewhat inconsistent in effect, I do include it in the exploratory analysis and in the time periods models, but I test the effect at the higher two-tailed level since the expected direction is conflicted. This five-point variable measures the justice's childhood social status based on the following coding: upper class (5), upper–middle class (4), middle (3), lower-middle (2), and lower class (1). The data are gathered from *The Supreme Court Compendium* (Epstein et al. 2003).[7]

Religion (Catholic)

Tate and Handberg note that voting and policy differences among major religious groups in the United States generally follow the pattern that Protestants have tended to be more conservative than Catholics, Jews, or those with no religious affiliation—especially in regard to civil rights and liberties positions (469). Brudney, Schiavoni, and Merritt (1999) found that judges and justices who were Catholic or Jewish were likely to take the liberal position on labor issues. They believe it is likely that such affiliation is "a rough proxy of social class among the instant population," at least for the middle decades of the twentieth century, when "Catholic and Jewish families were more likely than their Protestant counterparts to be working class in economic status and social perspective" (93). Nagel (1962) found that Catholic state and federal Supreme Court justices were more liberal than Protestant justices in criminal cases and business regulation. Tate and Sittiwong's Canadian study showed that Catholicism had a liberalizing influence in Canada as it does in the United States and the Philippines. This dichotomous variable demarks the justice's religious affiliation: Catholic is coded 1 and non-Catholic (Protestant and Jewish) is coded 0. The data are gathered from *The Supreme Court Compendium* (Epstein et al. 2003).

If hypothesis two is correct, then to the extent that these attributes (being Catholic and having an urban upbringing, and so forth) are linked to liberalism, then we would expect all to have a positive effect on nullification votes except the first, southern upbringing, which would be associated with conservatism. The direction of the effect of social status remains unclear. We would expect that the effect of Democratic Party would have the stronger affect of these attributes since it is a label that is accepted by the justice himself or herself that typically represents a broad set of policy preferences.

Career Experiences and Socialization

Studies of judicial attributes have also examined attributes related to adult socialization as well, particularly the different career experiences of lawyers who eventually become Supreme Court justices. Empirical evidence has supported this hypothesized link to some extent. Schmidhauser's work (1961) demonstrated that judicial experience was negatively related to adherence to precedent and that judicial inexperience and humble beginnings were correlated with dissent behavior. Goldman (1966) found judicial and political experience correlated with liberalism and also found that judges without judicial experience were more likely to dissent. Tate and Handberg found some evidence that prior judicial and prosecutorial experience affected the justices' liberalism on the bench. These effects have been demonstrated beyond the limited context of the United States as well; Tate and Sittiwong (1989) found in Canada that both types of prior experience were related to both types of liberalism, and in the Philippines political experience was positively related and judicial experience at the trial court level was negatively related to civil rights and liberties liberalism.

Judicial role theorists such as Gibson (1978) argue that a judge's activism or restraint is a function of the judge's beliefs concerning the appropriate behavior for judges. Although studies of the role orientation of judges have largely focused on the liberalism/conservatism or party dimension as explanatory factors, studies such as Wold (1974) have also theorized that a judge's professional experience will have socialized him or her towards certain norms. Wold expected that judges with prior judicial experience would be more socialized toward the norm of judicial restraint than judges without such experience. He did not find evidence to support his expectation, however. As we saw above, Goldman found some correlation between a lack of judicial experience and the proclivity to dissent, and Schmidhauser also found a correlation with dissent behavior. It is my expectation that judges with prior federal judicial experience were more socialized toward restraintist votes; however, the opposite may be true in regard to judges with *state*-level judicial experience because of the more political and partisan nature of judicial selection at the state and local level. Judges that hold positions on the bench, won or maintained through election or retention elections, may be more socialized toward seeing judicial decision making in political terms and thus may tend to be less deferential to the other branches.

Whereas Wold found no relationship between activism and a judge's prior experience in political office; political experience has been related to liberalism by Tate and Sittiwong. Brudney, Schiavoni, and Merritt (1999) however did find that judges and justices who had held elected office prior to joining the bench were more liberal in regard to labor union claims.[8] I expect that career experience in either state or federal political office will increase the likelihood of the justice toward striking a congressional statute because the career experience may have socialized the justice toward seeing judicial decision making in a more political context and thus tending to be less deferential to the other actors in the policymaking process. We might expect a stronger impact from these attributes that delineate adult socialization than those that relate to childhood socialization.

Federal Judicial Experience

Justices with any amount of prior federal judicial branch experience are coded (1) and justices without prior judicial experience are coded (0). The data are gathered from *The Supreme Court Compendium* (Epstein et al. 2003).

Federal Political Experience

Justices with any prior federal political occupation are coded (1) and justices without prior experience are coded (0). Political occupation includes holding elective or appointive political office. The data are gathered from *The Supreme Court Compendium* (Epstein et al. 2003).

State Judicial Experience

Justices with any amount of prior state judicial experience are coded (1) and justices without prior judicial experience are coded (0). The data are gathered from *The Supreme Court Compendium* (Epstein et al. 2003).

State Political Experience

Justices with any state or local political occupation are coded (1) and justices without prior experience are coded (0). Political occupation includes holding elective or appointive political office which could range from an occupation as state or local judges to being a state legislator or holding a state and local executive office. The data are gathered from *The Supreme Court Compendium* (Epstein et al. 2003).

Finally, I include one last attribute related to the justice's adult socialization: whether the justice had any level of experience as a law professor. Bork (1990) attributed the liberal activism of the New Deal and Warren Courts and the federal judiciary more broadly to "professors steeped in the revisionist liberal culture of law schools" who went on to become judges themselves (135). Of course, liberal critics of the conservative Rehnquist Court might counter that conservative former law professors from the University of Chicago, such as Justice Scalia, are the current activists on the bench.

Experience as Law Professor

This seven-point variable identifies the justices' experience as law professors according to the following coding: dean (6), professor (5), assistant professor (4), associate professor (3), lecturer (2), or instructor (1). If the justice served at multiple positions, code the highest number. For example, service as dean and professor would be coded as 6. The data are gathered from *The Supreme Court Compendium* (Epstein et al. 2003).

Other Independent Variables

Congruence between Justice Policy Preference and Direction of Statute

As discussed above, this dichotomous variable measures the congruency between the justice's policy preference, party affiliation in this analysis, and the policy direction of the statute. The score is calculated with one point if the justice is liberal (Democrat) and the statute is liberal, or if the justice is conservative (Republican) and the statute is conservative.[9] The score is calculated as a zero if the justice is liberal (Democrat) and the statute is conservative, or if the justice is conservative (Republican) and the statute is liberal.[10]

Congruence between Justice Policy Preference and Enacting Congress

This four-point variable measures the level of congruency between the justice's party affiliation and the party affiliation of the majority in the House, the majority in the Senate, and the president at the time the statute was passed. The score is calculated with one point for each party match with these three institutions; thus the scores range from 0 (no match) to 3 (match with both chambers of Congress and the president).

Divided Government

This variable is measured as follows: both majorities in Congress and the president are of the same party (0), the majority of one chamber of Congress and the presidency are of the same party (1), both chambers of Congress controlled by the party opposite to that of the president (2).

Justice Party Congruence with Sitting Congress

This four-point variable measures the level of congruency between the justice's party affiliation and the party affiliation of the sitting majority in the House, the sitting majority in the Senate, and the president at the time of the Court's decision. The score is calculated with one point for each party match with these three institutions; thus the scores range from 0 (no match) to 3 (match with both chambers of Congress and the president).

Congruence between Direction of Statute and Sitting Congress

This four-point variable measures the level of congruency between the policy direction of the statute (liberal or conservative) and the party affiliation of the majority in the House, the majority in the Senate, and the president at the time. The score is calculated with one point for each party match (liberal with Democrat or conservative with Republican) with these three institutions; thus the scores range from 0 (no match) to 3 (match with both chambers of Congress and the president).

Age of Statute

This variable is created by subtracting the year in which the statute was enacted from the year of the Supreme Court decision. The natural log of this number is then taken due to skewedness of the age variable, which as we saw in Chapter Four contained a few extreme outliers.

Solicitor General's Participation in the Case

This variable was originally coded to measure the level of the solicitor general's role in these cases in the following manner: cases in which the solicitor general was counsel (3), on the brief (2), on amicus brief (1), and played no role (0). Since the solicitor general's office was not created until 1870, the early cases contain missing data on this variable. Initial analysis suggested that the variable performed better a simple dichotomous measure denoting any level of participation of the solicitor general in the case.

Civil War and World Wars

This dichotomous variable marks the United States' most significant wars: the Civil War and World Wars I and II. The years during which the United States was engaged in one of these wars are coded 1 and all others are coded 0.

Role—Chief Justice of Associate Justice

This dichotomous variable denotes justices serving as chief justice (1) from those serving as associate justices (0).

Chief Justice Dummy Variables

A dichotomous variable was created to denote each of the chief justice courts under study here: John Marshall (1801–1835), Roger Taney (1836–1864), Salmon P. Chase (1864–1873), Morrison R. Waite (1874–1888), Melville W. Fuller (1888–1910), Edward D. White (1910–1921), William Howard Taft (1921–1930), Charles Evan Hughes (1930–1941), Harlan Fiske Stone (1941–1946), Fred M. Vinson (1946–1953), Earl Warren (1953–1969), Warren Earl Burger (1969–1986), and William H. Rehnquist (1986–2001 in the context of this study).

Judiciary Act of 1925 (Judge's Bill)

This dichotomous variable marks the passage of the Judiciary Act in 1925 in which the justices were given more control of their jurisdiction. All years from 1925 forward are coded 1 and all others are coded 0.

The Repeal of Section 1252 of Public Law 86-3 in 1988

This dichotomous variable marks the repeal of Section 1252 which required direct appeal to the Supreme Court of decisions invalidating federal laws. All years from 1988 forward are coded 1 and all others are coded 0.

Pro-Judicial Power Statute

This dichotomous variable denotes cases in which the primary constitutional challenge to the statute involved the issue of judicial authority (Spaeth's category 9). Statutes that fell under this category and supported judicial power were coded 1 and all others were coded 0.

Pro-National Supremacy Statute

This dichotomous variable denotes cases in which the primary constitutional challenge to the statute involved the issue of federalism (Spaeth's category 10). Statutes that fell under this category and supported or enhanced national power over states' power or rights were coded 1 and all others were coded 0.

Pro-Civil Rights and Liberties

This dichotomous variable denotes cases in which the primary constitutional challenge to the statute involved the issue of civil rights and civil liberties: a combination of his civil rights (category 2), First Amendment (category 3), non-economic due process (category 4 as modified in earlier chapters) and privacy issue areas (category 5). Statutes that fell under this category and supported rights claims were coded 1 and all others were coded 0.

Pro-Criminal Defendant's Rights

This dichotomous variable denotes cases in which the primary constitutional challenge to the statute involved the issue of criminal defendants' rights (category 1). Statutes that fell under this category and supported criminal rights claims were coded 1 and all others were coded 0.

Methodology

I estimate the models using logit in STATA Release 9 since the dependent variable in these analyses is the dichotomous decision of the justice to vote either to nullify or uphold the challenged congressional statute. I follow Lindquist and Solberg (2007) in clustering the data on the justice rather than on the case. They followed Zorn's (2006) advice that the decision of whether to cluster on the justice or on the case depends upon model specification; they concluded that their model, which included a number of case-related variables, did a reasonable job of capturing within case variation, and more importantly, they concluded that it was more appropriate to cluster on the justice rather than the case because the consistency lies within the justices' views on judicial review cases. I believe the specification of case-related factors within my models appropriately control for within the case variation and that the same latent dependence holds for these models, but as an empirical matter, I also ran the models clustered on the case, and found no substantive differences that would merit going against the above assumptions. The tables report the standard logit coefficients. I draw upon the work of Roncek and Swatt (2006) to interpret the coefficient; they demonstrate that for dichotomous or polytomous logit "if we multiply the *b* coefficient by 100, we can then interpret this new *b* coefficient as the percentage change in the cumulative odds for a change in the independent variable" (736). Thus, if the decimal point on the coefficients reported in each table were moved over two decimal points, we would have the percentage change in the cumulative odds of a justice voting to nullify a congressional statute given a unit change in the independent variable. Following Roncek and Swatt (2006) I report the untransformed logit coefficients but will interpret the data using their simple transformation.

Results

Table 5.1 reports the results for the full multivariate analysis across the entire two-hundred-year period.[11] Coefficients for the ten personal attributes variables are listed first in the table; eight of which are statistically significant at least at the .05 level of significance.

I had hypothesized that liberal justices would be more likely to vote to nullify congressional statutes, even controlling for the ideological consistency of the statute with the justice's policy preferences, and here we find strong support for the hypothesis in that our surrogate measure for the justice's policy preferences, party identification, produces the strongest effect of the attributes. The coefficient for Democratic Party affiliation can be interpreted as indicating a 50 percent change in the cumulative odds of a justice voting to nullify a congressional statute given a change in the justice's party affiliation. Three of the four other attributes that were hypothesized to represent experiences that would make the justice more liberal and therefore under the second hypothesis more likely to vote to nullify are statistically significant: a Catholic religious affiliation (29 percent change), a non-southern upbringing (23 percent change), and a lower social status (9 percent change). The coefficient for one of the attributes, the urban childhood surroundings, is contra to our hypothesis, and therefore cannot be considered significant, even though it earns a large *z*-score. In the analyses that follow I will see if the attributes continue to perform as well across the various time periods, and I will also examine interaction effects with the ideological direction of the statute under review. Four of the five experience measures produce statistically significant coefficients: federal judicial experience (–.22), federal political experience (.35), state judicial experience (.32), and state or local political experience (.30). These results suggest that the

Table 5.1 Logit Models of Justices' Votes to Nullify or Uphold in Judicial Review of Congressional Statutes

	Coefficient	Standard Error	Z-score	$p > z$
Democrat Party Identification (+)	.50	.13	3.91	.0001
Catholic Religious Affiliation (+)	.29	.13	2.22	.02
Childhood Surroundings (Urban) (+)	−.29	.12	−2.39	.01
Childhood Surroundings (Southern) (−)	−.23	.12	−2.02	.02
Childhood Social Status*	−.09	.04	−2.19	.01
Federal Judicial Experience (−)	−.22	.14	−1.61	.05
Federal Political Experience (+)	.35	.13	2.69	.01
State Judicial Experience (+)	.32	.12	2.64	.01
State or Local Political Experience (+)	.30	.12	2.51	.01
Experience as Law Professor (+)	.03	.03	.99	.16
Congruence between Justice Policy Preference and Direction of Statute (−)	−.16	.09	−1.82	.04
Justice Party Congruence with Enacting Congress (−)	−.05	.03	−1.50	.07
Divided Government (+)	−.08	.04	−1.84	.03
Justice Party Congruence with Sitting Congress (+)	−.01	.06	−.01	.45
Congruence between Direction of Statute and Sitting Congress (−)	−.09	.08	−1.22	.11
Chief Justice (versus Associate Justice)(−)	−.28	.18	−1.55	.06
Judges Act (+)	−.43	.15	−2.83	.01
War (−)	−.45	.16	−3.01	.001
Age of Statute (Natural Log) (−)	−.08	.06	−1.38	.08
Pro-Judicial Power Statute (−)	−.92	.27	−3.58	.0001
Pro-Civil Rights and Liberties Statute*	.20	.20	1.00	.15
Pro-National Supremacy Statute (−)	−.11	.26	−.41	.34
Pro-Criminal Defendants Statute (+)	−.34	.37	−.92	.17
Chief Justice Taney*	−.87	.33	−2.59	.01
Chief Justice Fuller*	−.54	.17	−3.21	.001
Chief Justice White*	−.48	.17	−2.80	.01
Chief Justice Stone*	−.47	.28	−1.66	.10
Chief Justice Vinson*	−.41	.25	−1.64	.10
Chief Justice Warren*	.91	.15	5.93	.0001

Table 5.1 *(continued)*

	Coefficient	Standard Error	Z-score	$p > z$
Chief Justice Burger*	.65	.17	3.91	.0001
Chief Justice Rehnquist *	1.21	.16	7.34	.0001
Constant	–.97	.23	–4.32	.0001
		N=7012	Wald chi^2 = 456.19	$p > .0001$

Note. Hypothesized direction in parentheses

*Variables are tested at the higher two-tail test of significance.

justices' career experiences do play an important role in the justices' socialization toward judicial norms, in this case judicial deference to the congress. Political experience may socialize the justice toward seeing judicial decision making in political terms, and thus the justice becomes less inclined toward being deferential to the Court's fellow political branches. State-level judicial experience appears to have the same effect, again perhaps because of the more political and partisan nature of judicial selection at the state and local level. Prior experience as a law professor was not statistically significant here, but we shall see in the subsequent analyses, during certain historic periods, experience as a law professor does have an impact on the justices' votes, although not exactly as Judge Bork would predict.

The other key attitudinal hypothesis was that a Supreme Court justice's vote on the constitutionality of a congressional statute will be influenced by the consistency between the policy direction of the statute and the justice's ideological preferences. I measured this in two ways using the justice's party affiliation as the indicator of the justice's policy preference: (1) congruence between the justice's policy preference and the ideological direction of the statute and (2) justice's party congruence with the enacting Congress. Both of these hypotheses are supported by the data. The coefficient for the first congruence is –.16, and the coefficient for the second congruence is relatively small at –.05 with a level of statistical significance that might be considered marginally acceptable (.07); we see that this variable is a less direct measure of ideological congruence than the other that was based on the ideological direction of the statute. Still, we can expect that a Republican justice will be more likely to strike statutes that passed by Democratic Congresses and vice versa and, but more importantly, that a Democratic justice will have a stronger proclivity toward striking conservative legislation and a Republican justice will have a stronger proclivity toward striking liberal legislation. These effects hold, even controlling for a variety of institutional and legal factors.

The next three hypotheses were derived from the strategic model which suggested that the justices would be constrained by policy preferences of the sitting Congress; in particular, justices would be less likely to vote to nullify in three circumstances: (1) when the level of party unification is greater among the sitting government (Congress and the president); (2) when there is ideological congruence between the justice and the sitting Congress (when the Court faces a friendly Congress); and (3) when there is ideological consistency between the direction of the statute and the sitting Congress. None of these hypotheses are supported; the coefficient for divided government is negative rather than positive, and the level of statistical significance is too low to be generally acceptable, and the coefficient for the friendly Congress produces a minimal coefficient that barely rounds to .01 and that is not statistically significant.[12] The third hypothesis is supported somewhat more by the data, producing a coefficient of –.09 that is marginally insignificant at the .11 level. Overall, though we must conclude at least in the full-time-period models that the strategic approach fails to contribute to our understanding of this narrow set of votes. We will return to these hypotheses in the period analysis.

The next four variables capture institutional influences. Only one is statistically significant at the standard level of .05, but two of the coefficients might be considered to achieve marginally acceptable levels at .06 and .08, the chief justice variable and the age of statute variable, respectively. The role of the chief justice does appear to enhance a justice's deference to Congress As we hypothesized, justices are less likely to strike laws the longer the statutes have been in effect, which is perhaps indicative of the enhanced legitimacy the statute takes on over time. As we saw in Chapter Two, the presence of the three major wars does lead to increased judicial deference to Congress. The coefficient indicates a –45 percent change in the cumulative odds of a justice voting to nullify a congressional statute given a change in the state of war. Finally, we had expected the Judges Act to have a positive effect on nullification votes, believing that the changes in the Court's jurisdictions made it more likely that the Court was accepting congressional challenges with greater merit than when its mandatory jurisdiction was broader and perhaps meant hearing challenges that were more likely to be frivolous. This does not prove to be the case as the coefficient is negative here.

Next are the set of dummy variables that control for the issue area and the ideological direction of the statute in the four key areas where we expected a strong institutional, ideological, or strategic influence. Three do not achieve statistical significance: the presence of a pro-national supremacy statute, a pro-criminal defendant statute, and a pro-civil rights and liberties statute.[13] We will see the effect of the latter two variables change across time periods, but the failure of the former effect will continue across time periods. The large coefficient (–.92) delineating the presence of a pro-judicial power statute rather strongly supports the hypothesis that a justice will be less likely to strike a statute that supports its own institution's power. Finally, I tested for the effect of the particular chief justice on the bench. I conducted preliminary exploratory analysis to determine which chief justice variables to include in the model. The model includes the eight chief justices that performed best in the multivariate full-time-period models. All are statistically significant at quite high levels, except for two which are statistically significant at the .10 level—Stone and Vinson. Five of the chief justice variables produce negative coefficients ranging from -.41 to -.87; these are the five earlier chief justices: Taney (-.87), Fuller (-.54), White (-.48), Stone (-.47), and Vinson (-.41). The three chief justices with positive coefficients are the three recent chief justices prior to Roberts: Warren (.91), Burger (.65), and Rehnquist (1.21). These results fit the analysis of Chapter Two that demonstrated the decreasing level of deference in the more recent courts. The coefficient for the Rehnquist Court indicates a 121 percentage increase in the cumulative odds of a nullification vote. Unlike in Chapter Two, however, the Chase and Waite courts did not even achieve a high enough level of statistical significance, once we control for a variety of other factors, to be included in the analysis other than as a part of the base category.

I conducted one final test on the full period model. Most early studies of the Supreme Court examined only nonunanimous cases assuming that those cases represented issues before the Court that were unsettled or in which the law was vague, and there was more room for the justice's attitudes to come into play (e.g., Pritchett 1954; Goldman 1966, 1975; Tate 1981; Tate and Handberg 1991). In regard to the earlier Supreme Court when the court did not control its docket, this delineation seemed especially relevant since the Court might be hearing substantial numbers of cases on which the law was well settled or a precedent strongly controlled the case—cases in which the justices might not have even chosen to docket a case. Studies of the early Supreme Court have shown that the justices' attitudinal patterns are more observable in the nonunanimous set of decisions (Wood et al. 1998, 2000). Therefore, I ran the model on just the nonunanimous decisions. The results remain the same, with only minor changes; for most variables the new results were just a matter of a few degrees of statistical significance lost or gained. Only four variables were affected substantively. Three of the chief justice variables lost their significance—Taney, Warren, and Burger—when the unanimous decisions were culled out. One variable achieved statistical significance that had not previously done so. The pro–criminal defendant statute produced a rather large coefficient (-1.54) that was statistically significant at the .001 level once the unanimous decisions were removed from the model.

Overall, when we examine the full set of votes across the entire time period, we see that attitudinal and institutional influences are better explanators than those associated with the strategic model. However, we must keep in mind that the model covers a rather long period of time, approximately two-hundred years, and while it scientifically desirable to be able to specify a model that is not time-bound, it is rather unlikely to be the case for such an extended period of time. Although the model attempts to control for institutional and personnel changes on the bench over time, it is likely, as with all models, that some unobservable influences are also at play. Tables 5.2 through 5.5 divide the Court into McCloskey's historical periods as was done in Chapter Two, beginning with the period 1865–1900, as the pre-Civil War period had an insufficient number of cases to analyze. It should be noted that the specification of the models varies somewhat across time as measures do not have enough variation to be included in some periods or have too much collinearity to be included in others.

Table 5.2 presents the results for the 1865–1901 period. In this early period the personal attributes do not perform as well generally.[14] The Democratic Party variable, our surrogate for liberal ideology, is not statistically significant at the .11 level. The three childhood socialization variables continue as in the full model, but the professional experience variables are only statistically significant except for state and local political experience (.57). Interestingly, in this time period, prior experience as a law professor does have an impact that would be statistically significant if we had hypothesized that such experience would decrease rather than increase the likelihood of a vote to nullify. Such a hypothesis might not be inappropriate for this period of time, which is prior to the legal realist movement, and thus perhaps law schools were more likely to advocate the norm of judicial restraint. Neither of the attitudinal measures of congruency is statistically significant nor are any of the strategic approach measures of congruency. Two are in the wrong direction: divided government and congruence between the direction of the statute and the sitting Congress. Neither of the two institutional variables is statistically significant; neither the age of the statute nor the role of chief justice makes a difference in this earlier set of votes. However, one of the issue area variables, a pro-civil rights and civil liberties statute, is highly significant and produces a large coefficient (1.68) which indicates a 168 percent increase in the cumulative odds of a vote to nullify. Overall, the model fits poorly compared to the full period and suggests that our current understanding of the Supreme Court may fail to explain a significant portion of the Court's history, at least in regard to this limited albeit significant set of cases. At the same time, we should keep in mind that even though this period represents a significant number of years, it only accounts for 119 of 896 cases,

Table 5.2 Logit Models of Justices' Votes to Nullify or Uphold in Judicial Review of Congressional Statutes (1865–1900)

	Coefficient	Standard Error	Z-Score	$p > z$
Democrat Party Identification (+)	.35	.29	1.19	.11
Childhood Surroundings (Urban) (+)	–.47	.15	–3.14	.001
Childhood Surroundings (Southern) (–)	–.34	.16	–2.13	.02
Childhood Social Status*	–.09	.03	–2.61	.01
Federal Judicial Experience (–)	–.16	.27	–.60	.27
Federal Political Experience (+)	.13	.15	.82	.21
State Judicial Experience (+)	.10	.14	.69	.25
State or Local Political Experience (+)	.57	.16	3.53	.0001
Experience as Law Professor (+)	–.16	.09	–1.71	.04
Congruence between Justice Policy Preference and Direction of Statute (–)	.03	.10	.29	.38
Justice Party Congruence with Enacting Congress (–)	–.09	.12	.46	.23
Divided Government (+)	–.18	.09	–1.86	.03
Age of Statute (Natural Log) (–)	.02	.10	.23	.41
Justice Party Congruence with Sitting Congress (+)	.04	.13	.29	.39
Congruence between Direction of Statute and Sitting Congress (–)	.26	.11	2.41	.01
Chief Justice (versus Associate Justice)(–)	.18	.20	.88	.19
Pro–Civil Rights and Liberties Statute*	1.68	.28	6.01	.0001
Pro-Judicial Power Statute (–)	.19	.32	.62	.27
Constant	–1.53	.56	–2.72	.003
		=802	Wald chi² = 46.9	.002

*Variables are tested at the higher two-tail test of significance.

only 22 of which nullified a congressional statute. As I reported in Chapter Two, if we take into consideration the size of the Court's docket during this period we see that the cases range from approximately 0 to 4 percent of the Court's caseload, on average 1.7 percent of the caseload. Still, it suggests that for a significant area of constitutional jurisprudence, the justices' votes appear not to be influenced by the factors we typically associate with their behavior in later years, which in turn suggests that the justices' votes in their earlier periods may be more easily attributed to the legal model. Wood, Keith, Lanier, and Ogundele (1998, 2000) found some evidence to support this observation even when only nonunanimous decisions were considered. Certainly, this period falls before the rise of dissensus on the Supreme Court (Haynie 1992) and prior to the Court's eventual control of its docket. To check for these possible influences I ran the model with only nonunanimous decisions; the Democratic Party coefficient increases (.73) and does achieve statistical significance at the .04 level. But for this one rather significant exception, the rest of the model largely remains unchanged. Thus, these influences do not appear to offer significant explanation for the failure of the model in this time period. McCloskey had argued that this period was one of increased but moderated activism, saying that the Court had realized that the "ambiguity of its mandate is both its limitation and its opportunity" (89) and thus we find a Court, at least in regard to these cases, that seems to be driven somewhat by concerns other than its own policy preferences.

Table 5.3 presents the next time period, 1901–1937. The model performs better here than in the previous time period. Democrat Party identification variable is highly significant ($p < .0001$) and produces a large coefficient (.68); however, none of the childhood socialization variables are statistically significant in this model. Federal judicial experience does not achieve statistical significance here; however, the other three are signed correctly and all are significant at the .01 level or better. In this time period none of the policy congruence variables are statistically significant because the coefficients are in a direction contra to our hypotheses.[15] Two of the institutional measures are statistically significant: war (−.66) and age of the statute (−.54) at least at the .01 level of significance. The coefficients for the chief justice and the Judges Act measures are in the correct direction but they do not achieve acceptable levels of statistical significance. Two of the statute variables produce large and statistically significant coefficients: pro-criminal defendant (1.16) and pro-civil rights and liberties statutes (1.00). These results support the hypothesis that justices are more likely to nullify laws that enhance or support fundamental rights, despite the expectations that judicial review be used to protect minority interests from majority incursions. The results support McCloskey's claim that "the question of civil rights in general, had been relegated to a minor and almost negligible place among the court's concerns" (90). In this period, the attitudinal and institutional influences appear to be stronger than in the previous time period, and the strategic approach continues to fail to have an impact on the votes.

Table 5.4 presents the results for 1937–1957, the period McCloskey referred to as the "modern court" in postwar America.[16] All of the personal attributes measures in this model are statistically insignificant except for Catholic religious

Table 5.3 Logit Models of Justices' Votes to Nullify or Uphold in Judicial Review of Congressional Statutes (1901–1937)

	Coefficient	Standard Error	Z-score	$p > z$
Democrat Party Identification (+)	.68	.19	3.63	.0001
Catholic Religious Affiliation (+)	−.10	.20	−.52	.31
Childhood Surroundings (Urban) (+)	.03	.10	.34	.37
Childhood Surroundings (Southern)(−)	.02	.19	.09	.46
Childhood Social Status*	−.09	.09	−1.03	.15
Federal Judicial Experience (−)	−.09	.14	−.67	.25
Federal Political Experience (+)	.46	.18	2.44	.01
State Judicial Experience (+)	.38	.15	2.64	.01
State or Local Political Experience (+)	.39	.14	2.86	.01
Experience as Law Professor (+)	−.02	.02	−.82	.41
Congruence between Justice Policy Preference and Direction of Statute (−)	.12	.05	2.51	.01
Justice Party Congruence with Enacting Congress (−)	.05	.04	1.30	.10
Divided Government (+)	−.29	.11	−2.73	.01
Justice Party Congruence with Sitting Congress (+)	−.13	.05	−2.51	.01
Congruence between Direction of Statute and Sitting Congress (−)	.32	.05	6.58	.0001
Chief Justice (versus Associate Justice) (−)	−.02	.14	−.14	.44
Judges Act (+)	.18	.13	1.41	.16
War (−)	−.66	.15	−4.50	.0001
Age of Statute (Natural Log) (−)	−.54	.11	−2.56	.01
Pro–Civil Rights and Liberties Statute*	1.00	.18	5.55	.0001
Pro–National Supremacy Statute (−)	.07	.19	.40	.35
Pro–Criminal Defendants Statute (+)	1.16	.45	2.56	.01
Constant	−1.42	.55	−2.56	.01
	$N = 2557$	Wald chi² = 3746.6	$p > .0001$	

*Variables are tested at the higher two-tail test of significance.

affiliation. Three of the career experience measures continue to be statistically significant; both political experience variables and state judicial experience. This is the first period in which a liberal/Democratic justice is not more likely to nullify than a conservative one. However, one of the party congruence measures

Table 5.4 Logit Models of Justices' Votes to Nullify or Uphold in Judicial Review of Congressional Statutes (1937–1957)

	Coefficient	Standard Error	Z-score	$p > z$
Democrat Party Identification (+)	.29	.54	.54	.29
Catholic Religious Affiliation (+)	1.72	.96	1.79	.03
Childhood Surroundings (Urban) (+)	−.07	.36	−.19	.42
Childhood Surroundings (Southern) (−)	.79	.65	1.21	.11
Childhood Social Status*	−.21	.21	−.99	.16
Federal Judicial Experience (−)	−.43	.67	−.64	.26
Federal Political Experience (+)	.30	1.02	.29	.39
State Judicial Experience (+)	−.32	.52	−.60	.27
State or Local Political Experience (+)	−.17	.76	−.22	.41
Experience as Law Professor (+)	.07	.08	.92	.18
Congruence between Justice Policy Preference and Direction of Statute (−)	−.35	.26	−1.35	.09
Justice Party Congruence with Enacting Congress (−)	−.22	.06	−4.02	.0001
Congruence between Direction of Statute and Sitting Congress (+)	.06	.15	.38	.35
Divided Government (+)	.16	.12	1.33	.09
Justice Party Congruence with Enacting Congress (−)	−.22	.06	−4.02	.0001
Justice Party Congruence with Sitting Congress (+)	.21	.20	1.03	.15
Chief Justice (versus Associate Justice) (−)	−.48	.71	−.68	.25
War (−)	−.49	.41	−1.18	.12
Pro–Civil Rights and Liberties Statute*	.70	.47	1.50	.07
Pro–National Supremacy Statute (−)	−.28	.39	−.73	.23
Age of Statute (Natural Log) (−)	−.13	.09	−1.51	.07
Constant	−1.81	.95	−1.91	.03
		$N = 1112$	Wald chi^2 = 401.07	$p > .0001$

*Variables are tested at the higher two-tail test of significance.

for the justices is statistically significant: congruence between justice and enacting Congress (−.22 $p < .0001$) and congruence between justice and policy direction of the statute is statistically significant at marginally acceptable levels (−.35 $p < .09$). These results clearly support the attitudinal model, while only one of the three strategic approach related congruence measures is even marginally statistically significant; the coefficient for divided government (.16) would be significant at the .09 level. One of the institutional variables, age of the statute, continues to be statistically significant in this model, as well. The pro–civil rights and liberties statute continues to be statistically significant, with justices again more likely to nullify pro–rights statutes than uphold them. These findings are somewhat interesting given McCloskey's assertion that during this period the Court was "smarting from the wounds incurred by its own rashness" just as were the justices in 1866 in the pre–Civil War period (121). The results suggest some evidence of a heightened awareness of needing to bow the strategic concerns in that the justices are less likely to vote to nullify unless facing an ideologically compatible Congress; however, the other strategic influences have no effect. In addition, the failure of the various surrogates for the justices' policy preferences, with the exception of religion, in this period suggests that attitudinal influences were somewhat suppressed. Those justices with political experience, however, are more likely to vote challenging Congress, suggesting perhaps less heightened awareness than the other justices may demonstrate. It is also interesting to note that in this period, where the Carolene Products footnote declares the preferred freedoms doctrine, and signals a significant change in the Court's agenda, the Court is still more likely to strike a rights-protective statute than uphold it.

Table 5.5 presents the results for the most recent Court, from 1958 to 2001.[17] The first notable difference in this period is that a liberal justice, the Democrat Party–affiliated justice, is no longer more likely to nullify than a conservative justice. This finding does not imply, however, that policy preference is not influential—to the contrary, three perhaps four of the party-based measures are statistically significant. Concomitantly, with Democratic Party affiliation's influence on "activism" ending, the regional influence of southern restraint ends as well; giving credence to the assertions of the rise of conservative activism (see Schwartz 2002; Keck 2002). Social status, along with state judicial and political experience, continues their same effect. Interestingly, experience as a law professor becomes statistically significant in this time period, just as Bork would predict, except that its influence is statistically significant even controlling for party affiliation and various measures of ideological concurrence. I ran the model with an interaction effect between law professor and Democratic Party identification as well, and the interaction was not statistically significant. Thus apparently the impact of being a former law professor holds for conservative Scalia as well as liberal Douglas. Both of the attitudinal model measures of congruence produce coefficients in the correct direction; the congruence between the justice's party identification and the direction of the statute (–.42) is statistically significant at the .0001 level and the smaller coefficient for congruence between the

Table 5.5 Logit Models of Justice's Votes to Nullify or Uphold in Judicial Review of Congressional Statutes (1958–2001)

	Coefficient	Standard Error	Z-score	$p > z$
Democrat Party Identification (+)	−.16	.36	−.45	.33
Catholic Religious Affiliation (+)	.29	.34	.84	.20
Childhood Surroundings (Urban) (+)	−1.00	.36	−2.81	.01
Childhood Surroundings (Southern) (+)	−.12	.30	−.40	.34
Childhood Social Status*	−.17	.10	−1.72	.04
Federal Judicial Experience (−)	−.30	.32	−.94	.17
Federal Political Experience (+)	.15	.23	.67	.25
State Judicial Experience (+)	.53	.28	1.87	.03
State or Local Political Experience (+)	.73	.23	3.21	.0001
Experience as Law Professor (+)	.20	.06	3.12	.001
Congruence between Justice Policy Preference and Direction of Statute (−)	−.42	.14	−3.18	.0001
Justice Party Congruence with Enacting Congress (−)	−.09	.07	−1.25	.11
Divided Government (+)	.05	.06	.82	.21
Justice Party Congruence with Sitting Congress (+)	.17	.11	1.56	.01
Congruence between Direction of Statute and Sitting Congress (−)	−.47	.11	−4.34	.0001
Chief Justice (versus Associate Justice) (−)	−.37	.66	−.56	.29
Age of Statute (Natural Log) (−)	.08	.05	1.75	.04
Pro-Civil Rights and Liberties Statute*	−.31	.33	−.94	.34
Pro-Judicial Power Statute (−)	−1.30	.78	−1.67	.05
Pro-National Supremacy Statute (−)	−.26	.46	−.56	.29
Pro-Criminal Defendants Statute (+)	−1.66	.56	−2.96	.01
Constant	−.56	.83	−.68	.25
	$N = 2464$	Wald chi^2 = 1247.0	$p > .0001$	

*Variables are tested at the higher two-tail test of significance.

justice's party and the enacting Congress would be statistically significant only at the marginal level of .11. Divided government continues to be insignificant.

In contrast to the full-period analysis, the two strategic approach congruence measures are statistically significant for the modern Court: party congruence between justice and sitting Congress (.17 $p < .01$) and congruence between direction of statute and sitting Congress ($-.47$ $p < .0001$). Both results provide support for the hypothesis that the justices are more likely to strike a congressional statute facing a friendly Congress and less likely to strike a statute that is ideological congruent with preferences of the sitting Congress. The two institutional measures are not statistically significant in this time period; being a chief justice has no impact on the odds of a nullification vote. The age of the statute produces a coefficient which if we had hypothesized non-directionally with a two-tailed test would have been statistically significant. In the full time-period model one of the directional issues, a pro–judicial power statute, was statistically significant; here it is the only statistically significant issue as well; however, the pro–criminal defendant measure produces a very strong coefficient (-1.66) that would have been statistically significant if we had not hypothesized a specific direction and had tested with a two-tailed test of significance. Overall, the model for this time period suggests that the recent Supreme Court justice act in ways that are consistent with both attitudinal assumptions, but that the attitudinal factors are not sufficient to explain the variation in the justices' behavior; they also appear to respond to strategic concerns such as the policy preferences of Congress, despite the fact that the justices are arguably less constrained in decisions of constitutionality than they are in statutory interpretation. In addition, they also appear to be influenced by institutional concerns, such as protecting the power of the judiciary; however, other institutional influences are not statistically significant.

Conclusions

In this analysis we have examined the justices' votes in the context of the key theoretical perspectives in studies of judicial behavior, and we have examined a variety of influences associated with each perspective. We have been able to identify a substantial number of influences on the justices' voting behavior across the two-hundred year period. Predominantly the influences have supported the assumptions of the attitudinal model, demonstrating strong effects for personal attributes of the justices that represent significant childhood and adult socialization. Most importantly, we have seen a liberal justice, here a justice with a Democratic Party affiliation, is more likely to nullify a congressional statute, even when controlling for the ideological congruence between the justice and the statute or the justice and the enacting Congress. At the same time a southern non-Catholic justice who grew up in an upper-class family was more likely to be restraintist than a non-southern Catholic justice who grew up with a more humble social status. In addition to the observed effects of the justices' childhood socialization, we also see strong influences from the justices' adult or career socialization. Justice who serve on the federal bench prior to joining the Supreme Court are more likely to show deference to Congress, but justices who spend time in political office, whether federal or state, prior to joining the bench or state judicial experience were less likely to defer to their coordinate branch, and justices with state judicial experience showed the same effect, reflecting perhaps socialization through the political or partisan process of judicial selection at the state and local level. Probably, the most significant finding in regard to the attitudinal approach is that a Supreme Court justice's vote on the constitutionality of a congressional statute is influenced by the consistency between the policy direction of the statute and the justice's ideological preferences, and to a smaller extent the congruence between the justice's policy preferences and those of the enacting Congress. Thus, a Republican justice will be more likely to strike statutes that passed by Democratic Congresses and vice versa and, more substantively, that a Democratic justice will have a stronger proclivity toward striking conservative legislation and a Republican justice will have a stronger proclivity toward striking liberal legislation. It was significant that these attitudinal effects held, even controlling for a variety of institutional and legal factors.

The evidence for the strategic model was quite weak. In the analysis above, I tested three hypotheses that were derived from the strategic model which predicted that the justices would be constrained by policy preferences of the sitting Congress; in particular, justices would be less likely to vote to nullify in three circumstances: (1) when the level of party unification is greater among the sitting government (Congress and the president); (2) when there is ideological congruence between the justice and the sitting Congress (when the Court faces a friendly Congress); and (3) when there is ideological consistency between the direction of the statute and the sitting Congress. None of these hypotheses were supported, and at least in examining the full–time period under study, we were left to conclude that strategic approach fails to contribute to our understanding of this somewhat narrow set of votes. In addition, only one of institutional influences demonstrated an effect that was statistically significant at the standard levels of significance; two achieved somewhat marginal levels. We saw that even controlling for a wide variety of influences, the justices were still less likely to vote to nullify congressional action during the Civil War or the two world wars. Also, we saw that the justices are less likely to strike laws the longer the statutes have been in effect which is perhaps indicative of the enhanced legitimacy the statute takes on over time. In addition, we saw that a justice serving as chief justice is less likely to vote to nullify, again suggesting the possibility of some strategic concerns or certainly the institutional concern that chief justice's votes might be affected by concerns over the continued legitimacy of the Court as an institution.

Finally, the analysis examined some influences that reflected both attitudinal and/or strategic concerns, testing distinctions in the justices' votes on statutes that were either pro-national supremacy, pro-criminal defendant, pro-civil rights and liberties or pro-judicial power. We saw that only the pro-judiciary statute had an influence on the justices' votes, with the justices much more likely to support a statute that enhanced or upheld judicial power generally. In addition, we saw that the likelihood of a justice voting to nullify or uphold Congress depended in part on the chief justice court on which the justice was serving; justices were much more likely to vote to nullify Congress on the three recent chief justice courts prior to Roberts—Warren, Burger, and Rehnquist. The effect of serving on the Rehnquist bench was about twice of that of Burger and a third more than Warren. The analysis also demonstrated that even controlling for a large number of institutional and attitudinal factors the justices were much less likely to vote to nullify Congress during five chief justiceships: Taney, Fuller, White, Stone, and Vinson.

We were also able to examine the model across various periods of time, using McCloskey's historical periods to demarcate the periods. We discovered that the model did not perform as well in the earliest period, the post–Civil War period, with only a few of the attitudinal influences observable and none of the strategic influences appearing to significantly affect the justices' votes. These results suggest that our current understanding of judicial behavior may indeed be somewhat time-bound. In the early twentieth century, we see a much stronger influence from the attitudinal and institutional factors than in the previous time period, but the strategic approach continues to fail to have an impact on the votes. In the mid-twentieth century period we see only some influence from the attitudinal model and slim influence from one strategic factor. As we noted above, this period represented a somewhat tenuous time for the Court's legitimacy and future power, and the attenuated results suggested some evidence of a heightened awareness of strategic concerns in that the justices are less likely to vote to nullify unless facing an ideologically compatible Congress. And yet, despite the failure of the various surrogates for the justices' policy preferences, with the exception of religion, those justices with political experience were more likely to vote challenging Congress, suggesting perhaps less heightened awareness for institutional concerns than the other justices may demonstrate. When we examined the most recent period, the evidence strongly suggested that these Supreme Court justice act in ways that are consistent with attitudinal assumptions, but that the attitudinal factors were not sufficient to explain the variation in the justices' behavior. We also saw strong evidence that the justices' votes are influenced by strategic concerns such as the policy preferences of the sitting Congress. In addition, they also appear to be influenced by institutional concerns, such as protecting the power of the judiciary; however, the other institutional influences are not statistically significant. Thus, as we move across time we see that neither of these preference-based approaches is as robust in the nineteenth century, but there is significant evidence of attitudinal influences, and certainly much more than that of the strategic influences in those period. As we move into the twentieth century, the attitudinal effects are stronger as we move across all three periods, but the strategic approach does not begin to show observable effects until the mid-twentieth century period, and then the influences grow much stronger in the current court period. So, we are left with some dissatisfaction with our theories' ability to explain judicial behavior beyond the past century. Obviously, the analysis is limited to some extent. It only examines one component of judicial review. It does not examine the larger set of review cases that consider the constitutionality of state statutes, nor does it examine the exercise of review over executive action, which is arguably a small, but potentially more significant set of decisions. In addition, the measures of policy preferences and attitudes are surrogates rather than direct measures, and the surrogates appear to have less validity in earlier periods of the Court's history, when our delineation of party affiliation and political ideology may be the most tenuous. I believe we must keep these limitations in mind, but at the same time respect the very fact that we are able to identify in many instances the influence of these factors, even while controlling for a broad range of other influences on the justices' votes. In the last chapter, I will discuss more fully the strengths of the analysis undertaken in this book, while also exploring more fully its limitations and the implications of each for future research.

Notes

1. Wold found, however, among his particular set of judges that Republicans were more likely to be innovators or activists than were Democrats. He attributed this unexpected finding to the narrow geographic representation among the set of east coast justices he interviewed.

2. In addition, they found that the cases in which there was no discussion of the other political actors' preferences were in large part criminal due process cases (18 out of 37), and they note that it is a given that Congress goes against the criminal defendant's rights. If these cases are removed, then they find the justices referred to

other political actors' preferences in approximately 60 percent of the constitutional cases (150).

3. *Schenck v. United States* (1919).

4. We would expect this distinction to hold for justices who go on to assume the role of chief justice; that they would have been more likely to vote to nullify when serving as an associate justice than after becoming chief justice.

5. Tate and Handberg also created a variable for the appointing presidents and their intentions to produce justices who behave in a particular way. Based on historical evidence, they identified presidents who had clearly demonstrated a very real concern that the justices' policy views reflect their own. I have not recreated this measure as I believe it improbable to create valid assessment for many of the early presidents.

6. For this dimension Tate and Handberg used whether the justice's father was a farmer or not. Those data are not available for the entire set of justices under study here.

7. Tate and Handberg constructed a measure of the family based on the father's occupation.

8. Comparativists argue that judges in civil law systems who are typically career judges with relatively narrow experience are ill-prepared in temperament and political experience to exercise the independent function of judicial review, particularly in declaring laws unconstitutional (Rosenn 1987, 33).

9. Liberalism of the statute follows the Spaeth delineation with the modification for federalism as described in the previous chapters.

10. A measure was created controlling for the possibility that Southern Democrats were more likely to be conservative and Northern Republicans were more likely to be liberal. This regional delineation was not statistically significant in the trial analyses, however.

11. After preliminary analysis of the multivariate model, I decided to eliminate the solicitor general variable from the model for two reasons. The measure was not available for the full-time period under study and it was not statistically significant when the other variables were added to the model regardless of whether the measure was the full four-point delineation or the dichotomous measure. In addition, I dropped the dummy variable that delineated the 1988 repeal of Section 1252 of Public Law 86-3 because it was too highly correlated with the Rehnquist chief justice measure.

12. I also tested divided government as a dichotomous variable as well and the results remained the same.

13. I would remind the reader that the civil rights and liberties hypothesis was tested at the higher two-tailed test of significance.

14. The Catholic attributes variable is not included in this analysis as only two justices (White and McKenna) were Catholic. Only two of the directional issue area variables are included in the analysis due to collinearity or a lack of variation.

15. I was somewhat concerned that the ideological switch on federalism across the political parties might affect the policy preference variables in this time period

since the demarcation of the switch was not absolutely linked to 1935, and could have been more gradual and the pace somewhat idiosyncratic among the justices. So I dropped the federalism cases from the model and re-estimated the coefficients. The results of the model still held.

16. In this period pro-criminal and pro-judicial statutes and the Judges Act were dropped due to high collinearity or lack of variation.

17. The Chief Justice dummy variables were dropped from the model because of high collinearity with other variables, such as the issue variables, that were deemed to represent more theoretically interesting hypotheses.

References

Adamany, David. 1969. "The Party Variable in Judges' Voting: Conceptual Notes and a Case Study." *American Political Science Review* 63: 57–73.

Aliotta, Jilda M. 1988. "Combining Judges' Attributes and Case Characteristics: An Alternative to Explaining Supreme Court Decisionmaking." *Judicature* 71: 277–81.

Bergera, Mario, Barak Richman, and Pablo T. Spiller. 2003. "Modeling Supreme Court Strategic Decision Making: The Congressional Restraint." *Legislative Studies Quarterly* 28: 247–80.

Bork, Robert. 1990. *The Tempting of America: The Political Seduction of the Law.* New York: Touchstone.

Brudney, James J., Sara Schiavoni, and Deborah J. Merritt. 1999. "Judicial Hostility Toward Labor Unions? Applying the Social Background Model to a Celebrated Concern." *Ohio State Law Review* 60: 1675–766.

Caldiera, Gregory A. and Donald J. McCrone. 1982. "Of Time and Judicial Activism: A Study of the U.S. Supreme Court, 1800–1973." In *Supreme Court Activism and Restraint*, eds. Stephen C. Halpern and Charles M. Lamb. Lexington, MA: Lexington Books.

Caldiera, Gregory A. and John R. Wright. 1988. "Organized Interests and Agenda Setting in the U.S. Supreme Court." *American Political Science Review* 82(4): 1109–1127.

Caplan, Lincoln. 1987. *The Tenth Justice: The Solicitor General and the Rule of Law.* New York: Knopf.

Carp, Robert A., Donald R. Songer, C.K. Rowland, Ronald Stidham, and Lisa Richey-Tracy. 1993. "The Voting Behavior of Judges Appointed by President Bush." *Judicature* 76: 298.

Danelski, David J. 1989. "The Influence of the Chief Justice in the Decisional Process of the Supreme Court." In *American Court Systems*, eds. Sheldon Goldman and Austin Sarat. New York: Longman.

Danelski, David J., and Jeanne C. Danelski. 1989. "Leadership in the Warren Court." In *American Court Systems*, eds. Sheldon Goldman and Austin Sarat. New York: Longman.

Epstein, Lee, Valerie Hoekstra, Jeffrey A. Segal, and Harold J. Spaeth. 1998. "Do Political Preferences Change? A Longitudinal Study of US Supreme Court Justices." *Journal of Politics* 60: 801–18.

Epstein, Lee and Jack Knight. 1998. *The Choices Judges Make.* Washington, DC: Congressional Quarterly Press.

Epstein, Lee, Jeffrey A. Segal, and Harold J. Spaeth. 2001. "The Norm of Consensus on the U.S. Supreme Court." *American Journal of Political Science* 45: 362–77.

Epstein, Lee, Jeffrey A. Segal, Harold J. Spaeth, and Thomas G. Walker. 2003. *The Supreme Court Compendium.* Washington, DC: Congressional Quarterly Press.

Eskridge, William N. 1991. "Overriding Supreme Court Statutory Interpretation Decisions." *Yale Law Journal* 101: 331–455.

Ferejohn, John. 1999. "'Independent Judges, Dependent Judiciary' Explaining Judicial Independence." *Southern California Law Review* 72: 353–84.

Ferejohn, John, Frances Rosenbluth, and Charles Shipan. 2004. "Comparative Judicial Politics." Manuscript available at: http://www.yaleuniversity.net/ polisci/rosenbluth/ Papers/comparative%20judicial%20politics.pdf.

Ferejohn, John A, and Charles Shipan. 1990. "Congressional Influence on Bureaucracy." *Journal of Law, Economics, and Organization* 6: 1–20.

Frank, Jerome. 1949. *Law and the Modern Mind.* New York: Coward-McCann.

Friedman, Barry and Anna Harvey. 2003. "Electing the Supreme Court." *Indiana Law Journal* 78: 123–39.

George, Tracey E. and Lee Epstein. 1992. "On the Nature of Supreme Court Decision Making." *American Political Science Review* 86 (3): 323–37.

Gibson, James. 1978. "Judges' Role Orientations, Attitudes, and Decisions: An Interactive Model." *American Political Science Review* 86: 323–37.

Glick, Henry R. and Kenneth N. Vines. 1969. "Law-making in the State Judiciary: A Comparative Study of the Judicial Role in Four States." *Polity* 2: 142–59.

Goldman, Sheldon. 1966. "Voting Behavior of the United States Courts of Appeals, 1961–1964. *American Political Science Review* 60: 374–84.

Goldman, Sheldon. 1975. "Voting Behavior of the United States Courts of Appeals Revisited. *American Political Science Review* 69: 491–506.

Gottschall, Jon. 1986. "Reagan's Appointments to the U.S. Courts of Appeals: the Continuation of a Judicial Revolution." *Judicature* 70: 50–4.

Gryski, Gerard S., Eleanor C. Main, and William J. Dixon, 1986. "Social Backgrounds as Predictors of Votes on State Courts of Last Resort: The Case of Sex Discrimination." *Western Political Quarterly* 39: 528–37.

Hansford, Thomas and David F. Damore 2000. "Congressional Preferences, Perceptions of Threat, and Supreme Court Decision Making." *American Politics Quarterly* 28: 490–510.

Haynie, Stacia L. 1992. "Leadership and Consensus on the U.S. Supreme Court." *The Journal of Politics.* 54: 1158–69.

Howard, Robert M. and Jeffrey A. Segal. 2004. "A Preference for Deference? The Supreme Court and Judicial Review." *Political Research Quarterly* 57(1): 131–43.

Howard, J. Woodford Jr. 1977. "Role Perceptions and Behavior in Three U.S. Courts of Appeals." *Journal of Politics* 39: 916–38.

Keck, Thomas. 2007. "Party, Policy, or Duty: Why Does the Supreme Court Invalidate Federal Statutes?" *American Political Science Review* 101: 321–339.

Keith, Linda Camp, Tate C. Neal, and Steven C. Poe. 2007. "Is the Law a Mere Parchment Barrier to Human Rights Abuse?" Unpublished manuscript.

King, Kimi and James Meernik. 1999. "The Supreme Court and the Powers of the Executive: The Adjudication of Foreign Policy." *Political Research Quarterly* 52: 801–24.

Lanier, Drew Noble and Sandra L. Wood. 2001. "Moving on Up: Institutional Position, Politics, and the Chief Justice." *American Review of Politics* 22: 93–127l

Lindquist, Stephanie A. and Rorie Spill Solberg. 2007. "Judicial Review by the Burger and Rehnquist Courts: Explaining Justices' Responses to Constitutional Challenges." *Political Research Quarterly* 60: 71–90.

Lipset, Seymour M. and Stein Rokkan. 1967. "Cleavage Structures, Party–Systems and Voter Alignments: An Introduction." In *Party Systems and Voter Alignments: Cross-National Perspectives,* eds. Seymour M. Lipset and Stein Rokkan. New York: The Free Press.

Maltzman, Forest, James F. Spriggs III, and Paul Wahlbeck. 2000. *Crafting Law on the Supreme Court: The Collegial Game.* Cambridge, UK: Cambridge University Press.

Marks, Brian. 1988. "A Model of Judicial Influence on Congressional Policymaking: *Grove City College v. Bell.*" *Working papers in Political Science*, 88-7, Hoover Institution, Stanford University.

McCloskey, Robert G. 1994. *The American Supreme Court.* Chicago: University of Chicago Press.

McGuire, Kevin. 1998. "Explaining Executive Success in the U.S. Supreme Court." *Political Research Quarterly* 51: 505–26.

Meese, Edwin. 1985. "The Attorney General's View of the Supreme Court: Toward a Jurisprudence of Original Intention." *Public Administration Review* 45: 701–4.

Murphy, Walter F. 1964. *Elements of Judicial Strategy.* Chicago: University of Chicago Press.

Nagel, Stuart S. 1961. "Political Party Affiliation and Judges' Decisions." *American Political Science Review* 55: 843–50.

Pacelle, Richard. 2003. *Between Law and Politics: The Solicitor General and the Structuring of Race, Gender, and Reproductive Rights Policy.* College Station: Texas A&M Press.

Pickerill, J. Mitchell. 2005. "Congressional Responses to Judicial Review," in *Congress and the Constitution,* eds. Neal Devins and Keith E. Whittington. Durham: Duke University Press.

Pritchett, C. Herman. 1954. *Civil Liberties and the Vinson Court.* Chicago: University of Chicago Press.

Rehnquist, William H. 1998. *All the Laws but One: Civil Liberties in Wartime.* Knopf: New York.

Reichley, James. 1992. *The Life of the Parties: A History of American Political Parties.* New York: The Free Press.

Rohde, David W. and Harold J. Spaeth. 1976. *Supreme Court Decision Making.* San Francisco, CA: W.H. Freeman.

Roncek, Dennis W. and Marc L. Swatt. 2006. "For Those Who Like Odds: A Direct Interpretation of the Logit Coefficients for Continuous Variables." *Social Science Quarterly* 87: 731–38.

Rosenn, Keith S. 1987. "The Protection of Judicial Independence in Latin America." *University of Miami Inter-American Law Review* 19: 1–35.

Sala, Brian R. and James F. Spriggs. 2004. "Designing Tests of the Supreme Court and the Separation of Powers." *Political Research Quarterly* 57: 197–208.

Scheb, John M., Thomas D. Ungs, and Allison L. Hayes. 1989. "Judicial Role Orientations, Attitudes, and Decision-Making: A Research Note." *Western Political Quarterly* 42: 427–35.

Schmidhauser, John. 1961. "Judicial Behavior and the Sectional Crisis of 1837–1860." *Journal of Politics* 23: 615–27.

Schubert, Glendon. 1965. *The Judicial Mind.* Evanston: Northwestern University Press.

Schwartz, Herman. 2002. *The Rehnquist Court: Judicial Activism on the Right.* New York: Hill and Wang.

Segal, Jeffrey A. 1988. "Amicus Curiae Briefs by the Solicitor General during the Warren and Burger Courts." *Western Political Quarterly* 41: 135–44.

Segal, Jeffrey A. and Albert Cover. 1989. "Ideological Values and the Votes of U.S. Supreme Court Justices." *American Political Science Review* 83: 557–65.

Segal, Jeffrey A. and Harold J. Spaeth. 1993. *The Supreme Court and the Attitudinal Model.* Cambridge: Cambridge University Press.

Segal, Jeffrey A. and Harold J. Spaeth. 2002. *The Supreme Court and the Attitudinal Model Revisited.* Cambridge: Cambridge University Press.

Segal, Jeffrey A. and Chad Westerland. 2005. "The Supreme Court, Congress, and Judicial Review." *North Carolina Law Review* 83: 101–66.

Segal, Jeffrey A., Lee Epstein, Charles M. Cameron, and Harold D. Spaeth. 1995. "Ideological Values and the Votes of U.S. Supreme Court Justices Revisited." *Journal of Politics* 57: 812–23.

Shapiro, Martin. 1981. *Courts: Comparative and Political Analysis.* Chicago: University of Chicago Press.

Slotnick, Elliot E. 1987. "The Place of Judicial Review in the American Tradition: the Emergence of an Eclectic Power." *Judicature* 71(2): 68–79.

Solberg, Rorie Spill and Stephanie Lindquist. 2006. "Activism, Ideology, and Federalism: Judicial Behavior in Constitutional Challenges Before the Rehnquist Court, 1986–2000." *Journal of Empirical Legal Studies* 3: 237–61.

Songer, Donald R. and Sue Davis. 1990. "The Impact of Party and Region on Voting Decisions in the United States Courts of Appeals." *The Western Political Quarterly* 43: 317–35.

Spiller, Pablo T. and Rafael Gely. 1992. "Congressional Control or Judicial Independence: The Determinants of U.S. Supreme Court Labor-Relations Decisions 1949–1988." *RAND Journal of Economics* 23: 463–92.

Spriggs, James F. III and Thomas G. Hansford. 2001. "Explaining the Overruling of U.S. Supreme Court Precedent." *Journal of Politics* 63: 1091–111.

Tanenhaus, Joseph, Marvin Schick, Matthew Muraskin, and Daniel Rosen. 1963. "The Supreme Court's Certiorari Jurisdiction: Cue Theory." In *Judicial Decision-Making*, ed. Glendon Schubert. New York: Free Press.

Tate C. Neal. 1981. "Personal Attribute Models of the Voting Behavior of U.S. Supreme Court Justices: Liberalism in Civil Liberties and Economic Decisions, 1946–1978." *American Political Science Review* 75: 355–67.

Tate C. Neal and Roger Handberg. 1991. "Time Building and Theory Building in Personal Attribute Models of Supreme Court Voting Behavior, 1916–1988." *American Journal of Political Science* 35: 460–80.

Tate C. Neal and Panu Sittiwong. 1989. "Decision Making in the Canadian Supreme Court: Extending the Personal Attributes Model Across Nations." *Journal of Politics* 51: 900–16.

Ulmer, Sidney S. 1972. "The Decision to Grant Certiorari as an Indicator to Decision 'On the Merits.'" *Polity* 4: 429–47.

Ulmer, Sidney J. 1973. "Social Background as an Indicator to the Votes of Supreme Court Justices in Criminal Cases: 1947–1956 Terms." *American Journal of Political Science* 17: 622–30.

Wahlbeck, Paul J., James F. Spriggs, and Forrest Maltzman. 1999. "The Politics of Dissents and Concurrences on the U.S. Supreme Court." *American Politics Research* 27: 488–514

Wahlbeck at al. "The Politics of Dissents and Concurrences on the U.S. Supreme Court."

Walker, Thomas G., Lee Epstein, and William J. Dixon. 1988. "On the Mysterious Demise of Consensual Norms in the United States Supreme Court." *Journal of Politics* 50: 361–89.

Wold, John T. 1974. "Political Orientations, Social Backgrounds, and Role Perceptions of State Supreme Court Judges." *The Western Political Quarterly* 27: 239–48.

Wood, Sandra, Linda Camp Keith, Drew Lanier, and Ayo Ogundele. 2000. "Opinion Assignment and the Chief Justice: 1888–1940." *Social Science Quarterly* 81: 798–809.

Wood, Sandra, Linda Camp Keith, Drew Lanier, and Ayo Ogundele. 1998. "The Supreme Court 1888–1940: An Empirical Overview." *Social Science History* 22: 204–24.

Yates, Jeff and Andrew Whitford. 1998. "Presidential Power and the United States Supreme Court." *Political Research Quarterly* 51: 539–50.

Zorn, Christopher. 2006. "Comparing GEE and Robust Standard Errors for Conditionally Dependent Data." *Political Research Quarterly* 59: 329–41.

6 | Conclusions

In writing this book, I set out to fill part of the gap in our understanding of the U.S. Supreme Court's exercise of one its most potent powers, the power of constitutional review of Congress, particularly from a behavioralist perspective. Much of the scholarly attention to the Court's exercise of judicial review is largely historical or doctrinal, and often carries a normative dimension, as well. Here, I have sought to examine the Court's behavior in rigorous quantitative analysis, systematically testing some of our theoretical assumptions in regard to the countermajoritarian nature of the power and in light of the competing explanatory theories of judicial behavior. I have also attempted to provide a fuller descriptive analysis of the Court's and of the individual justices' voting behaviors than is typically possible in political science journals, and I have sought to offer some new insights into the justices' behaviors.

As we examined the Court's exercise of this power over its two-hundred year history, we saw that overall the Court has exhibited a strong norm of deference to Congress across the entire history under study here, and it has done so at rates more deferential than those the president enjoys in his exercise of executive powers in regard to domestic policy and even more than in national security and foreign policy matters where the president typically enjoys stronger prerogatives. As we examined the patterns of deference overtime we observed the number of Supreme Court cases challenging Congress increase gradually following the Civil War and Reconstruction, with a concomitant increase in the number of nullifications of Congress. However, the dominant trend across the Court's history remained one of supporting Congress, with exceptions primarily during the decades of the 1960s and the 1990s. We saw that the Court typically increases its level of deference during times of national crises, specifically the two world wars, nullifying substantially fewer statutes. In addition, we observed that not only has the level of judicial review and nullification rates varied across chief justice courts, the ideological patterns of the outcomes have produced significant patterns, with most Courts supporting primarily one ideological position or other, but not usually both. Some Courts such as the Taney Court, the Stone Court, and the Burger Court have shown particularly high levels of ideological consistency, followed by the Warren and Rehnquist Courts. We have found that when the Court does decide to go against the norm of deference it usually does so in a single ideological direction that is quite extreme from the direction of its votes to uphold congressional statutes, suggesting that the Court rarely goes against its ideological preferences when nullifying Congress. Finally, we have seen that the Court treats issue areas before it somewhat differently at least at the aggregate level. The Court has been most likely to nullify Congress on First Amendment and criminal procedure issues, followed by issues of judicial power and federalism. Contrary to normative expectations that an independent judiciary armed with the power of judicial review is the best guarantor of constitutional rights, we find instead that across the broad category of civil rights and civil liberties (criminal procedure, First Amendment, civil rights and due process issue areas) the Court has been much more likely to vote against rather than in support of the rights claimed. In these congressional review cases the Court has also been much more likely to support judicial power, and to support federal power over state rights, and it has been more likely to vote in the liberal direction on issues regarding economic activity. When the Court does act against Congress and nullifies statutes, we find the Court more likely to support civil rights and liberties claims and also more likely to support business interests and property rights. Overall, the examination of the historical patterns provided initial evidence of the ideological dimension of the Court's behavior.

As we examined the question of the countermajoritarian nature of the power of judicial review we found that the Court is overwhelmingly deferential to Congress and does not frequently exercise the power against congressional statutes. We are also able to observe in simple bivariate analysis some evidence that suggest the Court's exercise of the power was not as counter-majoritarian as it could be given the inherent nature of the power that places the Court's judgment over the elected legislature. The overwhelming majority of cases review congressional statutes that are more than four years old, and which would seem to represent a somewhat different enacting Congress than the current sitting Congress. Almost half of the statutes are over eight years, which would clearly represent a different Congress than the enacting one. In addition, in only one-third of the cases that nullified a statute, were statutes four or less years old and only slightly over half were eight years or less. Thus, use of the power to nullify statutes appears to be somewhat countermajoritarian, but not as much as we might expect. In terms of their significance in the development of constitutional jurisprudence, only a small percentage of the review cases are considered to be landmark decisions, particularly among those upholding congressional statutes. Still, much less than half of even the nullification cases are considered to be landmark cases as distinguished here. Thus the evidence we examined seems to support Dahl's assessment somewhat more accurately than Casper's. In addition, the evidence we observed suggests that Funston's assertion about critical periods and partisan periods does not hold when the analysis is extended to include the full exercise of review of Congress and is extended in time; the Court is more likely not less likely to nullify during the longer stable party periods. Thus, the Court's counter-majoritarian exercise of judicial review does not appear to be limited to these briefer transitional periods. Funston's other significant assertion does however hold in the extended analysis here; the Court is less likely to strike newer laws in stable party systems and more likely to strike newer laws in briefer critical period years; again these laws presumably are more likely to have been passed by sitting majorities in Congress and their nullification is perhaps more appropriately considered counter-majoritarian than older statutes. Finally, we saw another piece of evidence that tends to support the countermajoritarian claim; the Court in its review decisions, whether nullifying or upholding, typically is not acting consistently in the general policy direction of the sitting Congress, unless the sitting Congress is controlled at least in part by Democrats.

We also examined a different dimension of the power's countermajoritarian nature; that of its role in protecting minority rights from tyranny of the majority. There we saw that the Court largely acts in a majoritarian role, not as the bulwark against intrusions against minority rights by the political majority. Instead, we saw that the Court has exercised the power to review congressional legislation in way that has produced outcomes that diminish or ignore rights claims, even though it has primarily voted to uphold rights when going against the norm of deference to nullify congressional action. We were left to conclude that the level of support for civil rights by the Court, the branch of government claimed to be the guarantor of rights, is only slightly better than the rights protection promoted in forums of direct democracy—initiative and referenda—when a self-interested majority has the opportunity to defeat the rights of the minority. Ultimately we are left to conclude that the concern about or conversely the optimism for the Court's countermajoritarian exercise of this power, at least, in regard to Congress, may be somewhat overstated. Although solving the normative debates concerning the power of judicial review lies beyond the interest of this type of work, perhaps the empirical assessments here will inform those debates to some extent.

When we examined the individual justices votes in detail with initial bivariate analysis we were able to observe several significant patterns across the justices' votes, examining as much as space limitations would allow each justices' particular behavior on the bench. First, we found that even though the justices on average are highly deferential to Congress, there are significant numbers of justices who depart from the norm. In addition, we found among the justices who are most willing to challenge Congress both liberals and conservatives, and both Democrats and Republicans. We saw that after Warren joins the bench very few justices have extremely deferential scores, and additionally, we saw all of the recent justices on the bench (excluding Roberts and Alito who are not included in this work) place within the top thirteen nullification rates. When we examined the ideological dimension of the justices' individual votes we found several significant patterns as well. First, we found that the majority of the justices' vote fall in the moderate range, with only small proportions of the justices earning scores that could be considered consistently liberal or conservative. This finding also has a time-related caveat, in that as we move into the appointees of Franklin Roosevelt and beyond, the moderate tendency disappears rather quickly. Overall, the ideological dimension of the justices' votes in congressional review cases tends to be moderated, in comparison to the liberalism scores based on the full set of the justices' decisions or key issue areas across the justices' tenure. We also find that when we separate out the justices' votes to nullify from those to uphold the statute, the nullification votes were more extreme ideologically. However, we observed an interesting movement; the movement in ideology was primarily in the liberal direction. In fact when we examine justices with large differences in their uphold votes and votes to nullify, we find that the difference was primarily with justices being more liberal in their nullifying votes than in their votes to uphold Congress. We also examined the justices' votes across issue areas and once again we found several significant trends. We found that on average, the justices were much less likely to support civil rights and civil liberties claims, despite the claim that judicial review is most legitimately exercised in regard to rights-based claims. We found the justices were much more likely to support national government claims over states' rights claims and against tax-payer claims. Finally, we found that justices on average were much more likely to vote against business claims in favor of government regulation. Thus, in general, we saw clear ideological components to the justices' votes, despite the overall adherence to the norm of restraint and despite the generally attenuated ideological effects in these review votes, relative to the general overall voting behavior of these justices.

Ultimately, we moved beyond the initial bivariate analysis to examine in fully controlled multivariate statistical models, the key theoretical perspectives in studies of judicial behavior, including a variety of influences associated with each perspective. We were able to identify a substantial number of influences on the justices' voting behavior across the two-hundred year period. Predominantly, the influences supported the assumptions of the attitudinal model, demonstrating strong effects from the personal attributes of the justices that represented significant childhood and adult socialization. Most importantly, we saw that a liberal justice, here a justice with a Democratic Party affiliation, is more likely to nullify a congressional statute, even when controlling for the ideological congruence between the justice and the statute or the justice and the enacting Congress. At the same time a southern non-Catholic justice who grew up in an upper class family was more likely to be restraintist than a non-southern Catholic justice who grew up with a more humble social status. In addition to the observed effects of the justices' childhood socialization, we also observed strong influences from the justices' adult or career socialization; a justice who serves on the federal bench prior to joining the Supreme Court was more likely to show deference to Congress, but justices who spent time in political office, whether federal or state, prior to joining the bench were less likely to defer to their coordinate branch, and justices with state judicial experience showed the same effect, reflecting perhaps socialization through the political or partisan process of judicial selection at the state and local level. Probably the most significant finding in regard to the attitudinal approach was that a Supreme Court justice's vote on the constitutionality of a congressional statute is strongly influenced by the consistency between the policy direction of the statute and the justice's ideological preferences, and to a smaller extent the congruence between the justice's policy preferences and those of the enacting Congress. Thus, a Republican justice was more likely to strike statutes passed by Democratic Congresses and vice versa and, more substantively, Democratic justice had a stronger proclivity toward striking conservative legislation and a Republican justice had a stronger proclivity toward striking liberal legislation. It was significant that these observed attitudinal effects held, even controlling for a variety of institutional and legal factors.

In contrast, the evidence for the strategic model was quite weak. We tested three hypotheses derived from the strategic model that predicted that the justices would be constrained by policy preferences of the sitting Congress; in particular justices would be less likely to vote to nullify in three circumstances: (1) the greater the level of party unification there is among the sitting government (Congress and the president); (2) when there is ideological congruence between the justice and the sitting Congress (when the Court faces a friendly Congress; and (3) when there is ideological consistency between the direction of the statute and the sitting Congress. None of these hypotheses were supported, and at least in examining the full time-period under study, we were left to conclude that strategic approach failed to contribute to our understanding of this somewhat narrow set of votes. In addition, only one of institutional influences demonstrated an effect that was statistically significant at the standard levels of significance; two achieved some-what marginal levels. We saw that controlling for a wide variety of influences, the justices were still less likely to vote to nullify congressional action during the Civil War of the two world wars. We saw that the justices are less likely to strike laws as the longer the statutes have been in effect which is perhaps indicative of the enhanced legitimacy the statute takes on over time, and may support indirectly strategic assumptions as well—that a justice would be less likely to strike a law that through the course of time had assumed greater legitimacy. In addition, we saw that a justice serving as chief justice is less likely to vote to nullify, again sug-gesting the possibility of some strategic concerns or certainly the institutional concern that chief justice's votes might be affected by concerns over the continued legitimacy of the Court as an institution.

Finally, the analysis examined some influences that reflected both attitudinal and/or strategic concerns, testing distinctions in the justices' votes on statutes that either were pro-national supremacy, pro-criminal defendant statute, pro-civil rights and liberties, or pro-judicial power. However, we saw that only the pro-judiciary statute had an influence on the justices' votes, with the justices much more likely to support a statute that enhanced or upheld judicial power generally. Last, we found that the likelihood of a justice voting to nullify or uphold Congress depended in part on the chief justice court on which the justice was serving; justices were much more likely to vote to nullify Congress on the three recent chief justice courts prior to Roberts—Warren, Burger, and Rehnquist. The effect of serving on the Rehnquist bench was about twice of that of Burger and a third more than Warren. The analysis also demonstrated that even controlling for a large number of insti-tutional and attitudinal factors the justices were much less likely to vote to nullify Congress during five chief justiceships: Taney, Fuller, White, Stone, and Vinson.

In the final analyses of the book, we were able to examine the model across var-ious periods of time, using McCloskey's historical periods to demark the periods. The general model did not perform as well in the earliest period, the post–Civil War period, with only a few of the attitudinal influences observable and none of the strategic influences appearing to significantly affect the justices' votes. These results suggested that our current theoretical understanding of judicial behavior may indeed be at least somewhat time-bound, or it may be that our ability to ferret out the various influences are hampered by data limitations backwards in time. But as we examined the early twentieth century we saw a much stronger influence from the attitudinal and institutional factors than in the previous time period, and the strategic approach continued to fail to have an impact on the votes. In the mid-twentieth century period we saw only some influence from the attitudinal model and slim influence from one strategic factor. As we noted above, this period represented a somewhat tenuous time for the Court's legitimacy and future power, and the attenuated results suggested some evidence of a heightened awareness of strategic concerns in that the justices are less likely to vote to nullify unless facing an ideologically compatible Congress. Yet, despite the failure of the various surrogates for the justices' policy preferences, with the exception of religion, those justices with political experience were more likely to vote challenging Congress, suggesting perhaps less heightened awareness or concern for institutional needs than the other justices may demonstrate. When we examined the last three chief justice courts period, the evidence strongly suggested that these recent Supreme Court justice act in ways that are consistent with attitudinal assumptions, but that the attitudinal factors were not sufficient to explain the variation in the justices' behavior. We also saw strong evidence that as we move into the modern Court, the justices' votes are influenced by strategic concerns such as the policy preferences of the sitting Congress. In addition, they also appear to be influenced by institutional concerns, such as protecting the power of the judiciary; however, the other institutional influences are not statistically significant. Thus, as we move across time we see that neither of these preference-based approaches is as robust in the nineteenth century, but there still is significant evidence of attitudinal influences, and certainly much more than that of the strategic influences in those periods. As we move into the twentieth century, the attitudinal effects are stronger as we move across all three periods, but the strategic approach does not begin to show effects until the mid-twentieth century period, and then the influences grow much stronger in the current Court period. So, we are left with some dissatisfaction with our theories' ability to explain judicial behavior beyond the past century.

The strength of the analyses presented here is the examination of both dimensions of judicial review of Congress, both votes to uphold as well as those to nullify, plus the longitudinal depth of the analysis, and the ability to examine a broad set of theoretically important questions over a near complete set of Courts and justices. However the analyses, as with all social science, are limited in other dimensions. The study only examines one component of the Court's exercise of judicial review. It does not examine the larger set of review cases that consider the constitutionality of state statutes, nor does it examine the exercise of review over executive action, which is arguably a small, but potentially more significant, set of decisions. In addition, the measures of policy preferences and attitudes are necessarily surrogates rather than direct measures, and while several of the surrogates appear to be quite robust, the surrogates as a whole appear to have less validity in earlier periods of the Court's history, when our delineation of party affiliation and political ideology may be the most tenuous. I believe we must keep these limitations in mind, but at the same time respect the very fact we are able to identify in many instances the influence of these factors, even while controlling for a broad range of other influences on the justices' votes. Future research should address the Court's additional exercise of review over the popularly elected branches beyond just the current Courts. In addition, scholars should seek to replicate measures, such as the Martin-Quinn scores, for the entire history of the Supreme Court which would also test the robustness of the surrogate measures used thus far. Although scholarly interest in explaining judicial behavior largely focuses on the modern Court, we should not neglect these earlier Courts as well. Ultimately, with the spreading influence of the U.S. model of constitutionalism, and subsequent variations, we should examine our experience, comparatively with the exercise of judicial review in other constitutional democracies, both those that are established and those that are newly developing, if we are to understand fully that which was once referred to as "an American peculiarity."

Bibliography

Abramowitz, Alan I., and Kyle L. Saunders. 1998. "Ideological Realignment in the U.S. Electorate." *Journal of Politics* 60: 634–52.

Ackerman, Bruce. 1991. *We The People Foundations.* Cambridge: Harvard University Press.

Ackerman, Bruce. 1998. *We The People: Transformations.* Cambridge, MA: Harvard University Press.

Adamany, David. 1969. "The Party Variable in Judges' Voting: Conceptual Notes and a Case Study." *American Political Science Review* 63: 57–73.

Aliotta, Jilda M. 1988. "Combining Judges' Attributes and Case Characteristics: An Alternative to Explaining Supreme Court Decisionmaking." *Judicature* 71: 277–81.

Arrington, Theodore S., and Saul Brenner. 2004. "Strategic Voting for Damage Control on the Supreme Court." *Political Research Quarterly* 57: 565–73.

Becker, Theodore. 1970. *Comparative Judicial Politics.* Landham, MD: University Press of America.

Bergera, Mario, Barak Richman, and Pablo T. Spiller. 2003. "Modeling Supreme Court Strategic Decision Making: The Congressional Restraint." *Legislative Studies Quarterly* 28: 247–80.

Bickel, Alexander. 1962. *The Least Dangerous Branch: The Supreme Court at the Bar of Politics.* Indianapolis: Bobbs-Merrill.

Blasi, Gerard J., and David L. Cingranelli. 1996. "Do Constitutions and Institutions Help Protect Human Rights?" In *Human Rights and Developing Countries*, ed. David Cingranelli. Greenwich, CT: JAI Press.

Bork, Robert. 1996. *Slouching to Gomorrah: Modern Liberalism and American Decline.* New York: Regan Books.

Brenner, Saul. 1979. "The New Certiorari Game." *Journal of Politics* 41: 649–55.

Brenner, Saul. 1989. "Ideological Voting on the Vinson Court: A Comparison of Original & Final Votes on the Merits." *Polity:* 22: 157–64.

Brenner, Saul and Harold J. Spaeth. 1995. *Stare Indecisis: The Alteration of Precedent on the Supreme Court, 1946–1992.* New York: Cambridge University Press.

Brenner, Saul and Theodore S. Arrington. 2002. "Measuring Salience on the Supreme Court: A Research Note." *Jurimetrics* 43: 99–113.

Brudney, James J., Sara Schiavoni, and Deborah J. Merritt. 1999. "Judicial Hostility Toward Labor Unions? Applying the Social Background Model to a Celebrated Concern." *Ohio State Law Review* 60: 1675–766.

Caine, Burton. 1988. "The Influence Abroad of the United States Constitution on Judicial Review and a Bill of Rights: Introduction." *Temple International and Comparative Law Journal* 2: 59–78.

Caldiera, Gregory A., and Donald J. McCrone. 1982. "Of Time and Judicial Activism: A Study of the U.S. Supreme Court, 1800–1973." In *Supreme Court Activism and Restraint*, eds. Stephen C. Halpern and Charles M. Lamb. Lexington, MA: Lexington Books.

Caldiera, Gregory A., and John R. Wright. 1988. "Organized Interests and Agenda Setting in the U.S. Supreme Court." *American Political Science Review* 82(4): 1109–127.

Caldiera, Gregory A., and John R. Wright. 1990. "Amici Curiae before the Supreme Court: Who Participates, When, and How Much?" *Journal of Politics* 52: 782–806.

Caplan, Lincoln. 1987. *The Tenth Justice: The Solicitor General and the Rule of Law.* New York: Knopf.

Carp, Robert A., Donald Songer, C.K. Rowland, Ronald Stidham, and Lisa Richey-Tracy. 1993. "The Voting Behavior of Judges Appointed by President Bush." *Judicature* 76: 298.

Casper, Jonathan D. 1976. "The Supreme Court and National Policy Making." *American Political Science Review* 70: 50–63.

Chambers, William Nesbit and Walter Dean Burnham. 1967. *The American Party Systems: States of Political Development.* New York: Oxford Press.

Champagne, Anthony and Stuart S. Nagel. 1982. "The Advocates of Restraint: Holmes, Brandeis, Stone, and Frankfurter." In *Supreme Court Activism and Restraint*, eds. Stephen C. Halpern and Charles M. Lamb. Lexington, MA: Lexington Books.

Chowdhury, Subrata Roy. 1989. *Rule of Law in a State of Emergency.* New York: St. Martin's Press.

Dahl, Robert A. 1957. "Decision-Making in a Democracy: The Supreme Court as a National Policy Maker." *Journal of Public Law* 6: 279–95.

Dahl, Robert A. 1967. *Pluralist Democracy in the United States.* Chicago: Rand McNally & Company.

Danelski, David J. 1989. "The Influence of the Chief Justice in the Decisional Process of the Supreme Court." In *American Court Systems*, eds. Sheldon Goldman and Austin Sarat. New York: Longman.

Danelski, David J. 1992. "Documenting the Establishment of Judicial Review: Japan and the United States." In *Comparative Judicial Review and Public Policy*, eds. Donald W. Jackson and C. Neal Tate. Westport, CT: Greenwood.

Danelski, David J., and Jeanne C. Danelski. 1989. "Leadership in the Warren Court." In *American Court Systems*, eds. Sheldon Goldman and Austin Sarat. New York: Longman.

De Tocqueville, Alexis. 1966. *Democracy in America*, ed. J.P. Mayer. New York: Harper and Row.

Devins, Neal and Keith E. Whittington, eds. 2005. *Congress and the Constitution*. Durham: Duke University Press.

Dilliard, Irving. 1959. *The Spirit of Liberty Papers and Addresses of Judge Learned Hand*. New York: Knopf.

Ducat, Craig and Robert L. Dudley. 1989. "Federal District Judges and Presidential Power During the Postwar Era." *The Journal of Politics* 51: 98–118.

Ely, John Hart. 1980. *Democracy and Distrust: A Theory of Judicial Review*. Cambridge: Harvard University Press.

Epstein, Lee and Jack Knight. 1998. *The Choices Judges Make*. Washington, DC: Congressional Quarterly Press.

Epstein, Lee, Valerie Hoekstra, Jeffrey A. Segal, and Harold J. Spaeth. 1998. "Do Political Preferences Change? A Longitudinal Study of US Supreme Court Justices." *Journal of Politics* 60: 801–18.

Epstein, Lee, Jeffrey A. Segal, and Harold J. Spaeth. 2001. "The Norm of Consensus on the U.S. Supreme Court." *American Journal of Political Science* 45: 362–77.

Epstein, Lee, Jeffrey A. Segal, Harold J. Spaeth, and Thomas G. Walker. 2003. *The Supreme Court Compendium*. Washington, DC: Congressional Quarterly Press.

Epstein, Lee and Thomas G. Walker. 2007. *Constitutional Law for a Changing America: Institutional Powers and Constraints*, 6th edition. Washington, DC: Congressional Quarterly Press.

Epstein, Richard. 2000. "Undue Restraint: Why Judicial Activism Has Its Place." *National Review* 52: 26.

Eskridge, William N. 1991. "Overriding Supreme Court Statutory Interpretation Decisions." *Yale Law Journal* 101: 331–455.

Ferejohn, John. 1999. "Independent Judges, Dependent Judiciary: Explaining Judicial Independence." *South California Law Review* 72: 353–84.

Ferejohn, John, Frances Rosenbluth, and Charles Shipan. 2004. "Comparative Judicial Politics." Manuscript available at: www.yaleuniversity.net/polisci/rosenbluth/Papers/comparative%20judicial%20politics.pdf

Ferejohn, John A., and Charles Shipan. 1990. "Congressional Influence on Bureaucracy." *Journal of Law, Economics, and Organization* 6: 1–20.

Frank, Jerome. 1949. *Law and the Modern Mind*. New York: Coward-McCann.

Friedman, Barry and Anna Harvey. 2003. "Electing the Supreme Court." *Indiana Law Journal* 78: 123–39.

Funston, Richard. 1975. "The Supreme Court and Critical Elections." *American Political Science Review* 69: 795–811.

Gamble, Barbara S. 1997 "Putting Civil Rights to a Popular Vote." *American Journal of Political Science* 41: 245–69.

Garro, Alejandro. 1993. "Nine Years to Democracy in Argentina: Partial Failure or Qualified Success?" *Columbia Journal of Transnational Law* 31: 1–102.

George, Tracey E., and Lee Epstein. 1992. "On the Nature of Supreme Court Decision Making." *American Political Science Review* 86 (3): 323–37.

Geyh, Charles Gardner. 2006. *When Courts and Congress Collide: The Struggle for Control of America's Judicial System.* Ann Arbor: University of Michigan Press.

Gibson, James. 1978. "Judges' Role Orientations, Attitudes, and Decisions: An Interactive Model." *American Political Science Review* 86: 323–37.

Glennon, Michael J. "The Use of Custom in Resolving Separation of Powers Disputes." *Boston University Law Review* 64: 109–48.

Glick, Henry R., and Kenneth N. Vines. 1969. "Law-making in the State Judiciary: A Comparative Study of the Judicial Role in Four States." *Polity* 2: 142–59.

Goldman, Sheldon. 1966. "Voting Behavior of the United States Courts of Appeals, 1961–1964. *American Political Science Review* 60: 374–84.

Goldman, Sheldon. 1975. "Voting Behavior of the United States Courts of Appeals Revisited. *American Political Science Review* 69: 491–506.

Goldman, Sheldon. 1982. *Constitutional Law and Supreme Court Decision-Making: Cases and Essays.* New York: Harper & Row.

Gottschall, Jon. 1986. "Reagan's Appointments to the U.S. Courts of Appeals: The Continuation of a Judicial Revolution." *Judicature* 70: 50–54.

Graber, Mark A. 1993. "The Non-Majoritarian Difficulty: Legislative Deference to the Judiciary." *Studies in American Political Development* 7: 35–73.

Gryski, Gerard S., Eleanor C. Main, and William J. Dixon, 1986. "Social Backgrounds as Predictors of Votes on State Courts of Last Resort: The Case of Sex Discrimination." *Western Political Quarterly* 39: 528–37.

Handberg, Roger and Harold Hill. 1981. "Court-curbing, Court Reversal, and Judicial Review: The Supreme Court versus Congress." *Law and Society Review* 14: 309–22.

Hansford, Thomas and David F. Damore. 2000. "Congressional Preferences, Perceptions of Threat, and Supreme Court Decision Making." *American Politics Quarterly* 28: 490–510.

Haynie, Stacia L. 1992. "Leadership and Consensus on the U.S. Supreme Court." *The Journal of Politics* 54: 1158–69.

Howard, Robert M., and Jeffrey A. Segal. 2004. "A Preference for Deference? The Supreme Court and Judicial Review." *Political Research Quarterly* 57(1): 131–43.

Howard, J. Woodford Jr. 1977. "Role Perceptions and Behavior in Three U.S. Courts of Appeals." *Journal of Politics* 39: 916–38.

Hurwitz, Mark S. and Joseph V. Stefko. 2004. "Acclimation and Attitudes: Newcomer Justices and Precedent Conformance on the Supreme Court." *Political Research Quarterly* 57: 121–29.

Ignagni, Joseph and James Meernik. 1994. "Explaining Congressional Attempts to Reverse Supreme Court Decisions." *Political Research Quarterly* 47: 353–71.

International Commission of Jurists. 1983. *States of Emergency: Their Impact on Human Rights.* Geneva: International Commission of Jurists.

Keck, Thomas. 2002. "Activism and Restraint on the Rehnquist Court: Timing, Sequence, and Conjuncture in Constitutional Development." *Polity* 35: 121–52.

Keck, Thomas. 2004. *The Most Activist Supreme Court in History: The Road to Modern Judicial Conservatism.* Chicago: University of Chicago Press.

Keck, Thomas. 2007. "Party, Policy, or Duty: Why Does the Supreme Court Invalidate Federal Statutes?" *American Political Science Review* 101: 321–39.

Keith, Linda Camp. 2002. "International Principles for Formal Judicial Independence: Trends in National Constitutions and Their Impact (1976 to 1996)." *Judicature* 85: 194–200.

Keith, Linda Camp. 2002. "Constitutional Provisions for Individual Human Rights (1976–1996): Are They More than Mere 'Window Dressing?' *Political Research Quarterly* (March) 55: 111–43.

Keith, Linda Camp. 2004. "National Constitutions and Human Rights Protection": Regional Differences and Colonial Influences." In *The Systematic Study of Human Rights*, eds. Sabine Carey and Steven C. Poe London: Ashgate Publishing.

Keith, Linda Camp. 2007. "The United States Supreme Court and Judicial Review of Congress: 1803–2001." *Judicature* (January/February 2007) 90: 1–14.

Keith, Linda Camp and Ayo Ogundele. 2007. "Legal Systems and Constitutionalism in Sub-Saharan Africa: An Empirical Examination of Colonial Influences on Human Rights." *Human Rights Quarterly* 29(4):1065–1097.

Keith, Linda Camp, C. Neal Tate, and Steven C. Poe. 2007. "Is the Law a Mere Parchment Barrier to Human Rights Abuse?" Unpublished manuscript.

King, Kimi and James Meernik. 1999. "The Supreme Court and the Powers of the Executive: The Adjudication of Foreign Policy." *Political Research Quarterly* 52: 801–824.

Knight, Jack and Lee Epstein. 1996. "On the Struggle for Judicial Supremacy." *Law and Society Review* 30: 87–120.

Ladd, Everett Carll, Jr. 1970. *American Political Parties: Social Change and Political Response.* New York: Norton Press.

Lamb, Charles. 1982. "A Preference for Difference?" *Political Research Quarterly* 57: 131–43.

Lamb, Charles and Stephen Halpern. 1992. *Supreme Court Activism and Restraint.* Lexington, MA: Heath.

Lanier, Drew Noble. 2003. *Of Time and Judicial Behavior: United Supreme Court Agenda-Setting and Decision-Making, 1888–1997.* London: Susquehanna University Press.

Lanier, Drew Noble and Sandra L. Wood. 2001. "Moving on Up: Institutional Position, Politics, and the Chief Justice." *American Review of Politics* 22: 93–1271

Larkins, Christopher M. 1996. "Judicial Independence and Democratization: A Theoretical and Conceptual Analysis." *American Journal of Comparative Law* 44: 605–26.

Lindquist, Stephanie A., and Rorie Spill Solberg. 2007. "Judicial Review by the Burger and Rehnquist Courts: Explaining Justices' Responses to Constitutional Challenges." *Political Research Quarterly* 60: 71–90.

Lipset, Seymour M., and Stein Rokkan. 1967. "Cleavage Structures, Party Systems and Voter Alignments: An Introduction." In *Party Systems and Voter Alignments: Cross-National Perspectives*, eds. Seymour M. Lipset,and Stein Rokkan. New York: The Free Press.

Llewellyn, Karl. 1931. "Some Realism about Realism—Responding to Dean Pound." *Harvard Law Review* 44: 1222–64.

Madison, James. 1789. "Federalist No, 48." In eds. Kurland and Lerner. The Founder's Constitution, http://press-pubs.uchicago.edu/founders/documents/v1ch10s15.html.

Maltzman, Forest, James F. Spriggs III, and Paul Wahlbeck. 2000. *Crafting Law on the Supreme Court: The Collegial Game.* Cambridge, UK: Cambridge University Press.

Marks, Brian. 1988. "A Model of Judicial Influence on Congressional Policymaking: *Grove City College v. Bell.*" Working papers in Political Science, 88–87, Hoover Institution, Stanford University.

McCloskey, Robert. G. 1994. *The American Supreme Court.* Chicago: University of Chicago Press.

McGuire, Kevin. 1998. "Explaining Executive Success in the U.S. Supreme Court." *Political Research Quarterly* 51: 505–26.

Meernik, James and Joseph Ignagni. 1997. "Congressional Attacks on Supreme Court Rulings Involving Unconstitutional State Laws." *Political Research Quarterly* 48(1): 43–59.

Meese, Edwin. 1985. "The Attorney General's View of the Supreme Court: Toward a Jurisprudence of Original Intention." In *Law and Politics,* Special Issue, ed. Charles Wise and David M. O'Brien. *Public Administration Review 45:* 701–04

Murphy, Walter F. 1964. *Elements of Judicial Strategy.* Chicago: University of Chicago Press.

Nagel, Stuart S. 1961. "Political Party Affiliation and Judges' Decisions." *American Political Science Review* 55: 843–50.

Nardulli, Peter F. 1995. "The Concept of a Critical Realignment, Electoral Behavior, and Political Change." *American Political Science Review* 89: 10–22.

Ogundele, Ayo and Linda Camp Keith. 2006. "The Supreme Court: An Empirical Overview." Paper presented at the annual meeting of the Southern Political Science Association, Jan. 3–6, New Orleans, LA.

Pacelle, Richard. 2003. *Between Law and Politics: The Solicitor General and the Structuring of Race, Gender, and Reproductive Rights Policy.* College Station, TX: A&M Press.

Parker, Richard. 1981. "The Past of Constitutional Theory—And Its Future." *Ohio State Law Review* 43: 233.

Perry, H.W. Jr. 1991. *Deciding to Decide.* Cambridge, Massachusetts: Harvard University Press.

Pickerill, J. Mitchell. 2005. "Congressional Responses to Judicial Review." In *Congress and the Constitution,* eds. Neal Devins and Keith E. Whittington. Durham: Duke University Press.

Poole, Keith T. and Howard Rosenthal. 1997. *Congress: A Political-Economic History of Roll-Call Voting.* New York: Oxford Press.

Powe, Lucas A. Jr. 2000. *The Warren Court and American Politics.* Cambridge, MA: Belknap Press.

Pritchett, C. Herman. 1948. *The Roosevelt Court: A Study in Judicial Politics and Values.* New York: McMillan Press.

Pritchett, C. Herman. 1954. *Civil Liberties and the Vinson Court.* Chicago: University of Chicago Press.

Rehnquist, William H. 1998. *All the Laws but One: Civil Liberties in Wartime.* Knopf: New York.

Reichley, James. 1992. *The Life of the Parties: A History of American Political Parties.* New York: The Free Press.

Rohde, David W., and Harold J. Spaeth. 1976. *Supreme Court Decision Making.* San Francisco, CA: W.H. Freeman.

Roncek, Dennis W., and Marc L. Swatt. 2006. "For Those Who Like Odds: A Direct Interpretation of the Logit Coefficients for Continuous Variables." *Social Science Quarterly* 87: 731–38.

Rosen, Jeffrey. 2006. *The Most Democratic Branch: How the Courts Serve America.* New York: Oxford University Press.

Rosenn, Keith S. 1987. "The Protection of Judicial Independence in Latin America." *University of Miami Inter-American Law Review* 19: 1–35.

Sala, Brian R. and James F. Spriggs. 2004. "Designing Tests of the Supreme Court and the Separation of Powers." *Political Research Quarterly* 57: 197–208.

Savage, David G. 1992. *Turning Right: The Making of the Rehnquist Court.* New York: John Wiley and Sons.

Scheb, John M., Thomas D. Ungs, and Allison L. Hayes. 1989. "Judicial Role Orientations, Attitudes, and Decision-Making: A Research Note." *Western Political Quarterly* 42: 427–35.

Schmidhauser, John. 1961. "Judicial Behavior and the Sectional Crisis of 1837–1860." *Journal of Politics* 23: 615–27.

Schubert, Glendon A. 1965. *The Judicial Mind.* Evanston IL: Northwestern University Press.

Schubert, Glendon A. 1974. *The Judicial Mind Revisited: Psychometric Analysis of the Supreme Court Ideology.* New York: Oxford Press.

Schwartz, Bernard. 1993. *A History of the Supreme Court.* New York: Oxford University Press.

Schwartz, Bernard and Steven Lesher. 1983. *Inside the Warren Court:* 1953–1969. New York: Doubleday.

Schwartz, Herman. 2002. *The Rehnquist Court: Judicial Activism on the Right.* New York: Hill and Wang.

Segal, Jeffrey A. 1988. "Amicus Curiae Briefs by the Solicitor General during the Warren and Burger Courts." *Western Political Quarterly* 41: 135–44.

Segal, Jeffrey A. 1997. "Separation of Powers Games in the Positive Theory of Congress and Courts." *American Political Science Review* 91: 28–44.

Segal, Jeffrey A., and Albert Cover. 1989. "Ideological Values and the Votes of U.S. Supreme Court Justices." *American Political Science Review* 83: 557–65.

Segal, Jeffrey A., and Chad Westerland. 2005. "The Supreme Court, Congress, and Judicial Review." *North Carolina Law Review* 83: 101–166.

Segal, Jeffrey A., and Harold J. Spaeth. 1993. *The Supreme Court and the Attitudinal Model.* Cambridge: Cambridge University Press.

Segal, Jeffrey A., and Harold J. Spaeth. 2002. *The Supreme Court and the Attitudinal Model Revisited.* Cambridge: Cambridge University Press.

Segal, Jeffrey A., Lee Epstein, Charles M. Cameron, and Harold D. Spaeth. 1995. "Ideological Values and the Votes of U.S. Supreme Court Justices Revisited." *Journal of Politics* 57: 812–23.

Segal, Jeffrey A., Robert M. Howard, and Richard J. Timpone. 2000. *Political Research Quarterly* 53: 557–573.

Shapiro, Martin. 1981. *Courts: Comparative and Political Analysis.* Chicago: University of Chicago Press.

Sherry, Suzanna. 1998. "Independent Judges and Independent Justice." *Law & Contemporary Problems* 61: 15–20

Slotnick, Elliot E. 1987. "The Place of Judicial Review in the American Tradition: the Emergence of an Eclectic Power." *Judicature* 71(2): 68–79.

Solberg, Rorie Spill and Stephanie Lindquist. 2006. "Activism, Ideology, and Federalism: Judicial Behavior in Constitutional Challenges Before the Rehnquist Court, 1986–2000." *Journal of Empirical Legal Studies* 3: 237–61.

Songer, Donald R., and Sue Davis. 1990. "The Impact of Party and Region on Voting Decisions in the United States Courts of Appeals." *The Western Political Quarterly* 43: 317–35.

Spiller, Pablo T., and Rafael Gely. 1992. "Congressional Control or Judicial Independence: The Determinants of U.S. Supreme Court Labor-Relations Decisions, 1949–1988." *RAND Journal of Economics* 23: 463–92.

Spiller, Pablo T., and Emerson H. Tiller. 1996. "Invitations to Override: Congressional Reversals of Supreme Court Decisions." *International Review of Law and Economics* 16: 503–21.

Spriggs, James F. III and Thomas G. Hansford. 2001. "Explaining the Overruling of U.S. Supreme Court Precedent." *Journal of Politics* 63: 1091–1111.

Stotzky, Irwin P. 1993. "The Tradition of Constitutional Adjudication." In *Transitions to Democracy in Latin America: The Role of the Judiciary*, ed. Irwin P. Stotzky. Boulder, CO: Westview.

Sunstein, Cass R. 2005. *Radicals in Robes: Why Right-Wing Courts are Wrong for America.* Chicago: University of Chicago Press.

Swisher, Carl b. 1974. *History of the Supreme Court of the United States, the Taney Period 1836–1864.* New York: Macmillan Publishing Co.

Tanenhaus, Joseph, Marvin Schick, Matthew Muraskin, and Daniel Rosen. 1963. "The Supreme Court's Certiorari Jurisdiction: Cue Theory." In *Judicial Decision-Making*, ed. Glendon Schubert. New York: Free Press.

Tate C. Neal. 1981. "Personal Attribute Models of the Voting Behavior of U.S. Supreme Court Justices: Liberalism in Civil Liberties and Economic Decisions, 1946–1978." *American Political Science Review* 75: 355–67.

Tate C. Neal and Panu Sittiwong. 1989. "Decision Making in the Canadian Supreme Court: Extending the Personal Attributes Model Across Nations." *Journal of Politics* 51: 900–916.

Tate C. Neal and Roger Handberg. 1991. "Time Building and Theory Building in Personal Attribute Models of Supreme Court Voting Behavior, 1916–88." *American Journal of Political Science* 35: 460–80.

Tushnet, Robert. 1999. *Taking the Constitution Away from the Courts.* Princeton: Princeton University Press.

Ulmer, Sidney S. 1972. "The Decision to Grant Certiorari as an Indicator to Decision 'On the Merits.'" *Polity* 4: 429–47.

Ulmer, Sidney S. 1973. "Social Background as an Indicator to the Votes of Supreme Court Justices in Criminal Cases: 1947–1956 Terms." *American Journal of Political Science* 17: 622–30.

Ulmer, Sidney S. 1981. *Courts, Law, and Judicial Processes.* London: Free Press.

Wahlbeck, Paul J., James F. Spriggs, and Forrest Maltzman. 1999. "The Politics of Dissents and Concurrences on the U.S. Supreme Court." *American Politics Research* 27: 488–514.

Walker, Thomas G., Lee Epstein, and William J. Dixon. 1988. "On the Mysterious Demise of Consensual Norms in the United States Supreme Court." *Journal of Politics* 50: 361–89.

Weschler, Herbert. 1959. "Toward Neutral Principles of Constitutional Law." *Harvard Law Review* 73: 1–35.

Whittington, Keith. 2005. "Interpose Your Friendly Hand: Political Supports for the Exercise of Judicial Review by the United States Supreme Court." *American Political Science Review* 99: 583–96.

Wold, John T. 1974. "Political Orientations, Social Backgrounds, and Role Perceptions of State Supreme Court Judges." *The Western Political Quarterly* 27: 239–48.

Wood, Sandra, Linda Camp Keith, Drew Lanier, and Ayo Ogundele. 1998. "The Supreme Court 1888–1940: An Empirical Overview." *Social Science History* 22: 204–24.

Wood, Sandra, Linda Camp Keith, Drew Lanier, and Ayo Ogundele. 2000. "Opinion Assignment and the Chief Justice: 1888–1940." *Social Science Quarterly* 81: 798–809.

Yates, Jeff and Andrew Whitford. 1998. "Presidential Power and the United States Supreme Court." *Political Research Quarterly* 51: 539–50.

Zorn, Christopher. 2006. "Comparing GEE and Robust Standard Errors for Conditionally Dependent Data." *Political Research Quarterly* 59: 329–41.

Index

Abramowitz, Alan I., 111, 123, 183
Ackerman, Bruce, 2, 3, 18, 55
Adamany, David, 142, 169, 183
Adams, John, 62
Age of statute, 109–10, 149, 155, 158, 160–63
Aliotta, Jilda, 141, 169, 183
Armed forces clause, 55
Arrington, Theodore S., 123, 183
Arthur, Chester, 63, 74
Ashwander principles, 24–45
Attitudinal model, 2, 7–16, 60, 128–41, 154–67, 179–81
Attributes, justices, 146–48, 152–67

Baldwin, Henry, 61–62
Barbour, Phillip, 61–62
Becker, Theodore, 3, 18, 95, 100, 106, 123, 183
Beckers v. Cummings Steel, 25
Bergera, Mario, 131, 169, 183
Bickel, Alexander, 1–2, 18, 183
Bingham v. U.S., 25
Black, Hugo, 65, 69, 72–73, 81, 89, 95, 96–97

Blackmun, Harry, 65, 69, 73, 77, 80–81, 93, 98
Blasi, Gerard J., 3, 18, 183
Blatchford, Samuel, 63, 70, 78, 84, 100
Bork, Robert, 2, 18, 128, 147, 154, 162, 169, 183
Bradley, Joseph, 63, 68, 70, 78, 84
Brandeis, Louis, 24, 64, 67, 71, 75, 79, 88, 97
Brennan, William, 65, 72, 76, 80–81, 91, 95, 97–98, 118, 139
Brenner, Saul, 12, 18, 123, 183, 184
Brewer, David, 63, 71, 78, 85
Breyer, Stephen, 66, 69, 73, 77, 80, 94–95, 100
Brown, Henry, 63, 67–68, 71, 78, 85
Brudney, James J., 144–46, 169, 184
Buchanan, James, 63, 66, 70
Burger, Warren, 9–10, 13–14, 23, 40–41, 44, 51, 65, 69, 73, 77, 80–81, 92, 96, 129, 135–36, 138, 150, 154, 156, 166, 176, 180, 190
Burnham, Walter D., 111, 123, 184
Burton, Harold, 67, 68, 72, 76, 79, 82, 91, 98

Bush, George H. W., 66, 73, 77
Butler, Pierce, 64, 68–69, 71, 75, 79, 89
Byrnes, James, 65, 67

Caine, Burton, 106, 123, 184
Caldeira, Gregory A., 27–28, 30–31,
    34–35, 52, 133, 135
Cameron, Charles M., 8, 21, 128,
    136, 140, 172, 190
Campbell, John, 63, 66
Caplan, Lincoln, 135, 169, 184
Cardozo, Benjamin, 65, 72, 75, 79, 89
Carp, Robert A., 141, 169, 184
Casper, Jonathan D., 3, 7, 18, 103,
    107–11, 123, 184
Catron, John, 62, 67–70, 74, 78, 81
Chambers, William N., 111, 123, 184
Champagne, Anthony, 918, 184
Chase, Salmon P., 40–43, 53, 61, 63,
    68, 70, 78, 83, 97, 150, 156
Chase, Samuel, 62
Chisholm v. Georgia, 16
Chowdhury, Subrata R., 18, 29, 55,
    101, 123, 184
Cingranelli, David L., 3, 18, 183
Clark, Tom, 65, 67, 72, 76, 79, 81, 91, 98
Clarke, John, 64, 71, 79, 81, 88
Cleveland, Grover, 63–64, 71, 74–75
Clifford, Nathan, 63, 66, 68, 70, 78, 83, 97
Clinton, William J., 66, 73, 77
Civil rights, 6, 8, 14, 36–38, 43, 45,
    54, 69, 75–76, 82–100, 117–24,
    133–46, 151, 153, 155, 158–65
Coin money clause, 55
Commerce clause, 55, 100
Consolidated Omnibus Budget
    Reconciliation Act, 97
Coolidge, Calvin, 64, 72, 75
Cover, Albert, 8, 21, 128, 136, 140,
    172, 190

Criminal procedure, 14, 17, 44–55,
    82, 100, 118–21, 152–67, 176, 180
Curtis, Benjamin, 63, 66, 74
Cushing, William, 61–62

Dahl, Robert A., 3, 7, 18, 103, 107–9,
    111, 123, 184
Damore, David F., 11–12, 19, 131,
    170, 186
Danelski, David J., 55, 69, 101, 105–6,
    123, 134, 169, 184–85
Danelski, Jeanne C., 134, 169, 185
Daniel, Peter, 61–62
Davis, David, 63, 70, 78, 83
Davis, Sue, 141, 143, 172, 190
Day, William, 64, 71, 79, 85
De Tocqueville, Alexis, 1, 18, 105,
    124, 185
Devanter, Willis, 64–65, 71, 79, 87
Devins, Neal, 19, 21, 125, 171, 185, 189
Dilliard, Irving, 2, 19, 185
District of Columbus clause, 55
Dixon, William J., 134–35, 141, 170,
    173, 186, 191
Douglas, William, O., 60, 65–66, 69, 72,
    74, 76, 79, 81, 90, 95, 97–98, 118,
    139, 162
Ducat, Craig, 17, 19, 185
Dudley, Robert L., 17, 19, 185
Due process, 14, 17, 45–54, 82, 100,
    118–20, 151, 167, 176
Duignan v. U.S., 24
Duvall, Gabriel, 61–62

Economic issues, 8, 17, 36–39, 42–54,
    69, 75–77, 82–100, 118–20, 128,
    136, 142–51, 176
Eisenhower, Dwight, D., 65, 72
Ely, John H., 1–2, 19, 185
Enemy Alien Act, 108

Epstein, Lee, 8, 11–13, 18–19, 19–21, 45, 53, 55, 60, 101, 109, 119, 124, 127–28, 130–31, 134–36, 139–42, 144–45, 147–48, 170, 172–73, 185–86
Epstein, Richard, 19, 186
Eskridge, William N., 11–12, 19, 130–31, 170, 185

Ferejohn, John, 5, 7, 11, 17, 19, 36, 104, 112–15, 118, 124, 130–32, 139, 170, 185
Field, Stephen, 62, 68, 70, 78, 83, 97
First Amendment, 14, 46–55, 100, 118–21, 136, 151, 176
Ford, Gerald, 66, 73
Fort Laramie Treaty of 1868, 108
Fortas, Abe, 65–66, 72, 74, 76–77, 80–81, 92, 95
Fourteenth Amendment, 16, 55
Frank, Jerome, 19, 170, 185
Frankfurter, Felix, 65, 67–68, 72, 76, 79, 90, 97–98
Friedman, Barry, 3, 5, 7, 12, 19, 104–5, 113, 124, 132, 170, 185
Fuller, Melville, 40–41, 43, 63, 68, 71, 78, 84, 150, 153, 156, 166, 180
Funston, Richard 3, 19, 103, 111–12, 124, 185

Gamble, Barbara S., 121, 124, 186
Garro, Alejandro, 3, 19, 95, 101, 107, 124, 186
Gely, Rafael, 11, 131, 173, 190
George, Tracey E., 19, 60, 101, 128, 141–42, 170, 186
Geyh, Charles G., 6–7, 19, 26–27, 36, 54, 56, 104–5, 124, 186
Gibson, James, 146, 170, 186
Ginsburg, Ruth Bader, 66, 69, 73, 77, 80–81, 94–95, 100

Glennon, Michael J., 26, 56, 186
Glick, Henry R., 129, 170, 186
Goldberg, Arthur, 65, 72, 76, 80, 92, 95
Goldman, Sheldon 9, 19, 37, 55–56, 101, 129, 136, 139, 142, 146, 156, 169, 170, 184–86
Gottschall, Jon, 141, 179, 186
Graber, Mark A., 4, 19, 103–4, 124, 186
Grant, Ulysses S., 42, 63, 70, 74
Gray, Horace, 63, 70, 78, 84, 97
Grier, Robert, 63, 68, 70, 78, 83
Gryski, Gerard S., 141, 170, 186

Halpern, Stephen C., 18, 55, 169, 184, 187
Hamilton, Alexander, 39, 105
Handberg, Roger, 3, 8, 22, 60, 102, 128, 136, 140–45, 146, 156, 168, 173, 186
Hansford, Thomas, 12–13, 19, 21, 131, 170, 173, 186, 190
Harding, Warren G., 64, 71, 75
Harlan, John Marshall I, 63, 70, 84
Harlan, John Marshall, II, 65, 67, 72, 76, 79, 84, 91
Harrison, Benjamin, 63, 71
Harvey, Anna, 3, 5, 7, 12, 19, 104–5, 113, 155, 124, 132, 170, 185
Hayes, Allison L., 129, 172, 189
Hayes, Rutherford B., 63, 70
Haynie, Stacia L., 134, 159, 170, 186
Hazardous Liquid Pipeline Safety Act of 1979, 97 *Hepburn v. Griswold*, 42
Hoekstra, Valerie, 8, 19, 127, 170, 185
Holmes, Oliver Wendell, Jr., 64, 67, 71, 79, 85, 97, 134
Hoover, Herbert, 65, 72, 75
Howard, Robert M., 10, 12–13, 17, 19, 21, 36, 53, 56, 95, 101, 106, 124, 128–29, 132–34, 138, 171, 186, 190

Hughes, Charles Evan, 40–44, 64, 71, 79, 97, 150
Hunt, Ward, 63, 70, 74, 78
Hurwitz, Mark S., 135, 186
Hylton v. U.S., 54

Ideology, 8–15, 37–42, 48–60, 76, 79–100, 128–29, 133, 138, 140–42, 157–67, 178, 182
Ignagni, Joseph, 3, 5, 11, 20, 131–32, 187, 188
INS v. Chadha, 6, 105, 110, 131
Institutional context, 8, 10–17, 67, 127–38, 154–59, 162–67, 179–81
International Commission of Jurists, 3, 20, 29, 56, 95, 101, 106, 124, 187

Jackson, Andrew, 17, 41, 62
Jackson, Howell, 64, 66, 70, 76
Jackson, Robert, 65, 67, 72, 76, 79
Jefferson, Thomas, 17, 39, 62, 111
Johnson, Lyndon B., 65, 72, 77
Johnson, William, 61–62
Judges Act, 153, 155, 159–60, 169
Judicial independence, 2, 6–7, 16, 26, 104–5, 113
Judicial power, 129, 136–37, 150, 153, 156, 158, 163–64, 166, 176, 180–81

Keck, Thomas, 20, 37, 56, 106, 124, 129, 137, 162, 171, 187
Keith, Linda Camp, 3, 20, 29, 42–44, 48, 52, 56–57, 75, 82, 95, 97, 101–2, 107, 124, 134, 138, 159, 171, 173, 187–88, 191–92
Kennedy, Anthony, 45, 65–66, 69, 72–73, 77, 80, 94, 97, 97, 130
Kennedy, John F., 65, 72
King, Kimi, 10, 20, 27, 56, 137–39, 171, 187
Knight, Jack, 11–13, 18–20, 119, 124, 130–31, 139, 170, 185, 187

Ladd, Everett C., 39–40, 56, 75, 187
Lamar, Joseph, 64–65, 71, 75, 79, 87
Lamar, Lucius Q.C., 63, 71, 74, 78
Lamb, Charles, 18, 55–56, 169, 184, 187
Lanier, Drew N., 43–44, 48, 56–57, 82, 97, 102, 134, 171, 173, 187, 191
Larkins, Christopher M., 3, 20, 95, 101, 107, 124, 137, 188
Legal Tender Cases, The, 42
Lesher, Steven, 68, 102, 190
Lincoln, Abraham, 39, 63, 70
Lindquist, Stephanie A., 10, 12–13, 20–21, 56, 102, 128–29, 132–33, 136, 138–39, 151, 171–72, 188, 190
Lipset, Seymour M., 143, 171, 188
Livingston, Brockholst, 61–62
Ludecke v. Watkins, 108
Lurton, Horace, 64, 71, 75, 79, 81, 85, 106, 135

Madison, James, 28, 62, 105, 124, 188
Main, Eleanor C., 141, 170, 186
Majoritarian issues, 2–4, 8, 15–18, 23, 103–23, 176–77
Maltzman, Forrest, 11–12, 20, 130, 134, 171, 173, 188, 191
Marbury v. Madison, 28, 105
Marks, Brian, 11, 20, 130, 171, 188
Marshall, John, 17, 28–29, 40, 42, 53, 61–62, 68, 74, 106, 150
Marshall, Thurgood, 8, 65, 72, 76, 77, 80–81, 92, 95, 98, 139
Matthews, Stanley, 63, 70, 78
McCloskey, Robert G., 28–32, 41–42, 53, 56, 101, 106, 124, 134, 159, 171, 188
McCrone, Donald J., 27–28, 30, 32, 52, 55, 135, 169, 184
McCurdy v. U.S., 24
McGuire, Kevin, 133, 171, 188
McKenna, Joseph, 64, 71, 75, 78, 86, 168

McKinley, John, 61–62, 64, 71, 111
McKinley, William, 64, 71
McLean, John, 62, 67, 70, 74, 78, 81
McReynolds, James, 64, 68–69, 71, 75, 79, 87, 97–98
Meernik, James, 3, 5, 10–11, 20, 56, 131–32, 137–39, 171, 187
Meese, Edwin, 128, 171, 188
Merritt, Deborah J., 144–46, 169, 184
Miller, Samuel, 63, 70, 78, 83
Minton, Sherman, 65, 67–68, 72, 76, 79, 91, 95
Monroe, James, 62
Moody, William, 64, 68, 71, 75, 79
Moor v. Texas, 24
Moore, Alfred, 61–62
Murphy, Frank, 65, 72, 76, 79, 81, 91, 95, 96–97
Murphy, Walter F., 11, 20, 130, 171, 188

Nagel, Stuart S., 18, 142, 145, 171, 184, 188
Nardulli, Peter F., 111, 125, 188
Natural Gas Pipeline Safety Act of 1969, 97
Necessary and proper clause, 55
Nelson, Samuel, 62, 70, 74, 78, 83
Nixon, Richard M., 65, 73

O'Connor, Sandra Day, 45, 66, 73, 77, 80, 93, 97
Ogundele, Ayo, 3, 20, 42–44, 48, 56–57, 75, 82, 95, 97, 100–2, 107, 124, 134, 159, 173, 187, 188
Oregon v. Mitchell, 6, 16, 105, 108, 131

Pacelle, Richard, 133, 171, 188
Parker, Richard, 1, 20, 188
Paterson, William, 61–62
Peckham, Rufus, 64, 71, 75, 78, 85, 95, 97
Perry, H.W., 13, 20, 189

Pickerill, J. Mitchell, 4, 6, 17, 21, 105, 125, 131, 171, 189
Pierce, Franklin, 63
Pitney, Mahlon, 64, 71, 79, 81, 87
Political party, 3–7, 10, 17, 38–39, 60, 70–74, 103, 111–16, 132, 139, 142–67, 177–82
Polk, James K., 63, 70
Pollock v. Farmer's Loan, 16
Poole, Keith T., 82, 101, 189
Postal powers clause, 55
Powell, Lewis, 66, 69, 73, 77, 80–81, 93
Pritchett, C. Herman, 8, 21, 156, 171, 189

Reagan, Ronald, 66, 73
Reed, Stanley, 65, 67, 72, 76, 79
Rehnquist, William H., 5, 8–10, 13–14, 17–18, 23, 34–37, 40–42, 44–45, 51, 66–67, 69, 73, 77, 80–81, 93, 97, 115, 123, 128–30, 134–36, 138, 148, 150, 154, 156, 166, 168, 176, 180
Reichley, James, 38–39, 57, 113, 116, 125, 172, 189
Reineche v. Northern Trust, 25
Richman, Barak 131, 169, 183
Roberts, Owen, 65, 69, 72, 75, 79, 89
Rokkan, Stein, 143, 171, 188
Roncek, Dennis W., 152, 172, 189
Roosevelt, Franklin, 15, 65, 72, 77, 98, 178
Roosevelt, Theodore, 27, 64, 71, 75
Rosenbluth, Frances 131, 170, 185
Rosenn, Keith S., 3, 21, 95, 101, 168, 172, 189
Rosenthal, Howard, 82, 101, 189
Rutledge, Wiley, 65, 72, 76, 79

Sala, Brian R., 9, 12, 21, 132–33, 172, 189
Sanford, Edward, 64, 71, 75, 79, 89, 97
Saunders, Kyle L., 111, 123, 184
Savage, David G., 37, 57, 189

Scalia, Antonin, 45, 60, 66–67, 69, 73, 77, 80–82, 93, 97, 129, 148, 162
Scheb, John M., 129, 172, 189
Schenck v. U.S., 168
Schiavoni, Sara, 144–46, 169, 184
Schmidhauser, John, 142, 146, 172, 189
Schubert, Glendon, 8–9, 21, 100–1, 136, 172–73, 189
Schwartz, Bernard, 37, 41–42, 44, 53, 57, 67–68, 74–75, 98, 101–2, 189–90
Schwartz, Herman, 37, 57, 162, 172, 190
Scott v. Sandford, 16, 42
Segal, Jeffrey A., 8–9, 11–13, 16–17, 19, 21, 36–37, 42, 45, 53, 55–57, 60, 82, 95, 101–2, 106, 109, 124, 127–28, 130–34, 136, 138, 140, 170–72, 185–86, 190
Shapiro, Martin, 137, 172, 190
Sherry, Suzanna, 106, 125, 190
Shipan, Charles, 11, 19, 130–31, 170, 185
Shiras, George, 64, 71, 78, 85
Sittiwong, Panu, 142–43, 146, 173, 191
Sixteenth Amendment, 16, 55
Sixth Amendment, 108
Skinner v. Mid-American Pipeline, 97
Slotnick, Elliot E., 106, 125, 138, 172, 190
Solberg, Rorie Spill, 10, 12–13, 20–21, 56, 102, 128–29, 132–33, 136, 138–39, 151, 171–72, 188, 190
Solicitor General, 12, 168
Songer, Donald R., 142–43, 169, 172, 190
Souter, David, 66, 69, 73, 77, 80–81, 94–95
Spaeth, Harold J., 8–9, 11–12, 16, 18–19, 21, 24–25, 37, 39–46, 48–49, 52, 54–55, 57, 60, 73, 82, 99–100, 102, 109, 124, 127–31, 136, 140, 168, 170, 172, 184–85, 189
Spiller, Pablo T., 11, 21, 131, 169, 173, 183, 190

Spriggs, James F., 9, 11–13, 20–21, 130–34, 171–73, 188–89
Statute age, 109–10, 149, 155, 158, 160–63
Stefko, Joseph V., 135, 186
Stevens, John Paul, 66, 69, 73, 77, 80–81, 93, 95, 97
Stewart, Potter, 65, 67, 72, 76, 80–81, 92, 95
Stone, Harlan Fiske, 14, 15, 40–41, 44, 51, 64, 72, 75, 79, 89, 97, 106, 138, 150, 153, 156, 166, 176, 190
Story, Joseph, 61–62
Stotzky, Irwin P., 3, 21, 95, 102, 107, 125, 191
Strategic approach, 2, 5, 7–8, 11–23, 127, 130–39, 155–67, 179–81
Strong, William, 63, 70, 78
Stuart v. Laird, 54
Sutherland, George, 64, 68–69, 71, 75, 79, 88
Swatt, Marc L., 152, 172, 189
Swayne, Noah, 63, 70, 78, 84
Swisher, Carl, 41, 57, 191

Taft, William H, 40–41, 43, 64, 69, 74–75, 79, 88, 135, 150
Takings clause, 45, 54
Tanenhaus, Joseph, 133, 173, 191
Taney, Roger, 14, 28–20, 40–42, 51, 57, 62, 67–68, 70, 74, 78, 81, 150, 153, 156, 166, 176, 180
Tate, C. Neal, 3, 8, 20, 22, 29, 56, 60, 74, 76–77, 82, 95, 101–2, 107, 123–24, 128, 136, 138, 140–46, 156, 168, 171, 173, 184, 187, 191
Tenth Amendment, 55
Thirteenth Amendment, 55
Thomas, Clarence, 45, 66–67, 69, 73, 77, 80, 94–95, 130
Thompson, Smith, 61–62

Timpone, Richard J., 17, 21, 190
Todd, Thomas, 61–62
Truman, Harry, Hoover, 65, 72, 76
Tushnet, Robert, 2, 22, 191
Tyler, John, 62, 72, 74

Ulmer, Sidney S., 133, 141, 173, 191
Ungs, Thomas D., 129, 172, 191
United Nations v. Sioux Nations of Indians, 108
United Surety v. American Fruit, 24

Van Buren, Martin, 62
Vines, Kenneth N.129, 170, 186
Vinson, Fred, 18, 36, 40–41, 44, 65, 67, 72, 76, 79, 81, 91, 96, 150, 153, 156, 166, 180

Wahlbeck, Paul J., 11–12, 20, 130, 134, 171, 173, 188, 191
Waite, Morrison, 40–43, 63, 70, 78, 100, 135, 150, 156
Walker, Thomas G., 45, 53, 55, 109, 124, 134–35, 140, 170, 185, 191
Warren, Earl, 9, 14, 17, 34–37, 40–41, 44, 51, 56, 65, 67, 69, 72, 76, 79, 81, 91, 95, 98, 118, 129, 135, 139, 147, 150, 153, 156, 166

Washington, Bushrod, 61–62
Washington, George, 62
Wayne, James, 62, 70, 74, 78,
Weschler, Herbert, 2, 22, 191
Westerland, Chad, 12, 21, 132, 172, 190
White, Byron, 65, 69, 72, 76, 80–81, 92, 97
White, Edward, 40–41, 43, 64, 71, 78, 85, 135, 150, 153, 156, 166, 168, 180
Whitford, Andrew, 10, 22, 27, 57, 137, 141–42, 173, 192
Whittaker, Charles, 65, 67, 69, 72, 76, 80–81, 92
Whittington, Keith E., 19, 21–22, 103–5, 113, 125, 171, 185, 189, 191
Wilson, Woodrow, 64, 71, 75
Wold, John T., 129, 1486, 167, 173, 191
Wood, Sandra L., 43–44, 48, 57, 75, 82, 97, 102, 134, 136, 157, 159, 171, 173, 187, 191
Woodbury, Levi, 61–62
Woods, William, 63, 70, 78, 100
Wright, John R., 133, 169, 184

Yates, Jeff, 10, 22, 27, 57, 137, 141–42, 173, 192

Zorn, Christopher, 151, 173, 192